This Old House complete
remodeling

This Old House Books
New York

THIS OLD HOUSE BOOKS
IN CONJUNCTION WITH SUNSET BOOKS

FOR THIS OLD HOUSE:

Editorial Director: Paul Spring
President, This Old House Ventures, Inc.: Eric Thorkilsen
Technical Consultants: General Contractor Tom Silva,
Master Carpenter Norm Abram, Plumbing and Heating Expert
Richard Trethewey, and Landscape Contractor Roger Cook

FOR SUNSET BOOKS:

Vice President and General Manager: Richard A. Smeby
Vice President and Editorial Director: Bob Doyle
Production Director: Lory Day
Operations Director: Rosann Sutherland
Retail Sales Development Manager: Linda Barker
Special Sales: Brad Moses

Managing Editor: Bridget Biscotti Bradley
Supervising Writer: Don Vandervort
Art Directors: Vasken Guiragossian and Amy Gonzalez
Writers: Louise Damberg, Patricia Freeman, and Michael Morris
Copy Editor: John Edmonds
Associate Editor: Carrie Dodson
Contributors: Joe Carter, Steve Cory, Mark Feirer,
Esther Ferington, and Curtis Rist
Illustrator: Ian Worpole
Page Production: Linda M. Bouchard
Photo Research: Robert Hardin and Anna Adesanya
Editorial Research: Gabriel Vandervort and Kit Vandervort
Prepress Coordinator: Danielle Javier
Proofreader: Meagan C. B. Henderson
Indexer: Mary Pelletier-Hunyadi

Cover: Photography by Alex Hayden (left); Brian Wilder (top right);
and David Duncan Livingston (bottom right)

For additional copies of *This Old House Complete Remodeling*
call Sunset Books at 1-800-526-5111 or visit us at www.sunset.com.

contents

LETTER
from This Old House

YOU'VE HEARD ALL THE HORROR STORIES FROM FRIENDS AND neighbors about the things that can go wrong when renovating your home. But what you seldom hear is advice from seasoned professionals that will guide you through the process. That's what we've assembled here: A walk through the different phases of remodeling—from the planning stages to completion—that spells out the options, opportunities, and pitfalls. It's really the distilled wisdom of all of us at This Old House.

In that spirit, let me share with you four things that will make everything else go more smoothly. First, do the homework: The more time you put into learning about your home, the better your decisions will be. Second, take the time to work out all the details with the design and building professionals you hire before construction begins. Third, know that your remodel, like all others, will run over budget, so hold at least 20 percent in reserve, and resist the "while we're at it…" add-ons. And fourth, always take the opportunity to improve the structure and systems of your house while the walls are open.

All of us at This Old House hope that your renovation, large or small, helps make your home all you want it to be.

Tom Silva

This Old House General Contractor

new directions

EXPLORE THE VARIOUS OPTIONS
TO MAKE YOUR HOUSE MORE LIVABLE

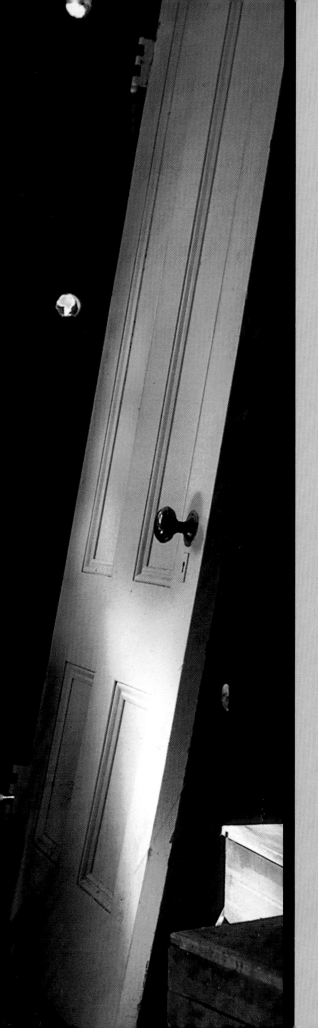

STACKS OF LUMBER, PICKUP TRUCKS LADEN WITH TOOLS and materials, haul-away dump bins: The signs can be seen on countless streets in communities nationwide. Remodeling is changing the face of America. Houses built in an earlier era are giving way to brighter, more lifestyle-focused homes adapted for the new millennium. It seems that every old house can use some modifications to accommodate growing and changing families.

Remodeling generally enhances the value of a house, likely the largest single investment most families make in their lifetime. But beyond the added value, we remodel to make our homes more comfortable. "When people think of comfort, they think of soft couches and thick-padded carpeting," says This Old House's Richard Trethewey. "But comfort goes far deeper than that, right down to the integrity of everything from the foundation to heating and cooling." This quest for comfort can only be achieved when all of the home parts and systems are considered in the remodeling process.

The following pages will get you started thinking about the possibilities. You'll also find stories of successful remodels that solved common problems, from cosmetic upgrades to major additions.

thinking about your remodel

Because you're reading this book, you've probably already thought quite a bit about how you'd like to improve your home. You may even know exactly what you want to improve. Often it's one or two rooms that look dated or don't function efficiently, or perhaps your home simply doesn't have enough space. But before you plunge headlong into a remodel, it's worth taking a step back and widening your focus, if you haven't already.

Reassess your home's strengths and weaknesses. Then think about all the things you really want in a home. This is the time to think big.

As you build your wish list, don't try to solve all of the problems. Just develop a collection of ideas that can be acted on or set aside. Leave the problem solving and final decisions for later, after you've begun working with design or building professionals who can help you refine your project.

getting to know your house

The magic of a remodel is taking a home that was originally built for somebody else and making it right for you. To accomplish this, you need to learn about how your home was originally built and clarify what will be involved in modifying it. Obviously, the less that's required to make this transformation, the faster, easier, and more affordable your remodel will be.

This cottage was transformed into a spacious retreat while staying within its existing footprint. The attic became a new living space and dormers were added for a more interesting roofline.

YOU'VE FORMED A WELL-CONSIDERED VISION OF HOW you'd like to improve your home. Giving shape to those dreams, however, can seem overwhelming—a word, says This Old House master carpenter Norm Abram, used a lot in the letters he receives from homeowners. "When I see it, I sympathize. But just remember, every project, no matter how large, involves solving a bunch of little problems one at a time," he says. "If you break a big job down into small, manageable steps and do them in a logical order, you'll eventually reach your goal."

Breaking down the process to reach that goal is precisely what this chapter is all about. Here you will learn about home design basics, which will help you visualize your project and gauge its difficulty. You will find out how to turn your ideas into an organized plan and how to choose and work with the right professionals for the job.

This chapter will also help you anticipate the realities of time, money, and the hassles involved in remodeling. You'll find information on controlling costs, financing a remodel, and living through the process of a renovation. Finally, you'll learn how to ensure the work has been completed satisfactorily before writing that last check.

planning and design

At this point, you've probably thought a lot about your home and what will or won't work for you. You may have collected ideas from books and magazines and noted features in other houses that appeal to you. Now it's time to take what you've learned and turn this information into a clearly defined design that satisfies your goals, conforms to zoning and code requirements, and stays within your budget.

In the planning stages, it is helpful to drive through comparable neighborhoods and study the houses you admire. You're bound to get some great design ideas for your own place.

developing a program

Getting from your wish list to actual construction plans begins with "the program"—essentially a collection of specific changes that define the scope of your project. For example, "our bathroom is too small" becomes "enlarge the bathroom 4 feet by tearing out the east wall." "The trim has no style" turns into "replace the clamshell molding with two-piece Colonial casing, crown, and base-

board." The program then grows into a design, which is typically born as rough sketches and ends up as full-fledged blueprints.

You may be able to put together the program yourself, but it's more likely that you'll want or need professional design help. If your project is relatively small and simple, involving neither major structural changes nor much electrical, plumbing, or mechanical work, you can probably pick out materials yourself and work with a contractor toward a final design.

Such a project might be a cosmetic makeover that mainly involves renewing or replacing trim, flooring, and wall surfaces. Even a project that includes moving a wall or doorway and putting in a window or two can be developed without a design professional. But do-it-yourself design can go only so far. A professional designer brings much more experience, expertise, and "eye" to a project to help ensure the best result.

Moving into a major project without design help can result in a plan that doesn't work well, looks marginal, or hides errors requiring expensive changes. Considering the cost of remodeling these days, it doesn't make sense to start with a haphazard design. Professionals who can help

you translate your dreams are discussed on the following pages.

Developing a program is a fluid process. As your design takes shape, you might find that the size or height of an addition must be reduced because of zoning constraints (see pages 36–37), or your remodel must be scaled down or accomplished in stages because of budget limitations (see pages 38–44). Even after construction begins, you can adjust your plans in small ways as the project takes shape. But plan carefully; major changes that occur after the work has begun are very costly.

It's not unusual to go through two, three, or more rounds of revisions, spread over several weeks or even months, to get to a final plan. Despite an understandable eagerness to reach the end of this progression, patience pays off. Changes on paper are far cheaper than those made to foundations, framing, or finish work.

types of blueprints

Blueprints are graphic representations of all aspects of a construction project. On sizable projects, they are necessary to solicit bids from contractors, gain financing from a lender, and apply for permits (though not all permits require professionally developed plans; check with your building department).

Because blueprints are key to planning a remodel, it is essential that you familiarize yourself with what they show.

Working with blueprints is a great way to visualize your remodel early on. Plus you can make changes quickly and easily, before the building begins.

plan views These are overhead views used for showing foundation, basement, floor, roof, and various room layouts and measurements. They typically indicate where existing construction is to be removed and where old will meet new construction. Plan-view details include all windows and doors with their sizes (or coded to a master list), all built-in cabinetry, kitchen and bathroom fixtures, and the dimensions of structural elements such as headers and beams. A simplified rendering of the floor plan is shown in a key plan, which leaves out measurements and other construction detailing so it's easier to see the design. Other plan views detail roof pitches, electrical and lighting systems, and heating and cooling systems.

elevations These are straight-on views—two dimensional so everything appears to be in the same plane—of walls, roofs, and other vertical elements. House plans include front, rear, and side elevations that show the placement of windows, exterior doors, siding, and so forth.

sections These drawings represent a slice through part of the structure, a cross section, to reveal how the structural components—walls, roofing, and flooring—go together. They also show windowsill heights and other essential dimensions.

details Plans typically need to include some areas enlarged to show exactly how certain construction elements are dimensioned and built. Details can range from structural elements such as foundations and roof framing to complex cabinetry or trim.

VISUALIZING YOUR RENOVATION

Indecision and uncertainty—common feelings when you are designing a renovation—usually stem from an inability to visualize the finished project by looking at a set of blueprints. How will a space really look and feel? Will it be big enough? Are the windows too small? How will the furniture fit in? Fortunately, there are a few aids.

perspective views Two-dimensional plan and elevation views can be turned into three-dimensional perspective views, called axonometrics, that provide a better representation of an inside space or an exterior

Architects and designers can create incredibly detailed perspective views using sophisticated computer software. These three-dimensional renderings allow for better visualization of the finished space.

shape. An architect may render these views himself or hire an architectural illustrator to not only picture the space but also include correctly scaled furniture and selected colors. Increasingly, such renderings are done with computer-assisted design (CAD) software.

models When the changes to a house are extensive, an architect will sometimes build a scale model that shows how new spaces will accommodate traffic and furniture and connect to existing spaces. Where additions, bump-outs, and roof raisings are involved, a model shows how the house's new proportions will look. Depending on the size and complexity, a whole-house model can cost $1,000 to $2,000, or more. Because of this, paying for a model usually makes sense only after you think you've arrived at a successful plan on paper.

virtual reality programs Some design firms offer a high-tech virtual reality computer tour of your future renovation, for a hefty price (often several thousand dollars). These tours allow you to look at the finished project

from photo-realistic renderings of colors, textures, and patterns to actual furniture and fixtures, all the while getting a sense of what it's like to walk from room to room. This computer-generated model usually starts with digital photographs of the existing house and then adds photo-realistic views of new elements such as windows or altered rooflines. With the computer's ability to knit together views of different elevations, it can turn the house on an axis and show how new elements relate to each other. For architects and other designers who've invested in these powerful programs, virtual reality can be a design starting point that gives clients a sense of their renovation results in a way that blueprints and models cannot.

home-design software Computer design programs made and priced for homeowners allow you to work up a finished renovation plan, complete with materials lists, or to at least noodle through your ideas before turning them over to a designer. Some programs employ a basic level of virtual reality, but their main strengths are in plotting floor plans and elevations, which can be turned into three-dimensional views. These software programs range from $20 to $150.

designers who can help

Most renovations of any complexity will benefit from a designer's experience and vision. Design help is offered by a variety of professionals, each with their own strengths.

◼ Architects have university training followed by apprenticeship at an established firm. They are licensed to practice at the state level. When "AIA" follows an architect's name, it means he or she has passed the architectural equivalent of the lawyer's bar exam and is registered with the American Institute of Architects. Fees typically run about 12 percent of the cost of building, or $100 per hour and up.

◼ Architectural designers are affiliated with the American Institute of Building Designers. AIBD members generally don't have the same depth of training as architects but may still bring strong talents and experience to their work. Hourly rates typically run less than $100 an hour. Since your choice boils down to one person, your search is for someone whose previous work includes a range of residential renovations, whose design style you like, and who is comfortable to work with.

◼ A design-build construction company offers everything from planning and design to construction.

Many discount the cost of design compared with architect or designer fees when a homeowner signs up for the complete service.

◼ Specialty designers handle specific projects such as kitchen and bathroom remodeling, deck and patio additions, landscape redesigns, or interior redecorating. Hourly rates can range widely from $40 to $150 or more for high-end designers.

◼ Home improvement centers typically offer in-house design services for projects such as kitchen or bath remodels. Most of these services don't extend to new plumbing, wiring, and so forth. Instead, they focus on the floor plan and replacement of cabinetry, flooring, and plumbing fixtures. The services are often free if you buy the products at the store.

Many designers will visit the site during construction to meet with the crew, review progress, and solve any design-related problems that may arise.

choosing a designer

Finding and choosing a good designer isn't always easy. The best ones often don't advertise because they have more than enough work that comes by word of mouth from satisfied clients. Here are a few ways to track down and a qualified designer.

search The best way to start your search is by asking family members, neighbors, and friends for referrals. You can also do some online searching at *www.aia.org* (for architects), *www.aibd.org* (for building designers), *www.nkba.com* (for kitchen and bath designers), *www.asla.org* (for landscape architects), and *www.asid.org* (for interior designers). Many have their own Web sites, which usually include their design philosophies and show completed projects.

initial contact When you call prospective designers, relate as much as you can about the scope of your project and when you'd like to start. Talk with as many candidates as you can to get a feel for what they are like, who's available and interested, and who will work for your price.

An experienced designer can guide you through the entire renovation process, from concept to completion.

interview A designer should be willing to spend about an hour, at no charge, at your home to present a portfolio and discuss your project. When you talk over the designer's past projects, discuss not only what was done but what problems were solved and what changes may have been made along the way and why. Be prepared to describe what you're aiming to have done, to what purpose, and the budget you have in mind. Ask about how the designer works with clients, including fee structure, and for some references. Even though the designer has not been hired yet, you should expect to hear some observations or ideas about your project.

references After narrowing the list of candidates based on experience, sensibilities, personality, scheduling, and fee structure, follow up on the references of those who interest you. Since you obviously won't be given references to dissatisfied clients, ask analytical questions, such as whether and how the designer came up with ideas, solutions to problems, and cost-saving measures. Be sure to ask how the completed project met the homeowners' needs and reflected their tastes. In other words, did the designer work to realize the homeowners' vision, not his or her own?

second meeting After narrowing the field to perhaps three or four candidates, propose to meet in their offices. You will get to see the operation, whom the designer works with, and the process by which a project goes from rough sketches to construction blueprints. Discuss your project in more detail and, if you remain interested, request a formal proposal. Ask that it outline the work to be done, the documents to be provided, the fee, and, most important, how many revisions are included in the fee.

Some designers include at least a few job-site visits in their bids, if only to make sure their design is being properly executed. A designer can also be your advocate in ensuring construction quality and code compliance. Extensive construction administration, in which the designer oversees the contractor's work while also specifying and ordering cabinets, fixtures, and other items, usually entails an additional fee. If you are not well-versed in house construction, having the designer occasionally on the job can be well worth the cost. But if you choose a contractor carefully, you shouldn't require full architectural supervision.

paying a designer

Designers generally get paid for their work in one of three ways.

hourly rate For smaller projects or ones on which you intend to act

as your own contractor, the best fee structure is usually an hourly rate. A good designer should be able to give you a ballpark estimate on how much time the work will take once you present the scope of your project.

flat fee This means one figure— quoted up front—for a complete design service that produces construction documents. For medium to large projects, flat design fees can make a lot of sense.

If a designer is integrally involved in the project, he or she should visit the site regularly and double-check the work being done.

percent of construction costs On jobs in which the designer is integrally involved, including construction oversight, this arrangement is common. Ranging from 5 to 15 percent of the total cost, this type of fee works only with projects that run on a fixed bid from the contractor you hire rather than on time-and-materials or some other basis.

getting it built

When your project's design is nearly complete, the next step is to find someone to build it. A general contractor is paid to deliver a completely finished project. His or her work includes scheduling and managing all the tradespeople necessary for every aspect, including demolition, framing, electrical, plumbing, and so forth. Typically, a contractor makes a profit by adding 15 to 25 percent to labor costs and possibly marking up the cost of materials.

If your project is fairly small and simple, you can opt to act as your own general contractor, hiring subcontractors directly. If you have the time and knowledge to oversee all of the work, you can reap significant cost savings, but be sure to factor in the value of your own time; acting as your own contractor can consume a tremendous amount of time and energy (see page 35).

The process of finding a contractor is similar to the one you went through to find an architect or designer.

choosing a contractor

"You wouldn't marry or start a business with someone without going over your choice with a fine-tooth comb," says This Old House general contractor Tom Silva. "When you hire a contractor, you're doing both those things. So the decision has to be made carefully." The following steps will help ensure a good relationship.

▪ Get no fewer than five and up to ten recommendations. Ask friends, family members, colleagues, and, most important, your architect or designer for names of builders they have worked with. A good designer-contractor relationship could help attract someone you otherwise would not be able to get.

▪ Call each candidate, mention who referred you, and spend 15 or 20 minutes trading information. Talk about the size and scope of your project (you will by now know how many square feet are involved) and when you'd like to start. First, ask how long they've been a general contractor and built in your immediate community—Tom Silva suggests a minimum of five years. Then ask about projects the contractor has completed, the size of the crew, available dates, and how many other jobs might be under way simultaneously. Finally, ask for references. Besides eliciting information, you want to hear confidence, forthrightness, and enthusiasm. Record your impressions.

▪ Pick the three or four strongest candidates to interview further. Invite each candidate to your home for an hour's worth of talk and a tour.

Be prepared to hand over a set of construction documents at this meeting, and ideally have your designer there as well. The documents and discussion will form the basis for the contractor's bid, so you want to hear lots of questions and see a distinct display of interest. You also want proof of license and bonding if required by your state (bonding is your protection against a contractor who leaves a job unfinished), plus at least a dozen references to past clients and at least one reference to a current client.

▪ Call at least three of the references. Be as direct as possible without getting too personal. How did the job go? Was the contractor on time and regularly on the job site? Did the contractor treat your property and your neighbors with respect? Was the crew courteous, and did they clean up every day? Was the project on schedule and on budget? What surprises were there? When there were disagreements, how did the contractor react? Were the disagreements generally about money or work quality? If all goes well with the conversation, ask if you can see the work that was done. The rest of your follow-up should include calls to your local Better Business Bureau and state consumer protection agency to uncover any history of complaints or actions taken. Finally, visit a job in progress to observe the crew's demeanor and habits.

■ So that you can compare bids, ask each contractor candidate to itemize costs for labor, materials, overhead, and profit, and detail the desired payment schedule. A good contractor should not hesitate to reveal his profit margin, which should be in the 10 to 20 percent range, and his overhead shouldn't be more than 5 to 10 percent of the total. However, contractors often have different labels for these categories or calculate them in different ways even if the final bid comes out the same. The payment schedule, as a rule, should not get ahead of the work. The initial payment—actually a deposit to secure the contractor—generally should not exceed 10 percent, though a higher percentage may be necessary if the contractor is ordering a significant amount of materials to start the job. Succeeding payments are made at defined milestones such as completion of rough framing, completion of drywall hanging (which means insulation and rough plumbing, electrical, and heating are in place), and so forth. The last payment should be a substantial sum, 10 to 15 percent, to be made when all inspections have been passed and you are 100 percent satisfied with the work that's been done.

■ If your designer has reviewed the bids with you, work with him or her on making your final selection. There's more to choosing a contractor than just comparing prices. In fact,

"Your home, whether you're remodeling, adding on, or building new, is the biggest investment that you make," says Tom Silva. "So be sure you pick the right contractors to work on it. The ones who offer the lowest bid and the quickest turnaround may not give you the quality craftsmanship you want."

the low bid may be the one to avoid, especially if it's a great deal lower than the others. "Throw out the lowball bid because he's probably cutting corners," Silva says. It's not uncommon for extra-low bidders to ring up a string of add-on charges for supposed changes. A low bid can also reflect the eagerness of a contractor just starting out, or an error that can produce an unhappy project later.

contract options

A construction contract should spell out all the details of the project, the responsibilities of the people involved, and the ways that any problems will be resolved.

There are two types of construction contracts: fixed-price and time-and-materials. The most common is fixed-price, which sets a flat fee for all the work (most often described as a "bid"). Only change orders can alter the number. In exchange for this certainty, the contractor usually pads the price for unforeseen problems.

In time-and-materials contracts, you pay only for actual hours worked and the cost of materials. The contractor generally adds a markup for profit and overhead, which could be 15 to 25 percent (this is often referred to as "cost-plus"). Materials receipts and the crew's hourly rate should be disclosed in all cases, although some contractors choose to quote an hourly rate for workers that includes their overhead and profit. The upside to this method is that if things go well, you can pay less than you would on a fixed-price bid. The downside is that there is no ceiling on the amount, which can be costly if workers are slow or run into serious problems. Some contractors will sign a "time and materials—not to exceed" contract that sets a high, outside limit.

Whichever type of contract you opt for, the contractor should give you a solid sense of the time needed for completion. As an incentive, you can build in a bonus if the contractor finishes the job in less time. This reduces the risk of a cost-plus arrangement and creates a win-win situation for both parties.

contract points

A good contract should cover many details. Standard contracts typically don't, so you may want a lawyer with construction contract experience to scrutinize yours. The AIA (*www.aia. org*) offers several contract forms for various projects. You can use the one that most closely matches yours and then tailor it to your specifications. A basic contract should contain:

■ The contractor's name, license number, phone and fax numbers, and business and e-mail addresses.

■ Project start and completion dates, with a provision for extensions due to delays that are beyond the contractor's control.

■ Detailed construction documents (a complete set of blueprints).

■ A detailed list of all materials and products the contractor will procure and/or install, including specific brands and model numbers; size, quantity, and grade of lumber; size, number, and defining features of all windows and doors; and so forth.

■ For a fixed-price contract, the project cost; for any type of cost-plus arrangement (and change orders for fixed-price contracts), the hourly rates for all workers.

■ The payment schedule.

■ The contractor's insurance documents, including personal liability, workers' compensation, and property damage coverage.

■ Lien releases from subcontractors, which free the homeowner of any responsibility to subcontractors in the event the contractor fails to pay them.

■ A hazardous-waste clause establishing who is responsible for testing and removing asbestos and lead-based paint (the homeowner is usually responsible).

■ Contractor and subcontractor warranties of workmanship and materials defects (usually good for one year after completion).

■ Procedures for change orders. For this, the contractor will typically present a document specifying the additional work, the materials, the price, and in some cases the completion time. It should be signed by both the homeowner and the contractor.

■ Other conditions specific to the project, such as daily start and quitting times; parking for trucks; and workers' access to a bathroom, telephone, and place to have lunch.

■ Procedures for dispute resolution and contract termination.

■ Confirmation of the homeowner's right to cancel for any reason within three days of the contract signing (like some other provisions, this is often required by your state's contracting laws).

SHOULD YOU BE YOUR OWN CONTRACTOR?

For most people, the allure of acting as one's own general contractor is all about saving money. With no markups on labor or materials and no add-ons for overhead or profit, a project can cost thousands less. Then again, if you acknowledge that time is money, the question becomes: Is the pay good enough? Here are some things you'll have to do.

- Find and schedule a core crew to handle demolition and construction, plus subcontractors for plumbing, electrical, and other trade work
- Schedule inspections
- Oversee progress and workmanship
- Answer questions and make decisions
- Handle the acquisition and delivery of special materials and products, including appliances and fixtures
- Write the checks
- Deal with anything unforeseen that comes up

Also consider whether you are qualified. You need a fair amount of construction knowledge, if not experience, and must be familiar with what subcontractors do. A key appointment will be your selection of a construction crew and the builder (often a foundation and framing contractor) who leads it. This work drives all the work the subcontractors will do, so you may be able to have the builder act as a sort of sub–general contractor, informing you of when the various subcontractors should be brought on.

In the end, you must weigh the money savings against the impact that taking on such a role will have. If you work at home some or part of the time, or if your office job allows some flexibility and you really like being extremely busy, it may well be worthwhile for you. But don't expect all the savings you imagine. Materials will typically cost you more than they do an established contractor, and job delays and rookie mistakes can take their toll too. Also recognize that the pace of your project and its quality depend on the skill and good will of subcontractors (electricians, plumbers, tilers, roofers, etc.). Unfortunately, it is often more difficult for a homeowner to hire and schedule top subcontractors since their loyalty goes to general contractors who will have work for them year after year.

keeping it legal

A renovation plan is subject to permit requirements, building codes, and zoning laws. These three are interconnected; you can't get a permit or pass ensuing inspections without conforming to local zoning and codes.

permits Cities typically require a permit to build when a project involves any structural, electrical, plumbing, or mechanical-system work (for example, heating and cooling). Requirements vary by region and even within a region, so check with your local building department on whether or not one is required for your job. In addition to a general building permit, you may need individual permits for work on the electrical, plumbing, and heating and cooling systems. Fees for permits frequently are based on the estimated project cost, which is all the more reason to build your budget carefully (see pages 38–44).

For the project to progress, it must pass a series of inspections, typically after the foundation is formed, the rough framing is up, the insulation is in place, the electrical is roughed in, the rough plumbing is installed, and so forth. After your project passes final inspection, a certificate of occupancy is issued acknowledging that all work has been done in accordance with both code and zoning requirements. The issuance of this permit is then registered with the city's tax assessors, who will often raise the property taxes because the improvements have increased the home's size or value.

While no one likes paying for permits, trying to duck under the radar can be much more costly if you get caught. The legal fees, fines, and potential cost of demolishing what was illegally built can be devastating. More important, the permit and inspection process protects you and future owners of your house from shoddy or unsafe work.

codes These requirements pertain to construction details, including foundation depth; rafter, joist, and beam spans; electrical capacities; and window and door placement. Any builder or tradesperson worth his or her salt knows the basic parameters of standard codes, though most towns and municipalities have nuances that vary from the basics. Any contract you sign should stipulate that all work must be permitted, inspected, and therefore code-worthy. The inspection process is intended to catch shortfalls or errors.

zoning These ordinances include restrictions on maximum height and minimum setbacks (how far a house must be from the front, side, and rear lot lines). When the economic boom of the 1990s spawned massive house expansions, some municipalities began limiting the size of the footprint—the area of the foundation—to a percentage of the lot size. Certain locales also have laws affecting a house's appearance (especially in historic districts), the way it can be used (for people contemplating a home-based business), or specific limitations such as the height of fencing, the width of a driveway, or even acceptable roofing materials.

In most municipalities, zoning regulations are too lengthy (and sometimes complicated) for a homeowner to know them all, so check with City Hall. If neighbors have completed similar remodeling projects, ask them about any out-of-the-ordinary restrictions they encountered or lessons they learned from going through the process.

When you apply for a permit, officials will scrutinize your plans. If the plans don't conform, you must change them so they do, or obtain a variance—a waiver of zoning rules.

Getting a variance is never a sure thing. It requires an application followed by a public hearing (immediate neighbors are usually notified of this hearing). This also typically requires a stiff fee. Officials on the review board and neighbors can question or comment on your plans, and you can explain and defend them. To win approval, you may have to prove that your project will not have a negative impact on the neighbors and/or that a financial or personal hardship will result from denial. Having your architect or designer with you is often helpful. As with permits, attempting to skirt zoning laws isn't worth it, especially since doing so could prevent you from selling your home.

Tom Silva always makes sure construction plans exceed the expectations of local building codes. He and Norm Abram are seen here double-checking the measurements before a new foundation is poured.

financial considerations

Most homeowners do not have unlimited funds to spend on a renovation. An important first step is cost control, which begins with putting the renovation in perspective.

First ask yourself how long you intend to stay in your house. If you plan to stick around indefinitely to enjoy the results of your renovation, you can invest more than you'd be likely to get back if you sold the house. But this is a risky approach. Smart financial planning dictates a few guidelines.

Scale your renovation to the size and style of your house. Don't put an ultramodern kitchen in a traditional house, for example, or a huge master suite in a modest-sized house. Overdoing your renovation in these ways will make the rest of your house look dated, shabby, or worse.

Also, scale and style your renovation to the neighborhood. A $100,000 addition in a neighborhood of

Not all remodels require depletion of savings or a second mortgage. If you're not ready to take a major leap, consider making cosmetic improvements. This kitchen was inexpensively updated with a fresh coat of paint on the cabinets and colorful diamonds of linoleum on the floor.

$200,000 houses may never yield a good return on the investment. The same holds true for putting high-end appliances and materials in a small house. Any buyers looking for these amenities would usually be looking in a different neighborhood.

Once you have created a design with a budget that you believe makes sense, consider some of the following questions and tips.

what's it going to cost?

A common, but not always reliable, way to ballpark renovation costs is by square footage. In many areas of the country, $100 per square foot will buy you a good remodel or new construction. But this figure can double in areas with expensive labor and a high cost of living, and it can rise dramatically based on materials and product choices. Hardwood flooring is more expensive than vinyl, a granite countertop more than plastic laminate, built-ins pricier than stock cabinetry, custom windows more costly than standard sizes, and so on. For kitchens and baths, national averages can exceed $200 per square foot, depending on the selection of appliances and fixtures, which vary widely in price. On the other hand, if you stick with cosmetic enhancements, you may get by with well under $100 per square foot.

When you start talking with designers and contractors, ask about prices per square foot based on the materials and products you are considering. This will quickly give you a general idea of how dramatically you may need to adjust. For example, if a marble countertop is at the top of your wish list, perhaps your existing refrigerator can give you a few more years of service.

In making the inevitable compromises, keep in mind that it will be much easier to upgrade appliances and furnishings in the future than it will be to tear up the flooring or change the tile in the shower.

Once you have your base budget for building, don't forget to add the costs for design fees, permit fees, expenses for storage if furniture has to be moved out, rental fees if

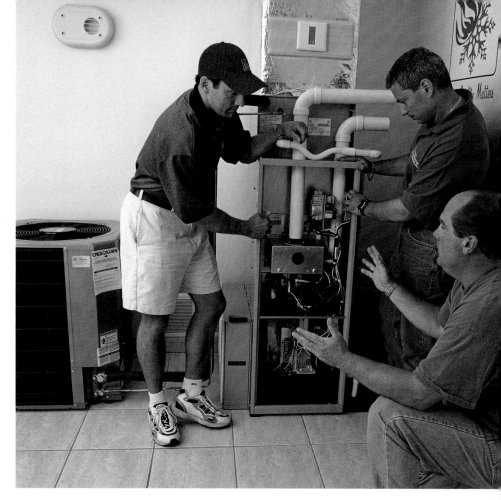

For major remodels, don't overlook the cost of system upgrades. This Old House plumbing and heating expert Richard Trethewey encourages homeowners to spend money on systems that will keep the house comfortable, such as this new gas furnace, not just the finishes that make it look good.

you must move out, restoring landscaping, and other miscellaneous expenses. Last but not least, build in a percentage for contingencies such as change orders, unforeseeable conditions, or delays. Tom Silva advises homeowners embarking on a remodel to expect the unexpected. "I always tell people to subtract 20 percent from the budget before making renovation decisions. Chances are good that you'll be spending some or all of it."

renovations that add value

For most homeowners, a house isn't just an investment. Neither should it be a money loser. Even if you have no foreseeable plans to move, it's still wise to be aware of which improvements are most valued by future buyers of your home and which they will be unwilling to pay for.

Because the kitchen and bathrooms often sell a house, it's no surprise that they top the list in renovation value. Master suites, family rooms, and two-story additions are also smart investments. In general, today's buyers increasingly favor finished, improved houses over taking on renovation or expansion costs and hassles themselves. They're also very space conscious and want maximum square footage for their money. For this reason, attic and basement conversions are a plus. Style matters too, so any addition should be completely in sync with the house, right down to such elements as ceiling heights and molding profiles.

At the other end of the value scale, swimming pools score low because they're seen as both a maintenance burden and a safety concern. And despite their rising popularity, home offices aren't strongly favored either.

But this doesn't mean you should nix the pool and eschew the office. Any house should serve its owners' wants and needs first. Even the top

BELOW: This bathroom gets its no-fuss, contemporary look from small glass tiles and the clean lines of the cabinetry. RIGHT: White paint, glass cabinets, and uncovered windows make this kitchen bright and airy, while the island ensures plenty of storage space.

improvements will rarely return more than their costs immediately. You simply want to avoid investing far more than you could ever realize from a sale. To that end, it's a good idea to consult with one or more real estate brokers to get a sense of what your house's post-improvement market value might be.

If you plan to sell soon, spending less can actually return more. For instance, doing a kitchen face-lift—

new counters, fixtures, appliances, flooring, and paint—is much less expensive than a full-bore remodel yet creates the aura of newness that buyers like. Often the smartest approach if you're planning to sell is to make cosmetic improvements.

Buyers increasingly favor large, updated master suites. A fireplace, adjoining master bathroom, and a glass door leading to a balcony add value to this bedroom.

controlling costs

Once construction begins, the money for a renovation goes out swiftly. If you can control the all too common urge to expand the project—the "while we're at it" syndrome—you may even be able to reduce costs. Here are some ways to save.

compare lenders If you are taking out a loan to pay for the renovation, look around for the lowest interest rate. When you're borrowing thousands, even a quarter point can save thousands of dollars in compounded interest (see page 44).

schedule seasonally Most contractors charge less when business is slow. When winter comes to cold climates, for instance, people are less apt to undertake a major renovation, especially if they have to live in the midst of it. If your remodel does not involve exposing parts of your house to the elements, consider booking the work during an off-season.

contract hourly Renovation contracts are most commonly based on a set price for a set amount of work. That price includes a contractor's profit and overhead along with the workers' salaries. However, in some situations, you can save money with a time-and-materials contract, whereby you pay an hourly labor rate plus the direct costs for all materials. To guard against runaway hours, set a limit on the total time. If it comes in under, you spend less; if it goes over, you don't spend more. (For more information on contract options, see page 34).

be a shopper Contractors spend lots of time buying fixtures, appliances, decorative hardware, lighting, and other items. If you make that your responsibility, you won't pay for the contractor's time or markups. Plus, you can shop by price and not just availability.

check the line items Instead of accepting lump-sum quotes for a suite of appliances, fixtures, or other products, insist on item-by-item breakdowns. The $400 faucet may be fine, but you may not want to spend $800 for a sink when you know you'll be happy with one for half that. Also, the very act of requesting itemized quotes signals to suppliers that they're making a competitive bid, which should push the total down even further.

You are your best consumer advocate. If you want high quality for the lowest price, do your own shopping instead of letting the contractor or design professional choose for you.

Put in a little sweat equity. If your contractor agrees to it in advance, pitch in on the work when the crew is at another job. You'll keep things moving without getting in their way.

request discounts Try to keep your vendors to a limited number and make all your purchases from each vendor at the same time. This increases the chances of your buying in greater volume. That fact alone may qualify you for a discount, because most suppliers will be hard-put to walk away from a large order.

put away the credit cards Credit card interest rates are high, and just a few thousand dollars can incur hundreds of dollars in interest in a short time. Treating your credit cards as if they were your child's college fund or your hard-earned retirement savings should keep you from using them casually.

put in some sweat equity Assess your do-it-yourself skills and see where you might be able to pitch in. Demolishing a wall, for instance, requires more time and energy than skill. Doing your own painting can save hundreds or even thousands. But be sure to make an honest assessment of your skill level, or your mistakes could end up costing you more. For more about this, see "Should you be your own contractor?" on page 35.

HOW NOT TO SAVE MONEY

Renovating for better appearance, space, or features that you can see and feel is always more appealing than upgrading the infrastructure—pipes, wiring, insulation, or ductwork. But scrimping on plumbing, electrical, and heating and cooling improvements also means scrimping on the various systems that make a house comfortable. By doing so, you will also miss out on the opportunity to make the house more energy efficient, along with the long-term cost savings such improvements can entail (see "Remodeling for Energy Savings" on page 45).

Neglecting system upgrades also risks costly repairs or improvements later. Better to replace old pipes when they're exposed than when they spring a leak inside a wall. Better to upgrade the electrical service from 100 to 200 amps now than to muddle along with an underpowered house. System upgrades offer other benefits as well. For example, consider running data and audio-video wiring—or at least the conduit that can carry it—through any room that could utilize such links now or in the future.

getting the money

When you purchased the home you're now planning to renovate, you probably became well versed in what's required to obtain a mortgage. The options for financing a renovation all follow similar procedures, and include the following.

cash-out refinancing As the name implies, you can re-mortgage your home for more than you currently owe, pay off the existing mortgage, and apply the extra cash to your renovation. Lenders typically offer such loans at up to 90 percent of a house's appraised value, though some may go to 100 percent. As with any refinancing, there are significant closing costs and points—often 1 to 2 percent of the mortgage amount. If you wish, you may be able to pay additional points to reduce the interest rate (this usually pays for itself in four to five years of reduced monthly payments).

renovation loan This lesser-known way to borrow uses the house's presumed post-renovation value as the loan's equity basis. The main limiting factor on how much can be borrowed is the owner's income. Because the bank is risking its money on improvements not yet done, it keeps very close tabs on the project to make sure it's done well, on time, and according to plan. You must hire, at your own expense, a renovation consultant who monitors progress and approves payments to the contractor (who must be licensed and bonded) from an escrow fund. Borrowers interested in doing much of the work themselves might be limited by the loan terms unless they can prove they have both the skills and the time to devote to the project.

home equity loan For a number of reasons, taking out a second loan has become a very popular way to fund renovations. Besides putting a lot of money at your disposal, these loans close quickly for very little or no cost, and the interest is tax-deductible. Plus, the bank neither controls nor monitors the money; you can use it to buy windows for the house or a vacation in Italy (though the latter won't raise your home's value). Equity loans and lines differ in that a loan is made in a lump sum and you immediately start paying interest on the entire principal; with an equity line, you write checks against a maximum amount, paying interest only on what you've borrowed from the time you borrow it. The longer the expected duration of the project, the better sense a home equity line of credit makes.

The Internet provides a quick and easy way to compare rates and apply for loans.

REMODELING FOR ENERGY SAVINGS

Renovations that entail opening walls and ceilings, stripping off siding, and/or replacing fixtures and appliances give you the opportunity to make your house more energy efficient at the same time. Houses with little or no insulation, lots of air leaks, and old single-pane windows can benefit enormously from improvements in these areas. In most cases, these improvements will pay for themselves in a few years via reduced utility bills. In addition, you can choose appliances, lighting, heating and cooling systems, and kitchen and bathroom fixtures that use less energy and water with no compromise in performance. Here's a look at the possibilities.

structure The older the house, the more likely heated or cooled air leaks out and outdoor air leaks in (termed "infiltration"). If your renovation calls for the home's siding to be stripped off, consider insulating exterior walls and/or covering the sheathing with housewrap (see page 63), which will block incoming air while still allowing moisture from inside to escape. This is also the time to caulk seams around obvious sources of infiltration, such as doors and windows.

insulation Current building codes typically require significant amounts of wall and ceiling insulation, so if they are being opened, you'll have to comply anyway. Walls should have R-19 batts as a minimum; ceilings should carry at least R-30 (see pages 62–63).

windows If you are replacing windows and live in a climate that pushes into winter or summer extremes, choose the most energy-efficient ones you can afford.

High-quality options have double glazing that's filled with an inert gas (usually argon) and treated with a special coating (low-E) to maximize insulation value. When they're installed, the gap between the window frame and the wall framing should be filled with an expanding foam sealant to prevent infiltration. If your window sash and frame are in good shape, adding or replacing storm windows will produce similar savings for less (see page 233).

heating pipes and ducts A great deal of energy can be wasted in simply delivering heat from the furnace or boiler to registers and radiators. Air ducts should be both sealed to block air leakage and wrapped with insulation. Water pipes should be encased in sleeves of foam insulation.

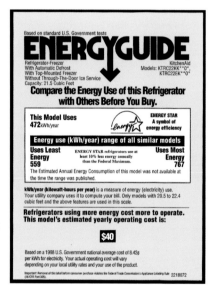

appliances The greatest efficiency gains in this area have been made with refrigerators, dishwashers, washing machines, and water heaters. If it's time to replace any of these, look for top-rated energy-efficient appliances that carry the federal Energy Star label (left).

lighting Fluorescent lights (below and right) use about one-fourth the electricity that standard bulbs consume, last longer, and now come in sizes, shapes, color tones, and output levels for virtually every type of fixture. Halogen lights are also very energy efficient, but the bulbs are expensive and can get very hot.

the remodeling process

The first day of construction usually brings a rush of excitement, but this can quickly subside if you have not properly prepared for the realities of the work to come. Will you be living with the renovation or moving out? How will you keep the work from disrupting daily life? What sort of job-site interaction should you have with the contractor and crew? How will you handle changes to the plans? These are just a few questions you need to deal with to ensure the project goes as smoothly as possible for you and your family.

living in or moving out

Moving out is disruptive all on its own, so unless your renovation is extensive, this should be a last resort. Even the loss of the kitchen isn't necessarily grounds for evacuation. Then again, if the only bathroom is being torn out, there's probably a short-term rental in your future.

The live-in option requires resilience, to be sure, but the right preparations can soften the blow of demolition and construction. First, try to keep daily routines intact, or set new routines in an organized fashion. Make a plan for storing the furniture and other items that will be disrupted by the renovation. If the work is extensive, consider using a

commercial storage facility or renting a portable container that's dropped at your property. Try to avoid cramming belongings into other rooms of the house. As it is, you are losing the use of the rooms involved in the renovation. You need the rest of your rooms to do double duty, not be unusable to you as well.

kitchen survival If you are about to lose your kitchen, summon your resourcefulness and a big helping of tolerance. Before demolition begins,

set up a temporary kitchen elsewhere. An adjacent dining room or, if it is large enough, the basement or laundry room is the best choice because of access to a water supply and drain lines. Avoid decamping in a bathroom unless it is large enough and can be devoted solely to kitchen activity.

Generally, the longer you'll be kitchenless, the more convenience you'll want. You'll need at least a sink with running water (not necessarily hot), storage and counter space, some select cooking appliances, and a refrigerator. Some of the cabinets and countertops being torn out of the old kitchen can be redeployed in the temporary space. Having a few

During a remodel, your kitchen will be full of safety hazards and contractors—plus the electricity and water will often be shut off—so you'll want to find someplace else to prepare meals.

tabletop appliances, including a microwave, can open up a surprising range of cooking options. One caution: Never use a barbecue or unvented gas appliance indoors; the vapors are deadly. See page 146 for more information on living without a kitchen during a remodel.

managing the mess

In addition to noise and the presence of workers around the clock, a major remodeling challenge is keeping a tide of dust from invading every room. Nearly every phase of work involves dust, from demolition to drywall or plaster finishing. You will not be able to eliminate the invasion entirely, but you can minimize it.

Ask your contractor to drape 4-mil plastic between the work area and the rest of the house and tape it firmly to the ceiling and walls. Where possible, create an air lock by separating two plastic curtain walls by about 3 feet. Stuff old towels in the threshold gaps under doors, and tape shut doors that will not be used. If your house has forced-air heating or cooling, seal off any return registers in the workspace to avoid recycling dust through the system (discuss this with your heating contractor).

If a bump-out, addition, or extensive exterior work is part of the plan, your landscaping will inevitably be affected. Mature plants are worth a lot of money, so take the time to move them out of harm's way before

work begins. "It's well worth the effort to save your plants," says This Old House landscape contractor Roger Cook. "It's better to take them out than assume they won't get hurt." Shrubs that are a modest size can be carefully dug out and replanted in temporary locations. To ease the shock, choose areas with the same general soil and sun/shade conditions and avoid transplanting in very hot weather. Cook suggests setting up a temporary sprinkler system for plants that have been relocated so they are sure to get plenty of water. Cordon off trees, giving them a wide berth, especially in areas that will receive vehicle traffic, since the weight of the trucks and heavy equipment can compress the soil and harm the roots.

Don't worry too much about the grass; it will likely succumb to worker and vehicle traffic. When the renovation is complete, aerating or

Before remodeling begins, pack up everything of value and store it away from the mess.

turning and amending the compacted soil and seeding the area should quickly return it to lush turf. Just be sure workers don't rinse their buckets used for painting, plastering, or similar work on your lawn.

Protection from the elements is another order of business. If a roof or exterior wall is being torn off, waterproof tarps must be properly secured. In fact, you might want to stipulate in the contract that any damage resulting from project-related leaks will be the contractor's responsibility.

Finally, be very clear with your contractor about maintaining a neat job site. It is the contractor's responsibility to clean up and haul away all construction debris. Make sure it gets taken care of, as your regular trash service will not accept it.

be involved
and stay involved

Before construction begins, agree on a work schedule with your contractor. Crews often like to start early—6:30 or 7 A.M., for example—to take best advantage of daylight in winter or cool weather in summer. It's in your best interest to accommodate their hours in order to speed up the work, but check on municipal codes that may restrict start and finish times, particularly on weekends. It's also a good idea to talk with your neighbors, who may not appreciate waking to the sounds of banging hammers and screaming power saws.

Regular, frank communication with your contractor is a critical part of maintaining steady progress and desirable results. Schedule regular meetings, particularly if your contractor is working on other jobs. Depending on the pace of progress, meetings could be as often as every day but should be at least once a week. Have your architect or designer attend some of them if possible. These sessions should be an open forum, where all parties can ask questions, air concerns, and work out any changes.

Coming prepared to these meetings means regularly walking through the job site, occasionally with your architect. Note anything and everything you see that you have questions about. Be sure to check whether walls are plumb and square, exterior siding joints are tight, all gaps and intersections are caulked, and weatherstripping and flashing is in place. Feel free to check the work, but if you find you have concerns, put them as questions—rather than accusations—to your contractor to begin the dialogue.

Keeping in close communication with your contractor is a must. Here, Tom Silva talks with the home-owners while his crew continues to make progress on the house.

Check detail work before making your final payments. Inspect trim and molding for flaws. Everything should be smooth and seamless.

To avoid interfering with work in progress, the best time to ask questions is after the crew has gone home.

Keeping the communication regular will also make it easier to work through any serious issues, such as changes to the plans, without incurring change orders. The earlier you make changes, the better. For example, framing, wiring, and plumbing changes are far easier to make before walls have been covered with drywall or plasterboard.

If a major change does come up, involve your architect or designer in redesigning and in helping negotiate the cost of the alteration with the contractor. When everything is settled, have the contractor draw up the change order, including a description of the work to be performed and the price, for both of you to sign. Be sure to keep a copy of the change order.

Last but not least, the work crew that you'll effectively be living with will benefit from a bit of "goodwill management." Providing a few comforts will pay off not only in good relations but also in productivity. Workers will, of course, need a bathroom; in many cases, the contractor will supply a port-a-john. Lunches and breaks are typically taken wherever there's a place to sit, but if you can supply a table and chairs, they will be much appreciated. If the area is in a warm place during a winter project, you will be all but loved. A water source for drinking and washing up should also be made available. Though you may be tempted to pass out drinks and snacks, ask the general contractor about this policy first. Some may not appreciate the interruption of work or the blurring of the client-worker relationship.

before you write the last check

The final phases of any renovation can be the most difficult as work slows, homeowners get antsy for completion, and contractors turn more of their attention to their next projects. Also, detail work such as installing trim and cabinet hardware, putting in lights, and prepping walls for painting goes much slower than other processes, such as framing. As eager as you might be to reclaim your house, now is not the time to lose patience, particularly if you've maintained a watchful eye over your project thus far. You have to keep checking the overall fit and finish of everything and make sure things work.

As your project winds down, inspect the work more frequently in order to catch minor flaws or errors and report them to the contractor right away.

With the finish line in sight, make a punchlist, a listing of everything that still needs to be handled. Everything on the list should be done to your complete satisfaction before you make that final payment.

paint If the walls and ceilings were prepped well, they will be smooth and show no evidence of drywall screws or joint lines. All seams formed by painted trim should be caulked to eliminate "black line" gaps. If your project involved new framing, be aware that the lumber can shrink in a year or less, pushing out screw heads or even causing cracks. It's no one's fault, but the contractor should agree to repair such flaws if they appear.

trim Look for tight joints between trim pieces and tight seams where it meets the walls, ceiling, or floor. If the trim is painted, small gaps can be closed with caulking. Natural wood trim should have been scribed and cut to fit bows or other irregularities in the wall or whatever surface it meets. All nail or screw holes should be filled and sanded smooth so as to be practically invisible.

ABOVE: Look closely at kitchen details. Cabinets should have a smooth finish, and all hardware should be firmly attached. Tile should lie flat and show no signs of grout haze. RIGHT: Test all new fixtures. They should not leak from the pipe connection or drip while turned off.

cabinets and other built-ins

Make sure all new cabinetry is unblemished and in good working order. Custom cabinets should have paint or a clear finish on the inside surfaces and on all drawer parts. Doors and drawers should operate smoothly and close tightly. All shelves and any storage hardware or systems should be in place, and the latter should be adjusted for proper operation.

flooring

A solid wood floor that's not factory finished should have been installed, sanded, and given several protective coats before the room is finished. At job's end, the floor should be lightly screened again and given at least one more coat. The wood should show no sanding marks. Tile should lie perfectly flat from one piece to the next and have consistent grout lines. Linoleum and vinyl sheet or tile should fit tight and lie flat.

appliances and fixtures

Sinks should sit on or under the countertop with no gaps that could admit water. All faucets should work smoothly. Cooking appliances should be perfectly level and operate correctly.

lighting Make sure the right switches operate the right lights. If there are recessed lights, inspect the ceiling trim to ensure there are no gaps between trim and ceiling.

doors and windows Any new door or operable window should open and close without great effort and with no sticking. Any entry door should seal tightly against weatherstripping along all the edges. Lock mechanisms should work easily. Window locks should be effortless to engage, and all cranks should be installed on casement or awning operators.

roofing, siding, and gutters Besides doing a visual inspection of the general installation quality, wait for a rainy day to look for roof leaks in the attic and to check that gutters are diverting water correctly and have no leaks at the seams. If no rain is in sight, test the roof with a hose.

ABOVE: New windows should be airtight and operate seamlessly. LEFT: New roofing should be free of leaks and gutters should drain completely.

finalizing the job

When you are fully confident that the punchlist tasks have been accomplished satisfactorily, the contractor should obtain releases of all liens that may have been (or still could be) applied by subcontractors who worked on the job. All printed matter and warranty information related to new products and materials should be handed over to you.

Finally, it's a good idea to formally end the job with a letter of completion signed and dated by both you and the contractor. In addition to confirming that all the contract and payment requirements have been met, the letter starts the clock on the contractor's materials and workmanship warranty.

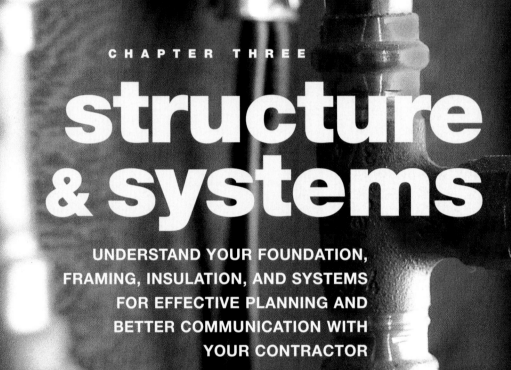

CHAPTER THREE

structure & systems

UNDERSTAND YOUR FOUNDATION,
FRAMING, INSULATION, AND SYSTEMS
FOR EFFECTIVE PLANNING AND
BETTER COMMUNICATION WITH
YOUR CONTRACTOR

THOUGH IT'S TYPICAL TO FOCUS ON THE VISIBLE ELEMENTS of a house during a remodel, the parts that really make a home tick are hidden in the walls, ceilings, and floors. Electrical, plumbing, heating and cooling systems, structural framework, insulation—these do the hard work of making a house comfortable, safe, and energy efficient.

"The stuff behind the walls is by far the most important, and the smartest place to put your money," says This Old House general contractor Tom Silva. If your remodel entails tearing open the walls or other surfaces, this is the time to look carefully at these systems. Before you get to that point, however, it's crucial to have a basic understanding of how these systems work so you will know what impact they may have on your renovation and how you might improve them.

Understanding your home's systems helps you to converse more knowledgeably with designers and builders and to make better-informed decisions, which can ultimately save you money.

On the following pages, we'll peel open the walls and surfaces of a house to look at its anatomy.

structural systems

The most fundamental system to a house's primary purpose—to provide shelter—is the structure. Structural elements, such as the foundation and the framing for floors, walls, and roof, provide the skeletal support for all the other layers.

foundations

Knowing the nature and depth of your house's foundation is essential only if your plans include an addition or a substantial second story, or if your remodel has been inspired by signs of a substandard foundation, such as cracked walls or buckling floors.

A solid, well-built foundation is by far the most permanent part of the house and therefore the most difficult to change. "There are no shortcuts when it comes to a foundation," Silva says. "It's a 'do it right, or don't do it at all' proposition."

The type and size of the existing foundation depend on the house's age, construction, and location.

Foundations beneath older homes might be of stone, brick, or other masonry, but most homes have foundations made of concrete block or poured concrete. For a new foundation, building codes call for poured concrete footings and steel reinforcing bar (rebar) in the foundation walls. "The rebar and the concrete work together to provide the strongest and most flexible material imaginable," Silva says. He points out that perimeter foundations made of concrete block filled with poured concrete are more prone to cracking and leaks.

Another type of foundation system is the concrete slab. The slab itself should be reinforced with wire mesh and poured over foam insulation, sand, a vapor barrier, and a 4- to 6-inch bed of compacted gravel. It must be supported on the perimeter by a steel-reinforced concrete footing common to all foundations.

Pouring a foundation demands precise work, from excavating the site to finishing the concrete. Climate dictates how deep the foundation must go. In a cold climate, such as New England's, a full foundation typically extends 4 to 8 feet into the ground. "This gives the base of the foundation, called the footing, a solid hold in ground that does not freeze, no matter how cold it gets," Silva says. Otherwise, a foundation can heave and ruin the house's structure

TYPICAL FOUNDATION

Labels: rim joist, mudsill, foundation wall, anchor bolt, waterproofing membrane, top fill, backfill, ¾-in. crushed stone, filter fabric, perforated drainpipe, rebar, keyway, footing, rebar

as the seasons change. In frost-free parts of the country, footings are placed only a few feet into the ground.

Most important is the consistency of the concrete, which is a mixture of gravel, sand, Portland cement, and water. Too much water will weaken the concrete, while not enough will make it difficult to pour. The forms should be filled evenly, then troweled smooth on top. The resulting foundation walls must be level and plumb, and free of voids and discoloration that are characteristic of weak concrete.

A concrete form should be filled during a single pour to prevent a "cold joint" that is likely to crack and leak. By the next day, the concrete is hard enough for the forms to be removed, but the concrete must be kept damp for at least three days with plastic wrapping or misting to ensure that it will cure properly. Curing too quickly will weaken the concrete.

KEEPING A FOUNDATION DRY

When water penetrates a foundation and seeps into or floods a basement or crawl space, it can cause serious damage. Beyond the obvious harm to anything stored in these areas, moisture leads to mold and mildew and creates a hospitable environment for wood-devouring insects.

To keep ground moisture and runoff from penetrating a new foundation, particularly important for basements and lots where drainage is an issue, the foundation walls must be waterproofed. There are a number of systems and coatings for foundations, but most provide only dampproofing, not true waterproofing. The TOH crew prefers an approach that utilizes a rubberized membrane that is sprayed onto the foundation walls. This material spans any hairline cracks that may form in the concrete. A contractor uses a power sprayer to apply a 60-mil-thick coat of this viscous,

blue-green coating to every part of the foundation that will contact the soil (shown below left).

Even if your house is not positioned at the bottom of a slope, water that accumulates at the base of the foundation needs to be pulled away from the house by a French drain. These footing drains are gravel-filled trenches containing perforated pipe; they rely on gravity to carry water away. "These are simple to install when you're building an addition, but they become harder and messier to retrofit into a house," Silva says. "I wouldn't build a foundation without one."

ANATOMY OF FRAMING

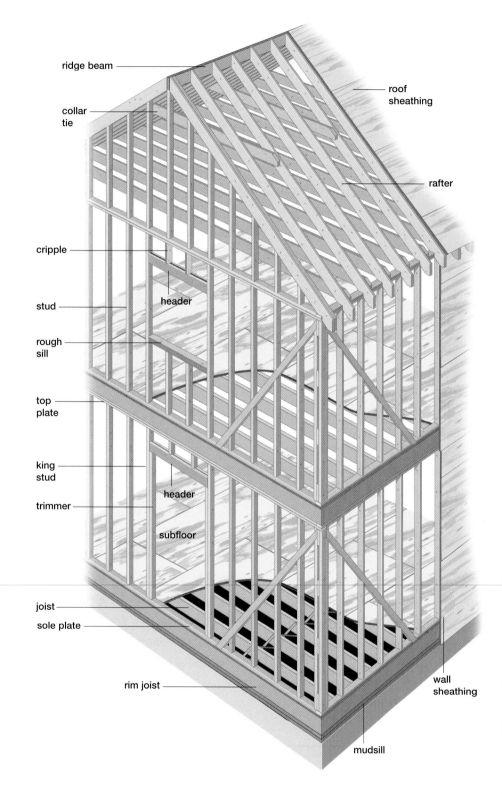

ridge beam

collar tie

roof sheathing

rafter

cripple

stud

header

rough sill

top plate

king stud

trimmer

header

subfloor

joist

sole plate

rim joist

wall sheathing

mudsill

framing

Homeowners often regard framing as something too technical to comprehend. It's really quite logical, though there are a few terms to learn. Familiarizing yourself with the language and methods of framing is important because you should be involved in the decisions of what materials and specifications are used, and in overseeing how well they are put together. What's at stake is an addition (or reinforced existing framing) that will feel more solid and support all finish materials with fewer cracks and failures. In an earthquake or a hurricane, the frame's integrity can actually make the difference between survival and disaster.

Most American homes have a framework of wood studs, joists, rafters, and similar lumber components. This framing gives a house its shape and its strength.

There are four methods of wood framing: platform (or Western), brace, balloon, and post-and-beam. Of these, platform is by far the most common. With this method, the floor and walls for each level of a multistory house are framed one at a time (the second-story floor sits on top of the first-story walls), as shown at left.

Wall, ceiling, and roof framing is composed almost entirely of 2-by dimension lumber spaced 16 or 24 inches apart from center to center. In older homes, these components may be unsurfaced, full-dimension lumber. The lumber for almost all homes built in the past few decades was surfaced before construction, so actual dimensions are less than nominal size. A 2 by 4, for example, is actually $1\frac{1}{2}$ by $3\frac{1}{2}$ inches.

Good framing produces a stronger house and makes applying all subsequent layers of finish easier. "The framing should not be taken lightly," Silva says. "It is important for the joints to be tight. Make sure seams between sheathing panels do not line up with the seams between panels below or above. It's always good to stagger them at least two studs, joists, or rafter bays."

When cut and nailed properly, two pieces of wood should join fully where they meet. While this is easy to accomplish when wood is nailed at right angles, it becomes more of a challenge when other angles are involved, particularly where roof rafters join at the ridge beam or where they attach to the top of a wall. The lower end of a rafter typically has a notch, called a bird's mouth, that rests on the wood plate at the top of the wall. When the bird's mouth is cut at the proper angle, there should be no gap between the rafter and the plate. Tom Silva also prefers to see a double top plate, two horizontal 2 by 4s or 2 by 6s, on top of the studs for every bearing wall. This helps keep walls straight and strong.

This is an up-close look at the bird's-mouth cut into a rafter resting on top of a wall's double top plate.

BUILDING TO CODE

When it comes to following a building code, Tom Silva is the first one to ignore it in favor of more stringent requirements. "I refuse to follow the building code," he says. "It's good enough for safety, but it doesn't make rock-solid houses." By going above and beyond code requirements, he and other builders can make an addition much stronger.

A case in point is the floor. Built only to code, floors bounce slightly when they're walked on, which can be annoying. To create a sturdier floor, Silva reduces the spacing between joists, sometimes increases the size of the joists, and installs thicker subflooring. For example, if he were building a 16-by-24-foot addition and the code called for 2-by-10 Douglas fir joists spaced 24 inches apart, he would reduce the spacing to 16 inches. And instead of using $\frac{5}{8}$-inch plywood for the subfloor, he would install $\frac{3}{4}$-inch tongue-and-groove plywood. The total additional cost of the materials would be just a few hundred dollars—a bargain price for a bounce-free floor.

Fourteen-inch-deep wooden I beams undergird a 22-foot-wide kitchen, giving solid support. Although the building code allowed a joist spacing of 19.2 inches, the I beams were installed every 12 inches for maximum floor stiffness.

57

Rafters and joists should be laid out directly over the wall studs whenever possible. This method of stacked framing helps to reduce settling by transferring the load of the house straight down.

Rafters and joists form the ceilings and floors in a house and rest across the top plates on the walls below. Some carpenters don't align these horizontal pieces with the vertical wall studs. This Old House master carpenter Norm Abram, however, recommends a framing practice called stacking (shown above). In stacked framing, the rafter and joist layout coincides with studs of the wall below, and the studs on different floors line up with each other. The idea is to transfer the load of the house straight down, to reduce settling and any cracks it might cause in the walls. Stacking also simplifies the task of running plumbing and ductwork between floors, since there is less need to cut through the framing to make connections. Depending on the house design, it may be impossible to stack all the framing, but whenever framing can be stacked, it should be.

species and quality Douglas fir is the best framing lumber. Insist on it unless it simply isn't available in your region. Within all species, there is a wide range of grades. Most building departments require "standard" or "better" for structural framing. Higher grades cost more and are not necessarily available at all lumberyards, but it is worth the premium to buy framing lumber that is straight, kiln-dried, and free of excessive knots.

Mudsills or any framing in contact with foundation concrete should be pressure-treated with preservative for rot and insect resistance. Cut ends should be soaked with preservative before installation.

Engineered lumber such as wood I beams and laminated beams can span longer distances with fewer support posts, producing not only a stronger frame but also more open interior spaces.

wall framing Walls framed with 2 by 6s are sturdier, reduce sound better, and accommodate more insulation than walls framed with 2 by 4s. Their increased interior room is especially important if they are to contain drain or vent pipes or heating ducts. In some regions, 2-by-6 exterior wall framing is required by building codes to meet insulation requirements. Where these considerations are not of concern, 2-by-4 framing will suffice and is less costly.

The key to wall framing is that it provide a flat, plumb surface so that when drywall or plaster is applied to it, the wall will be flat and true. Crooked walls are a sure sign of shoddy framing. When a new wall snakes or bows from one end to the other or is out of plumb, installing doors, windows, trim, cabinets, and countertops becomes an unnecessary ordeal. The trick is to make sure the framing is plumb and straight after it is upright but before the joists or

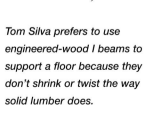

Tom Silva prefers to use engineered-wood I beams to support a floor because they don't shrink or twist the way solid lumber does.

rafters are nailed to the top plates—something all framers should do. Keeping the bottom plate straight requires merely nailing it down along a chalk line snapped onto the subfloor. For the top of the wall, most framers nail two pieces of scrap 2-by lumber to the two corners and then stretch a mason's line between these blocks. Sliding a test block along the gap between the string and the top plates to make sure the top plate is equidistant from the string will reveal any places where the wall isn't straight (see photo at right).

Norm Abram's favorite method for adjusting a wall so it's straight and plumb is to make a springboard.

For a typical 8-foot-high wall, he temporarily nails the ends of a 12-foot-long 1-by-8 springboard to the subfloor and the wall's top plate. Then he nails one end of a 4-foot-long 1-by-8 brace to the subfloor at a joist and props it against the underside of the springboard at a 45-degree angle. As Abram holds a level on the wall, a helper slides the top of the brace up or down along the springboard to move the top of the wall in or out with precision. When the wall is plumb and straight, he drives nails through the springboard and into the end of the brace to hold it in place.

Walls must be not only braced in a plumb position but strung to be sure they are straight.

FRAMING FOR HIGH WINDS AND EARTHQUAKES

In certain parts of the country, it's not enough to have a solid addition; you need an addition that can withstand the rumble of a mighty earthquake or the winds from a tornado or hurricane. "For this, you need more than just nails and extra-sturdy joists," Silva says.

Under normal circumstances, a building is affected primarily by gravity, a constant, stable, and predictable force that pulls in only one direction—downward. But during earthquakes, as well as in the hurricanes, tornadoes, or floods that afflict certain regions, houses are

exposed to forces moving parallel to the ground. "A building not securely attached to its foundation can hop or slide off its base," Silva says. Building codes implemented in some of these areas require stronger foundations, sturdier framing

connections, and better house-to-foundation anchoring than were required in the past to guard against disaster. The key in resisting both wind and earthquakes is to attach each part of the frame to the next with metal connectors from foundation to roof; and to make sure walls are braced well against lateral movement. Discuss any special framing requirements for your region with your contractor ahead of time.

A structural engineer who specializes in seismic resistance designated every hold-down and brace for this earthquake-resistant framing.

floor framing Unlike a floor set directly on a concrete slab, a raised wood-frame floor is resilient underfoot and allows room for insulation, heating ductwork, plumbing, and other system equipment.

Floor and ceiling joists from 2 by 8s, 2 by 10s, or larger members placed on 16- or 24-inch centers generally span foundation floors, beams, and walls. Flooring and ceiling materials are fastened to them. Plywood subflooring, nailed on top of the joists, provides a flat, solid base for finish flooring. (In older homes, subflooring may consist of 1-by-6 or 1-by-8 boards nailed diagonally across the joists.) The undersides of the floor joists for upper stories serve as backing for ceilings.

The sizes of joists and beams required are governed by the length of their spans and the loads placed on them. Central bearing walls often shoulder the loads midway, essentially dividing spans. Ceiling joists that don't carry live loads, such as those directly beneath an attic that isn't used as a living space, are of smaller-dimension lumber than the joists that also support a floor.

Joists are doubled up around stairways or other openings in the floor. Bridging between joists prevents them from twisting; solid blocking does the same, plus it provides backing for nailing subflooring and helps evenly distribute loads.

Floors that creak and groan may give old houses a certain charm, but they're certainly not what you want in new construction. Nails alone cannot create a squeak-proof floor. For better construction, Tom Silva uses a caulking gun to apply construction adhesive along the top edges of floor joists. He then moves each sheet of ¾-inch tongue-and-groove plywood subflooring into position, one at a time, and applies a thin bead of adhesive along the tongue edge. He centers the end joints over joists, never allowing two adjacent joints to line up. Then, using a nail gun, he nails the plywood to the joists every 6 to 8 inches. It's important to work quickly so that each sheet is placed before the adhesive skins over. "Nail guns are only as good as the person driving them," Silva says. "The nails should hit the centers of the supports and not be driven too deep. A nail's head should stop at the surface of the sheathing or just a hair below."

insulation and weatherproofing

No matter how well sealed a conventionally framed wall is, it needs to be insulated to become an effective barrier against outside air temperature fluctuations and humidity. "You need insulation whether you live in the hot South, where you air-condition in the summer, or in the cold North, where you can't get by without heating," says This Old House plumbing and heating expert Richard Trethewey. "Good insulation is an art, but the payoff is a home that will be far more comfortable to live in."

Insulation restricts the exchange of air between the inside and the outside. Any one of an assortment of insulating materials (see page 62) can be used—fiberglass being the most common—but all work the same way. "The important thing is to make sure that every part of a wall is insulated," Silva says. "Any gaps or holes are like holes to the outdoors. It's not enough for walls and ceilings to be almost completely insulated; they need to be completely insulated."

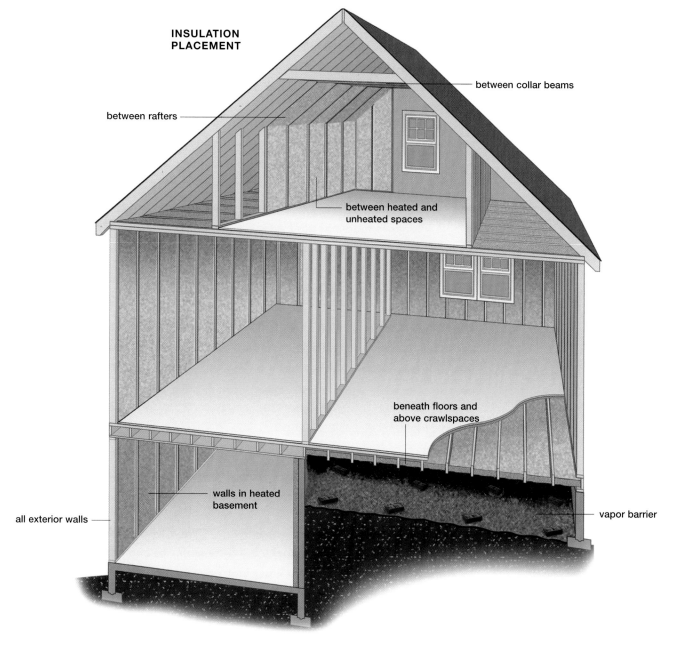

INSULATION PLACEMENT

between collar beams

between rafters

between heated and unheated spaces

beneath floors and above crawlspaces

walls in heated basement

all exterior walls

vapor barrier

TYPES OF INSULATION

FIBERGLASS BATT

FIBERGLASS WITH MIRAFLEX®

POLYURETHANE FOAM

POLYICYNENE FOAM

EXPANDED POLYSTYRENE
FOAM BOARD

CELLULOSE

Insulation comes in a number of materials, some of which are available only through contractors. The right one to choose depends on a number of variables, including access to the cavities or surfaces being insulated, required R-value (see page 63), cost, the need for an integral vapor barrier, and more. Tom Silva is a fan of liquid (spray-in) foam insulations because "they take the sloppiness out of the installation." It's critical for insulation to fit tightly and completely. "Is it going to cost you more? Absolutely. But you either pay now or you pay forever," Silva says.

fiberglass batts (and blankets) The least expensive type of insulation, fiberglass batts don't settle or disintegrate with age. Though they cause itching upon contact with skin, they are still the most popular choice among contractors because they are easy to install—but they must be installed correctly to be effective. They produce an R-value between 2.9 and 3.8 per inch. Batts that utilize Miraflex® fibers are virtually itch-free.

spray-in foam Spray-in foams such as polyurethane and polyicynene fill up every nook and cranny of a surface, so they insulate completely. Because they are all but impermeable to moisture and air movement, they eliminate the need for housewrap or an additional vapor barrier. They are two to three times as expensive as fiberglass batts but have a higher R-value per inch of thickness—from 3.6 to as high as 6.2. Because polyurethane is sprayed in with an agent that can damage the ozone layer, consider polyicynene foam instead. It's sprayed in with an environmentally friendly water-based blowing agent.

foam board Several types of foam-board insulation products are available. Expanded polystyrene, typically used for basement masonry walls and floors, offers an R-value between 3.9 and 4.2 per inch. Extruded polystyrene is applied over exterior walls under construction, insulating the studs as well as the cavities. It offers an R-value of about 5.0 per inch. Polyisocyanurate ("polyiso") and polyurethane foam boards are applied to exterior walls when you are adding siding, so they also insulate the entire wall; they provide a higher R-value, between 5.6 and 7.0 per inch. The need for a vapor barrier depends upon the "perm rating" of the specific material; polyiso is generally used with an aluminum foil facer.

wet-spray cellulose This type of insulation is made mostly of recycled paper treated with a fire retardant to make it inflammable, and boric acid to kill insects. Its R-value is between 2.9 and 3.4 per inch when installed properly. It is relatively inexpensive, but must thoroughly fill cavities (it has a tendency to settle).

understanding R-value The insulating value of a wall is measured by its R-value. The higher the R-value, the better the wall's insulation. Minimum required R-values are governed by local building codes.

Mild-climate areas usually call for R-11 in the exterior walls and under floors above unheated crawl spaces, and R-19 in the ceilings below ventilated attics. Cold-climate houses demand much higher R-values, such as R-19 in exterior walls and floors and R-38 or more in ceilings below attics.

The particular type of insulation and its thickness determine the R-value it delivers when properly installed. The value should be listed clearly on the product or packaging.

Installation can dramatically affect the insulation's performance. Insulation relies on tiny air cells to retard air movement, so it should not be tightly packed or its insulating value will decrease. "If you see workers squeezing it in place, then you know that it is not being installed well," Silva says. And it's critical that the insulation remain dry before installation; otherwise it won't perform well and can encourage the growth of mold and decay inside the structure.

foam and vapor barriers A good insulation job also involves sealing gaps around windows and door frames, usually with an expanding spray foam. Most insulation must also be accompanied by a water-impermeable vapor barrier that keeps moisture from condensing inside walls and ceilings (foam types generally do not require this).

"The vapor barrier always goes towards the warm side," Silva says, which usually means it goes on the inside of walls and ceilings. (In hot climates, the reverse is true.) Similarly, under an insulated first floor, the insulation's vapor barrier faces up toward the underside of the floor (see illustration, page 61). In a crawl space a vapor barrier of plastic sheeting should be spread over the ground so moisture has less chance of entering the insulation. A foam insulation that doesn't require an additional vapor barrier, such as polyurethane or polyicynene, is a good choice for insulating above a crawl space.

housewrap

In new construction, exterior wall studs are usually covered with plywood sheathing. Then, depending upon the construction method and the type of siding that will be used, the plywood is covered with either builder's felt, rosin paper, or housewrap (a spun-olefin barrier that provides an extra layer of protection against water and air infiltration). Tom Silva prefers to use a layer of 15-pound builder's felt or rosin paper in combination with spray-foam insulation, which completely repels water and air infiltration.

Where other types of insulation are used, housewrap is a good option as long as it's installed correctly. Housewrap seams should be taped after sheets from the rolls are stapled to the walls. In addition, the perforations around doors and windows need extra attention to protect against water. Silva staples strips of waterproofing membrane or builder's felt around window and door openings.

The key, Silva says, is not to count on the material to make up for sloppy building techniques. "I never stopped doing any of the other things I've always done to keep water out," he says. "It's the guys who skip these and count on the housewrap to do everything who go wrong."

Where wind-driven rain is a problem, Silva also seals the top of the flashing above each window and door with a self-sticking asphalt membrane. This serves as a backup in case the metal flashing fails to repel the water.

Tom Silva adds strips of waterproofing membrane or builder's felt wherever extra protection from rain is needed.

plumbing

The term "plumbing" encompasses water supply, gas supply, and drain-waste-vent (DWV) systems. Here's a closer look at each one.

water supply system

The water supply system carries water from an underground water main (or a storage tank or well) to the house and distributes it to sinks, showers, toilets, the washing machine, dishwasher, and other water-using fixtures and appliances.

As a rule, the supply line that runs from the water meter at the street to the house is a 1-inch-diameter pipe. In older homes, the main supply may be ¾-inch, which may not be large enough to serve additional bathrooms or a heavy water user such as a spa shower. If this is the case and you intend to make these types of improvements, you'll need to have the main supply pipe upgraded.

Once the main enters the house, it branches out to smaller pipes that deliver cold water to the fixtures and water-using appliances. One branch goes to the water heater and, from there, delivers hot water to the faucets and appliances that require it. The primary hot- and cold-water pipes routed through the house are usually ¾ inch in diameter (inside), particularly if there is more than one

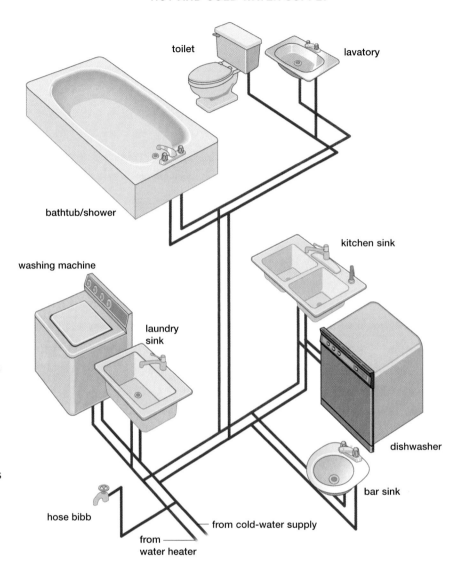

bathroom. Smaller branches that feed individual fixtures are generally ½-inch pipe unless a fixture requires a heavy flow.

Galvanized steel, copper, and plastic are used for supply piping. Local codes and the age of your house will indicate the kinds of pipe and fittings you're likely to find and will determine what you are allowed to use when remodeling. For hot- and cold-water supply lines, copper pipe is preferred.

A good water supply and drain system is all about materials and execution. Shortfalls in either area may lead to a failure to pass inspection, and if problems are not caught, you could be left with an unreliable, noisy system.

There are ways to prevent this. Hot-water lines should be insulated along their entire length to minimize heat loss. Insulating cold-water pipes is also a good idea because insulation helps eliminate condensation and

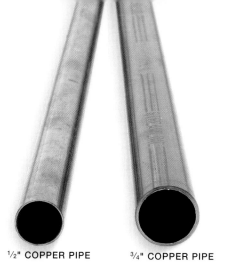

½" COPPER PIPE   ¾" COPPER PIPE

½" PLASTIC PIPE   ¾" BLACK PIPE
(FOR GAS)

ticking noises caused by the pipe's expansion and contraction. When pipes pass through framing, holes should be drilled large enough for bushings (or grommets) that allow the pipes to expand and contract.

gas piping

Gas pipe can look very similar to water pipe; it is typically black steel with threaded fittings. The best way to identify a gas pipe is to locate its points of origin and termination. Gas pipe runs from the gas meter (or a branch of the main gas pipe) to gas appliances and/or the heating system. Each gas pipe should have its own shutoff valve near each appliance it serves in case of emergencies, but this isn't always the case.

Because the natural gas that runs through a gas pipe is under pressure and its fumes are toxic and highly combustible, working on gas pipes and fittings is best left in the hands of a plumber. Never work on gas pipe without turning off the control valve.

Richard Trethewey decides how high to place the shower fitting while the walls are still open.

drain-waste-vent (DWV) system

Unlike the supply system, which brings in water under pressure, the drain-waste portion of the DWV system gets rid of water and waste via gravity. The vent system emits sewer gases. At 1½ to 4 inches in diameter, the pipes for this system are much larger than conventional supply pipes, and they are not under pressure (unless clogged). They may be made of copper, steel, cast iron, or plastic (as shown on page 65 and above).

For drain lines, many plumbers use PVC plastic, which is strong and reliable but noisier than the traditional cast iron. Because it's quieter, cast iron is the best material for pipes that run through the walls or ceiling around a living space.

Each plumbing fixture has a trap—a bend of pipe that remains filled with water at all times to keep toxic sewer gases from rising up and through the drain. Each fixture is connected to the vent system by a pipe that allows toxic sewer gases to exit through the roof. This also maintains atmospheric pressure so water doesn't siphon out of the traps.

The main pipe in the DWV system is the soil stack, which is a large vertical pipe that carries waste from toilets (and often other fixtures) down to the main house sewer drainpipe in the basement or crawl space. The vent portion of this pipe (the part above where the fixtures drain) usually goes up and out the roof. The main stack is typically 4 inches in diameter.

If large-diameter drain lines pass through floor joists to get where they're going, the holes cut for them should be centered in the width of each joist and the joist may have to be reinforced to avoid weakening the structure. Building codes dictate the allowable size and location of penetrations.

Because creating a new main soil stack is a big job, you can save money when remodeling by planning for fixtures to be placed within a few feet of the existing stack. Local codes also specify the horizontal distances vents are allowed to run from the fixtures to the stack.

"The paradox of plumbing is that no one notices it unless it isn't done right," Trethewey says. "It shouldn't be seen, and it shouldn't be noisy."

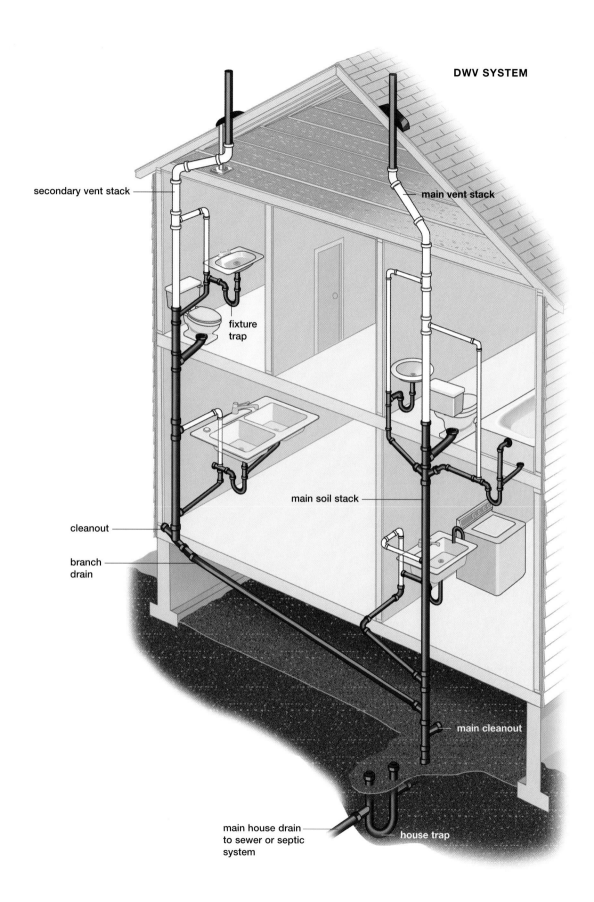

DWV SYSTEM

secondary vent stack

main vent stack

fixture
trap

main soil stack

cleanout

branch
drain

main cleanout

main house drain
to sewer or septic
system

house trap

electrical

Electrical work is nearly always involved in a remodel. Houses built before the past decade rarely have electrical systems that can meet the needs of the 21st-century household. Oversized refrigerators, microwave ovens, whirlpool baths, computer and entertainment systems—there is a veritable army of power-hungry appliances now on active duty.

Because new wiring has to meet current electrical codes, a remodel presents the perfect time to update all of a home's wiring to meet those standards.

electrical service

The power company delivers electricity through two or three wires to the main electrical service panel, where

SERVICE PANEL

- conduit from meter base
- hot service entrance conductors
- neutral service panel conductor
- 240-volt circuit
- 120/ 240-volt circuit
- 120-volt circuit
- main disconnect
- circuit breakers
- hot bus bars
- neutral bus bar
- continuous grounding electrode
- ground rod
- ground clamp

Note: Touching a service panel with the inside cover removed, as shown, poses a serious danger of shock or electrocution.

the meter is. Three-wire service provides both 120- and 240-volt capacities. Two-wire service allows only 120-volt power, which is substandard anywhere.

The control center for an electrical system is the service panel (left), sometimes referred to as the fuse box or main panel. This metal cabinet, often gray, usually houses the main disconnect (fuses or circuit breaker) that shuts off power to the entire house, although the main disconnect is sometimes located in a separate box. It may also contain the fuses or circuit breakers that protect the individual circuits that run throughout

the house to deliver electricity to receptacles, lights, appliances, and other power users. In some cases, a large circuit runs to a subpanel that feeds an individual appliance, such as an air conditioner, or a series of regular circuits.

The size of the main panel governs the number of electrical circuits that are available and their total capacity (amperage). A house with 60- or even 100-amp service is likely to need more power; in most cases, it should be upgraded to 200-amp service. Upgrading when your walls are opened up is far less expensive and disruptive than waiting until later.

circuits

Current codes require separate circuits for outlets, lights, and appliances. All circuits must be properly grounded, and circuits that serve bathrooms, kitchens, garages, and other potentially wet areas must be protected by ground-fault circuit interrupters (GFCIs).

Because incorrect or sloppy wiring can result in fire or electrocution, hire an experienced electrical contractor to plan and install wiring. Then make sure the work is inspected by your town's building department, who will make sure all code

requirements are met. You will want to spend time with your electrician on a wiring plan that works for your house. You don't, for instance, want to walk through a dark room to get to a light switch.

Here are a few recommendations:

■ Remember that, for maximum convenience, lighting can often be controlled from more than one location. A 3-way switch controls a light from two places; a 4-way switch can do the same from three or more locations.

■ Don't forget to ask for closet lights; they can be controlled by a switch that goes on when the door is opened and off when it's closed.

■ Take the opportunity while remodeling to convert all pull-chain controls to wall switches, which can more conveniently and precisely regulate ceiling fans and light levels.

■ Be sure that all wiring passages through framing are protected from nails and sealed with fireproof caulk, as required by code.

Circuit breakers protect wires from overheating by preventing them from drawing too much current.

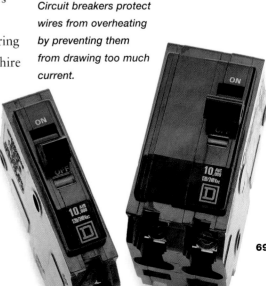

hvac

The systems that make a house comfortable—notably heating, ventilation, and air conditioning—are grouped under the acronym HVAC. Properly planning these systems is an essential part of any remodel.

forced-air heating

More than 70 percent of America's homes are heated by forced-air heating. With this type of system, room air is pulled into a furnace through large return-air ducts. The furnace warms the air and then sends it back to rooms throughout the house through a different set of ducts and registers.

Most forced-air furnaces burn natural gas, though some use oil, propane, electricity, and even coal or wood. Forced-air heating systems are popular, but if poorly designed or installed they can be noisy and inefficient.

One benefit of a forced-air system is that a humidifier and/or an ultra-fine air filter can be added easily. And the furnace's air-handling and duct system can double up to deliver central air conditioning.

When you are remodeling, relocating or adding ducts and heating registers to an existing system can be tricky. The installation is usually relatively simple, but the changes can affect airflow rates and thus the heat output from a given register.

An HVAC pro can determine the proper duct size and number of registers a room addition will need based on the room's volume, insulation levels, window sizes, and other factors. For a large addition, he or she can also determine whether the existing heating system can handle the increased heating load or whether a larger furnace will be needed.

Once walls, floors, and ceilings are opened up, seams and joints in all ductwork—old and new—should be totally sealed to prevent energy loss through leaks (up to 25 percent of heated or cooled air can be lost through improperly sealed joints). All air ducts should be insulated.

tip: dust When dusty interior work is under way, seal any return registers (which send air back to the furnace) in nearby areas. If weather or circumstances permit, shut down the system entirely to keep any dust from being blown through it.

A TYPICAL FORCED WARM-AIR SYSTEM

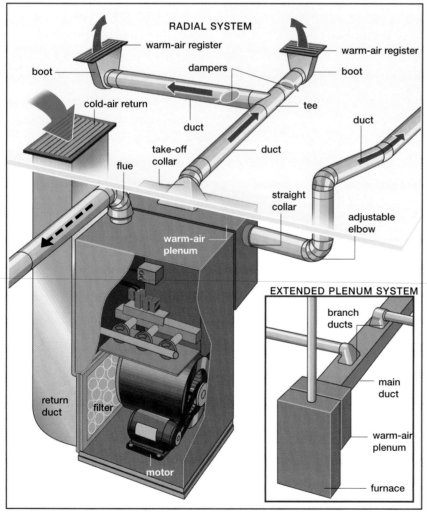

RADIAL SYSTEM

warm-air register · boot · dampers · warm-air register · boot · cold-air return · tee · duct · duct · take-off collar · duct · flue · straight collar · adjustable elbow · warm-air plenum · return duct · filter · motor

EXTENDED PLENUM SYSTEM

branch ducts · main duct · warm-air plenum · furnace

central air conditioning

If a house has forced-air heating with insulated ductwork, it can be relatively easy to add central air conditioning during a remodel. The installation requires putting an outdoor unit, called a condenser (right), near the house, placing an indoor unit, called an evaporator, on top of the furnace, and connecting the two with refrigerant-filled copper tubing.

hot-water and steam heating

Some houses, particularly older homes and many in the greater Northeast, are heated by hot water or steam. These systems employ a boiler to heat water. With a hot-water (hydronic) system, this heated water circulates through pipes or tubes to radiators, baseboard registers, or circuits of tubing or pipes under the floor that radiate heat into the rooms. You also can obtain sleek, flat, panel-style radiators that can be custom sized to meet both heating and space require-

ments and custom colored to work with a particular decorating scheme. With a steam system, the boiler heats the water until it becomes steam, which rises through pipes into radiators that then get hot and radiate heat into the room.

"Hot-water heat is the most comfortable heat for cold-weather climates," Trethewey says. "There is little air movement and no noise." Hydronic-heating pipes can be shifted, extended, or added to accommodate modest floor-plan changes. If floor space is increased significantly, a heating engineer should determine whether or not the existing boiler can handle the additional load and what the maximum length of each plumbing run should be. If a larger boiler is required, it pays to buy a high-efficiency unit with computer-chip controls that get the most out of every bit of fuel.

Placement of outdoor condenser units always involves a job site discussion. "You need to keep condensers free of obstructions, preferably on the north side of the building, and within 50 to 75 feet of the air handler," Trethewey says.

Because steam systems are noisy and irregular in their delivery of heat, they are no longer installed in homes. If your home has a steam system that you want to extend, be sure the boiler can handle the additional load. You may also decide to match your cast-iron radiators, which can be quite elegant.

BEWARE OF BACKDRAFTING

Many remodeling projects that involve extensive changes to the house can benefit from energy-efficiency upgrades such as installing thicker insulation, putting in better windows, and closing off air leaks in exterior walls. Though all are worthy improvements, they can negatively affect the operation of furnaces, boilers, and water heaters that get their combustion air from inside the house. A tight house can starve a burner for air. When another burner comes on, such as the one in a

water heater, furnace exhaust air can actually be drawn from the chimney back into the house. This dangerous condition, called backdrafting, can fill your house with carbon monoxide and other toxic combustion byproducts. Fortunately, the solution is simple and is being required by more communities: Feed outside air to the burners through exterior wall vents or ducts. A good HVAC contractor will make sure this is accomplished.

heat pumps

Heat pumps can both warm and cool a house using components similar to those for an air conditioner. During warm weather, a heat pump operates just like an air conditioner. But in cold weather, it runs in reverse to extract heat energy from outside air (or underground water). Most heat pumps are electric, a plus where gas and oil are not available.

Heat pumps are most effective in moderate climates, where winter temperatures don't regularly dip below freezing. When a heat pump can't extract enough heat from outdoors, it automatically shifts over to an internal electric heating coil. Using this as a heat source can be expensive.

radiant-heat floor systems

This type of heating system continues to grow in popularity. It consists of runs of tubing looped back and forth under the surface of the floor. As hot water courses through the tubing, heat is released and the entire floor becomes a low-temperature radiator.

Though radiant-heat floor systems have been used for many years, early types were expensive and unreliable. With today's systems, however, reliability has been greatly increased through the use of a special plastic tubing called PEX (a type of polyethylene) that doesn't corrode or become brittle.

Radiant floors cost more than other types of hot-water heat, but many homeowners say the "feet first" approach to warming a room is the only way to go. The TOH crew believes that adding radiant-floor heating to a bathroom in particular is a great investment, though experienced installers can be hard to find.

Still, this type of system isn't right for all situations. Radiant tubing is most appropriate for new slab floors that incorporate a layer of insulation to keep heat from uselessly migrating into the ground. The tubing is most effective when it's in contact with a thermal mass like concrete or an aluminum transfer plate placed beneath the finish flooring. It's least effective under a floor with a thick carpet because the carpeting slows heat transfer.

Today's radiant-heat floor systems are much more reliable because of plastic tubing called PEX, which doesn't corrode or become brittle.

New ductwork for a hydroair system is easily placed while the walls are open.

hydroair system

With a hydroair system, hot water is pumped to air handlers (water-to-air heat exchangers) in different parts of the house. A blower forces air across the heat exchanger, and the resulting warm air is distributed to rooms through standard ductwork. Experts say this system is especially appropriate for larger houses because it makes the long-distance distribution of heat more efficient. Because of the circulating hot water used to heat the air, it's also an excellent way to bring a little bit of radiant heat to a room such as a bathroom or kitchen.

ventilation

As discussed in both the Bathrooms and Kitchens chapters (see pages 150–151 and 200–201), proper ventilation is crucial in a house, especially in rooms where high levels of humidity are generated. Where ventilation is substandard, humid air can condense inside walls, where it can cause decay, mold, and related problems.

Proper ventilation will also rid the house of unwanted odors and vapors from cooking smells, cleansers, and household chemicals.

Tightly insulated houses don't "breathe" as well as older homes with leaky walls. While this is good for energy conservation, it isn't so good for ventilation. The air in a house should be replaced with outdoor air regularly. The Home Ventilating Institute offers guidelines at its website, *www.hvi.org.*

attic ventilation When fresh air circulates through an attic, unwanted moisture-filled air is efficiently carried away. Soffit vents along the eaves, coupled with a ridge vent, will adequately ventilate most attics. Turbine roof vents and attic fans can increase circulation. Be sure insulation does not block any vents.

foundation vents The unheated crawl space beneath a house that stands on a perimeter foundation also needs ventilation. Foundation vents prevent ground moisture from accumulating beneath the house and being drawn up into the living spaces.

room fans A variety of fan types and models are available (see pages 179–180 and 200–201). All should be vented to the outdoors. The quietest types have the fan motor mounted in the attic or near where the ductwork terminates. Choose rigid, insulated ductwork, and be sure there is a damper that prevents cold air from entering from outdoors.

HOUSE VENTS

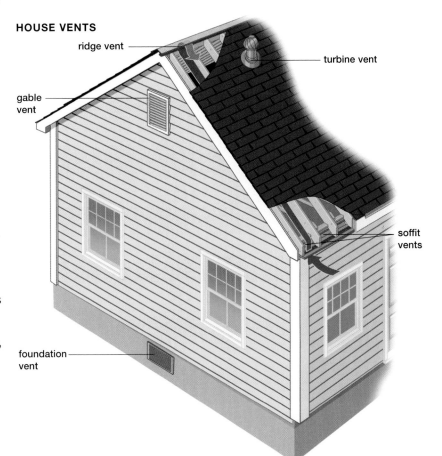

ridge vent

turbine vent

gable vent

soffit vents

foundation vent

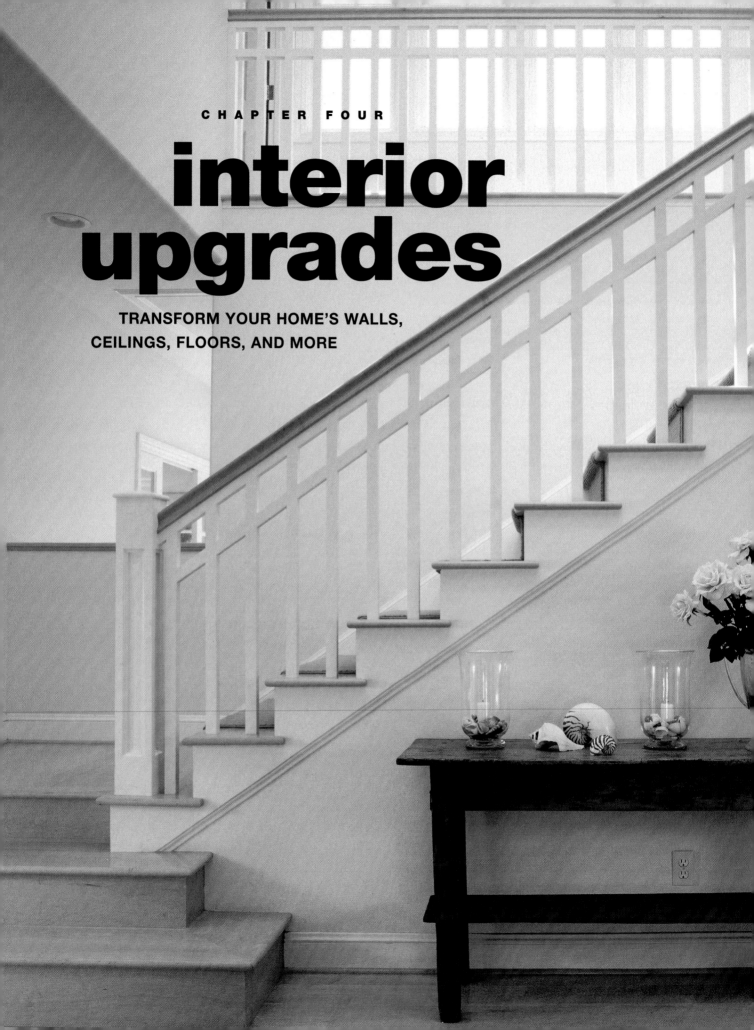

CHAPTER FOUR

interior
upgrades

**TRANSFORM YOUR HOME'S WALLS,
CEILINGS, FLOORS, AND MORE**

AS THE PREVIOUS CHAPTER DISCUSSES, A HOUSE'S INVISIBLE systems are vital. But the parts that you live with the most are interior surfaces such as walls, floors, ceilings, and doors. When these elements are at their best, your home feels beautiful, comfortable, and sound, making interior surfaces critical to a successful remodel.

This chapter walks you through the processes of making choices and overseeing high-quality workmanship. It tells you how to choose between drywall and plaster, paint and wallpaper, hardwood and vinyl, and more. Within each of these areas, This Old House general contractor Tom Silva and the rest of the crew provide a look at each element, offering insight and installation recommendations gleaned from their experience over the years.

One piece of advice Silva cannot stress enough is to take care of the fundamentals—electrical, plumbing, heating, and especially structural work—before making any surface changes or improvements. Often, problems that lead to the deterioration or failure of finish materials are hidden in the walls or under the floor. Addressing these first will save you headaches—and dollars— in the years to come.

walls and ceilings

If you plan to alter walls and ceilings, you should first know how they were constructed. In the mid-1900s, changes in the way homes were built were so fundamental that to this day people still refer to prewar and postwar construction. Prewar houses were built when labor and natural resources were unlimited, with framing lumber cut to full measure and walls made of plaster applied over wood, metal, or gypsum lath. Postwar homes, on the other hand, were constructed with surfaced lumber planed slightly smaller, and prefabricated, lighter-weight materials and sheet goods, such as plywood and drywall, to speed construction.

Plaster and drywall surfaces each have their advantages and drawbacks. Drywall is far more common than plaster these days because it requires less skilled labor and time to install, making it much less costly. Plaster, however, can't be beat for its good looks and solid feel.

drywall

A chalklike core of gypsum plaster bonded between two sheets of paper, drywall is the most common interior wall material today. Though it doesn't offer the solidity of plaster or have the same finished surface, drywall is easy to work with and comes in a

Graceful curves can be achieved with flexible ¼-inch drywall.

variety of types to suit different interior situations. Drywall contractors typically charge from $1.50 to $2.50 per square foot for installation and finishing (but not painting) of standard drywall. For a small job or special finish, you'll pay a 25 to 30 percent premium.

Standard drywall, ½ inch thick and light gray in color, is suitable for most walls and ceilings framed on 16-inch centers. More flexible ¼-inch panels are available for wrapping curved surfaces, and ⅜-inch-thick sheets are useful for resurfacing existing drywall or plaster that's too flawed to repair. Building codes usually require ⅝-inch fire-resistant drywall, identified as Type-X, in places such as walls between a house and an attached garage. Type-X is also more resistant to abuse. Type-MR (for moisture resistant), commonly known as green board, is used in damp, humid locations such as bathrooms and laundry rooms.

Most drywall sheets are 4 feet wide by either 8 or 12 feet long. Wider and larger sheets are also available. Professional installers like the bigger sheets because they make the work go faster and reduce the number of joints to finish. However, a 4-by-12-foot sheet requires two fairly strong people for installation

---

tip: hiring a drywall contractor If you hire a drywall contractor directly, ask for references from a general contractor or your neighbors. If possible, visit previous jobs to inspect the work. The walls should be smooth, without wavy spots or bumps over seams and screws. Your contract should specify that the final payment will be made after the walls have been painted with the prime coat, when defects are easiest to spot.

SAVING CLASSIC PLASTER

Any homeowner facing extensive plaster repairs first needs to do a reality check: Is the home's value worth the relatively high cost required to do this work? Drywalling over old plaster is less expensive, and even the next-best alternative—veneer plastering over new blue board—can be more cost-effective than complete restoration.

Of course, there are older and even historic homes with original plasterwork that deserve saving. "Once you've removed part of the building's original fabric," says Rory Brennan, a TOH historic plaster consultant, "it's gone forever." In cases like this, Brennan has a technique that can help. He drills multiple small holes through the plaster surface, into which he injects an adhesive that rebonds and reinforces the crumbling plaster. He also drives screws to tighten the plaster against the lath until the adhesive dries. Later, he removes the screws and patches the holes.

is secure, he trowels joint compound into the cracks, adding fiberglass joint tape to cover the gaps or, for wider cracks, fiberglass window screening. "The mesh creates a bridge over the crack, to bond to the stable plaster around it and reinforce the mud that repairs it," Silva says. Then, as with drywall finishing, more layers of compound are applied and each one is allowed to dry before being sanded smooth.

Crumbling, badly deteriorated plaster that's beyond a quick fix

After covering seams with fiberglass tape, Silva applies a skim coat of joint compound. Each of three coats of compound is applied, allowed to dry, and then sanded before the surface is ready for paint.

usually requires replacement. Silva removes the loose material as far back as necessary, until he reaches firm, well-anchored plaster. He then fills in the exposed area with blue board, which he screws to the lath and framing, if possible. Finally, he mists the rough plaster edges and applies a plaster veneer coat.

Master plasterers trowel on a thin coat of veneer plaster over blue board in this master bedroom. Just one coat of this material hides all screw heads and seams between panels.

veneer plaster

The TOH crew likes to use veneer plaster because it combines the best of modern materials with traditional craftsmanship, producing surfaces that look and feel like built-up plaster walls and ceilings. "It's a harder surface than drywall," Silva says, "and actually adds some rigidity to the wall."

This method, also called skim coating, is easier and requires far less work than built-up plaster. The process delays a project's progress less than drywalling—a room can usually be done in a day, as opposed to several days—and "there's no sanding,"

Silva notes, "which can be the messiest job in the world." Because of the skill required, however, veneer plastering costs from $3 to $5 per square foot, and finding someone to apply it can be difficult. This is a fairly new technique, and relatively few practitioners have taken up the trade.

It may take persistent inquiry to find a well-qualified veneer plasterer. In addition to checking the telephone listings, you can inquire at your local building department. The plasterer you hire may install the blue board or recommend a drywall subcontractor to do this part of the job. Be sure to ask about finish options, especially for ceilings. Plaster can be finished smoothly, or in several textures ranging from spattered to rough and stuccolike. A textured finish often

PIGMENTED PLASTER

Though plastering is no longer a mainstream construction method, decorative plaster is gaining in popularity. It still requires a skilled tradesperson—often a decorative painter—who has mastered an artistic technique that infuses pigments and other materials into plaster to create one-of-a-kind finishes. Depending on the skill of the artist and the type of finish desired, the result is a glassy, lustrous surface that can mimic polished stone or suede. This treatment can run about $8 per square foot, but remember you're getting an all-in-one finish.

costs you less than a cue-ball-smooth surface because there's less work involved.

Veneer plastering begins just like drywalling. The ceiling and walls are first covered with ½-inch-thick blueboard panels (an improved type of drywall developed in recent years that has a textured paper surface). Then wafer-thin skim coats of plaster are applied. Imperfections can be touched up before the plaster dries. "The beauty of the process is that it's clean, fast, and effective," Silva says. "When it's done just right, the final look is fantastic."

As beautiful as it can be, veneer plaster has some disadvantages, such as a hard, almost ceramic surface that reflects rather than absorbs sound.

When finished, the same bedroom (shown in progress on the opposite page) boasts smooth, rich walls.

"The acoustics of drywall are more pleasing," Silva says. In one TOH project, veneer plaster was used in every room except the media room, where the stereo and television were. There, standard drywall was used to minimize reverberation.

interior painting

Painting interior walls and trim is one of the easiest improvement projects a homeowner can undertake. But getting the job done right involves knowing the tricks and techniques of the trade. Which types of paint to choose, how to match colors, what goes into preparing surfaces correctly, and how the paint should be applied are all crucial to ensuring a good job.

Choosing colors is the first decision; give yourself plenty of time. It may take some trial and error and several trips to the paint store before you're satisfied. Consider how your chosen color will work with furniture, carpeting, and artwork, and what effect it will have on the finished room. Do you want to visually enlarge a small space with light tones or make an expansive space feel cozier with darker hues? Put some color chips on the walls or, better yet, buy quarts of the paints you are considering and brush on a sample of each (some paint stores offer sample vials with brush or sponge applicators, but only for premixed colors). See how they look at different times of the day, in natural light and under room lighting. And don't forget that you'll have to decide on a surface finish, or sheen, which makes a difference in the way the paint reflects or absorbs light, as well as in its durability and washability.

Whatever colors and types of paint you choose, invest in top quality, Tom Silva says. "Buy the best you can get. The extra expense is insignificant if it saves you from an early repainting job." A high-quality gallon of paint will cost between $20 and $30.

Picking just the right color for every room in your home is a challenge, but the results of careful planning can be breathtaking.

matching existing colors Paint dealers can custom blend just about any color you can imagine, or match any existing color through manufacturer codes (if you saved the color code or a can from the last paint job). Many stores can also analyze a chip of color and come up with an exact match. If you're color-matching a repair, remove a chip at least an inch or two square from a spot near the damaged area. If you want to replace the original, full-toned color, take a chip from a place where sunlight hasn't faded it, such as from inside a closet. Even when you think you have the perfect match, order a quart first and try it before having the rest custom mixed.

Painting contractors will not only do this job for you, but they will determine what type of paint is needed, what was used before, and whether remedial work such as re-priming or stain sealing is required.

priming and sealing Materials like wood and drywall that have never been painted require a coat of primer to seal their surfaces. This will ensure that subsequent topcoats adhere well and go on smoothly and evenly. Painting contractors typically cover new walls and ceilings with one coat of primer and two coats of finish paint.

A new prime coat is not always necessary over clean, well-bonded paint, but it is always required before an application of latex paint over oil or alkyd surfaces. In this case, sanding, scuffing, or applying a chemical agent to knock down any sheen on the previous layer, especially if gloss oil or alkyd paint was used, is also recommended. Special stain-killing primers should be used on surfaces with hard-to-remove grease stains or water marks from leaks, or on woodwork such as knotty pine that may bleed resins.

oil versus water For homes, there are two broad categories of paint, each having advantages and shortcomings. Oil-based paints contain resins of natural or synthetic alkyds. Water-based or latex paints are made with vinyl or acrylic resins. Both have undergone many changes in recent years as technology and environmental concerns have commanded improvements in their formulations.

Though oil paints contain volatile solvents required for thinning and cleanup, they are still recommended where a smooth, hard, glossy surface is desired, such as on interior or exterior woodwork and trim. Latex paints are typically nontoxic, low-odor, and easily cleaned up and thinned with water. Those with 100 percent acrylic resins offer the most vibrant, fade-resistant colors, even outdoors. Because they are so easy to work with, water-based paints are most popular for use on interior walls and ceilings.

choosing a sheen Ranging from dull to shiny, paint sheens are categorized as flat, eggshell, satin, semi-gloss, and gloss. The difference is not just aesthetic. Shinier, high-gloss paints are generally more durable, and most can withstand a good scrubbing. Flat paints hold dirt and are easily marred, so Tom Silva recommends using them only on ceilings. He uses semigloss paint on the moldings in his own home, and eggshell paint on the walls.

tip: before the painter paints First, walk the job to spot any problems or needed repairs. It's the painting contractor's responsibility to prepare the area thoroughly—sanding where necessary and fixing minor imperfections like nicks in drywall or plaster—before painting begins. Prep is a critical stage of any paint job and may account for more than half the time the job requires. You should agree upfront on the type and grade of paint, whether a primer is needed, and how many topcoats will be applied. Also ask how the room and its contents will be protected. A good painter will tape construction paper to floors, spread drop cloths over furnishings, drape plastic over doorways, and carefully mask areas that don't get paint.

wallpaper

The term wallpaper is actually a catchall word for a broad range of wall coverings, including many that are not made of paper. But all of them are applied in generally the same way: glued to the wall in strips or sheets.

Homeowners have been adorning their walls with printed paper coverings for centuries. Wallpaper continues to be a popular way to add color, design, texture, and personality to interiors. While wall coverings go in and out of fashion, they do offer a versatile solution for all kinds of interior-decorating challenges.

Historically accurate wallpapers are available for period restorations. Washable, water-resistant types are well suited to kitchens, baths, nurseries, and children's playrooms. Fabric-faced coverings are frequently used to add texture to otherwise featureless walls. And whimsical prints and patterns can brighten up overlooked areas of a home.

choosing materials Most wallpaper sold in the United States is actually vinyl with a paper backing. Paper wallpapers are available, but they stain easily, disintegrate when scrubbed, and are difficult to apply. Vinyl is more durable, and easier to hang and clean.

An even sturdier option is fabric-backed vinyl, which makes stripping, or removal, easier. Yet another type is expanded vinyl, which has a heavily textured surface good for covering imperfect surfaces. Most vinyl wallpapers come pasted so you don't have to mix and apply adhesive, a messy procedure.

Specialty wallpapers include metal foil and flocked paper. Foils tend to amplify even minor surface imperfections. Both types are distinctive but difficult to hang. Textile wallpapers include silk, linen, jute, burlap, and grass cloth. All require extra care during installation, as there is no way to wipe off paste that might get on the surface.

Before you hire a contractor who specializes in applying wall coverings, you should have some idea of what you want to put on your walls. Home centers, paint dealers, and decorating stores keep sample books with vast selections of types, styles, and colors. Decorating services can help steer you toward a design and color scheme that suits your needs. Be aware that wallpaper contractors will charge extra

Floral-patterned wallpaper adds Victorian charm to this bedroom.

These textured walls were created with expanded vinyl wallpaper that was painted over.

for wall coverings or patterns that are difficult to install.

When buying wall coverings, always purchase at least one roll more than the space requires so you'll have extra in case any is ruined during installation or if repairs become necessary. This is true especially for unique or hard-to-get patterns. Also check for lot and batch numbers on the rolls to be sure colors and repeating patterns match. It's a good idea to unroll and compare them at the store to see that the patterns are consistent.

The average price of conventional wallpapers ranges from 35 cents to 55 cents per square foot for materials, but prices can run to $2.75 or more per square foot for specialty coverings.

Though wallpapers are available in a bewildering variety of colors and designs, there are essentially two basic patterns. Straight patterns have repeating vertical or horizontal lines. In general, they are easier to hang and match. Drop patterns have designs that repeat at angles. They can be tricky to line up, especially in rooms with complex shapes and lots of obstacles, such as bathrooms, so they require extra paper to allow for more waste.

layout and hanging Because good adhesion is critical to any wallpaper job, careful preparation is essential. This includes ensuring that the walls are clean, smooth, and dry. Old wallpaper should be removed whenever possible. The only exception is when the paper is permanently adhered to unprimed drywall. It's almost impossible to remove wallpaper in this case without pulling off parts of the wall surface. Better to seal right over the old paper with a coat of sizing, then install the new wallpaper on top of it.

Your wallpaper contractor should spot-patch minor drywall or plaster imperfections and touch up the repairs with an oil-based primer. New drywall and plaster require a complete coat of primer. After this dries for 48 hours, an acrylic sizing is applied. Wallpaper paste can take up to six weeks to dry under vinyl papers, and the sizing protects the wall from the water in the adhesive. A coat of sizing also makes it easier to strip off the paper when the time comes to redecorate.

Another important part of a good wallpaper job is properly planning the layout to make allowances for all the room's peculiarities, including walls that are out of plumb. The key design element should be centered in the most prominent place on the wall, and all seam locations should be measured and marked so that none fall in awkward or difficult spots.

During installation, wallpaper can be allowed to overlap door and window edges and then trimmed with a razor knife.

trim, molding, and paneling

Over the past three centuries, decorative molding and other trim in American homes have ranged in style from rustic to classic to modern, from overblown to austere. Regardless of a home's décor, most architects would agree that interiors aren't finished until they're "trimmed out."

Molding and trim add both dimension and depth to interior surfaces, bridge a line or separation between materials, and/or serve as a transition between materials. Though the two terms are frequently used interchangeably, molding and trim are distinct elements.

Technically, moldings are trim pieces that have been planed or molded with distinctive ornamental profiles. Trim refers to any type of material—shapely or unadorned—used to provide visual relief or to cover gaps, edges, corners, or other imperfections between walls and floors, and walls and ceilings.

materials

Most trim today is made of wood or a material such as medium-density fiberboard (MDF) that looks and functions like wood. The most expensive wood trim is solid hardwood, which is usually reserved for matching hardwood paneling. Hardwood veneer moldings, bonded to a urethane or particleboard core, are another option. More stable and less likely to warp than solid wood, they take stains well and are virtually indistinguishable from the real thing once installed.

For a high-quality installation that doesn't call for stained trim, poplar is the top choice. It is relatively hard, stable, and inexpensive, and it machines well. It also takes paint beautifully. Pine is the most common wood trim found in lumberyards and home centers. An inexpensive, easily worked wood, it may be stained or painted. However, because much of the pine trim sold

An assortment of intricate moldings, from tall wainscoting to a plate rail used for displaying photos, gives this entry area classic style and visual interest.

today is fast-growth farmed wood, it is relatively soft and can dent easily, so it is best for low-traffic areas. If it is to be stained, look for pieces that have the most figuring and grain. Finger-jointed trim, made from many short lengths spliced together, is unsuitable for staining and can even show the joints over time when painted. Poplar, pine, and similar softwood moldings cost from 30 cents to $5 per foot, depending upon the complexity of their profile.

For trim that is to be painted, factory-primed wood and composite moldings such as MDF are available. MDF moldings cost from 35 cents to $2.50 per foot, depending upon the complexity of the profile. Tom Silva recommends these primed moldings because they eliminate much of the time and effort spent on

sanding and prepping. They also usually come primed on all faces, front and back—a necessary step many amateurs and even professionals skip. Incomplete priming can allow moisture to seep into the pieces, causing the wood to swell, shrink, and warp. Eventually, joints open and the trim can shift out of place.

PLASTER OR URETHANE?

Most molding in homes today is actually wood trim. The term "molding" was first used to describe the ornate, beautifully figured plasterwork found in homes and commercial buildings before the twentieth century. At each job, workers created molds shaped in classical patterns, filled them with wet plaster, and applied the moldings above doors and windows, where walls intersected with ceilings, or as decorative medallions around chandeliers and sconces.

If you own an older home that has plaster molding that needs repair, minor touch-ups can be made with joint compound and a small

pointed trowel or putty knife. Larger repairs may require creating a mold to match the existing trim profile and replacing sections with new plaster—a job for a specialized pro.

An alternative developed in recent years is foam-plastic urethane molding. This material is very stable, and high-quality castings easily pass for solid plaster moldings—so much so that they are often employed in the restoration of historic buildings, including the White House. Urethane moldings are lightweight and easy to apply, but they are not as hard or durable as plaster, so they are typically installed on ceilings or high on walls, out of harm's way. Urethane moldings range in price from about $4 to $16 per foot, depending upon the complexity of the profile.

Trim and molding can be used to create a wide variety of looks. Study pictures of homes built in the same era as yours to choose the style of molding that is historically appropriate.

If you wish to replace original moldings or just want a unique trim profile and know you'll need more than 100 feet or so, you may want to consider having them custom-made by a millwork shop. Molding cutter-head knives can be made to match a sample, a sketch, or one of many existing patterns. The knives and setup charge typically run from $150 to $300, and the molding itself is then priced by the foot according to the wood you choose. Or, if you want something unique, a skilled carpenter can often combine stock profiles to make one-of-a-kind assemblies.

styles

Up until the 1930s, virtually all of the trim in American houses was based on the classic Doric, Ionic, or Corinthian forms. With a far wider range of choices available today, and fewer builders and designers trained in classic period styles, modern molding combinations bear little relation to the formal patterns of the past.

Dramatic moldings in a remodel or new construction can turn the ordinary into the extraordinary. If your house is of an identifiable period style, as most prewar homes are, choose trim that stays within that style. Don't put clamshell mold-ing in a bungalow, for example. Take the time to research historically appropriate types at the library if you're not sure which style is correct. If you own a postwar home or one without a distinct period style, you have more options.

Avoid a hodgepodge molding plan by choosing one general style for the entire home. But that doesn't mean installing the same trim in the same way everywhere. Consider more elegant combinations for public areas, such as a main entrance or living room, and simpler versions in spaces like hallways, bedrooms, and baths. This strategy is also cost-effective.

crown molding This typically large, generously detailed molding is used at the junction of walls and ceilings, and often in smaller versions on door and window head casings and cabinet tops. It adds a formal, sculptured look to a room. Because of its size and expense, it was once found only in richly appointed houses, but single-piece crown is now widely available and not prohibitively expensive. More elaborate, and more costly, are crown moldings composed of several individual trim pieces stacked together. Urethane-foam moldings (right) achieve the look of custom-made crown without the expense. "I once used a large, one-piece urethane crown that, if done in wood, would have taken six built-up pieces," Silva says.

Tom Silva uses a pneumatic finish nailer to attach crown molding to angled nailing base he installed earlier.

URETHANE
CROWN MOLDING

Crown molding installation requires a skilled practitioner able to think in several dimensions at once. Miters must be cut upside down and at an angle that corresponds to the crown's position, when right side up, on the wall.

Inside corners are joined with a coped cut because wood shrinkage would eventually cause a mitered joint to open. Walls that are out of square or wavy—common in older homes—can add yet another layer of complication. Tom Silva rips lengths of blocking from 2-by-4 lumber, cutting it to the same angle that the crown will follow from wall to ceiling, and uses it to fill the intersecting joint to provide a straight, stable nailing base for the molding.

Crown molding creates a finished look and unifies different areas of large rooms.

COMBINING STOCK MOLDINGS

The most beautiful, elaborate, and unique moldings are often built up from many separate trim profiles. Look at stock pieces as parts of a kit rather than individually. Given the dozens of stock profiles available, the number of possible combinations is limited only by your imagination. Multi-piece assemblies are typically used for large crown moldings, chair rails, and fireplace mantels. The soon-to-be-painted mantel below, for example, combines a wide pine crown molding with maple casing.

window and door trim

Nowhere is molding more prominent or important than around windows and doors. Doors and windows are installed in frames, or jambs, that are carefully leveled, plumbed, and shimmed in place, which requires a space between the jamb and wall. This necessary gap must be covered with trim called casing.

Casing has grown narrower and less interesting over the past century. Historically, window casing was at least 3½ inches wide—particularly for double-hung windows—to hide the sash counterweights that ran in wide channels on either side of the window. But with the production housing that followed World War II, windows lost their sash weights and the width and embellishment

Wide casing helps make this window the focal point of a small bathroom.

of trim—inside and out—were reduced greatly to make homes more affordable.

Restoring original moldings in a home that has lost them through previous remodels is one of the best ways to revive an old house. Even in a postwar home of no specific style, you can impart some visual interest by replacing standard window and door trim with moldings that lend style and character.

installing trim

A week or more before the work begins, wood trim should be stacked inside the home, allowing it to acclimate to the temperatures in its new environment. This will help prevent warping and shrinkage after it is installed. In warm, humid weather, air-conditioning the space will encourage drying. Otherwise the wood will shrink in winter once it's installed, and gaps will open at the joints.

Trim installation should follow traditional, time-honored woodworking techniques, though today those skills are facilitated by power miter

saws, digital angle calculators, and pneumatic finish nailers. Air-powered nailing, in particular, yields better results because the process doesn't damage plaster walls, eliminates the need to pre-drill hardwoods, and avoids hammer marks in softwoods.

Continuous, unbroken molding runs are always preferable to multiple lengths of trim butted together. Where moldings must be joined, a scarf joint, or lapped splice, is preferred to a butt joint. A power biscuit joiner and wood glue can be used to make up joints and outside corners before they are fastened in place. Outside corners are mitered, but inside corners require a coped joint. After the trim is installed, nail holes and small imperfections are filled with paintable or stain-matched wood filler.

Many homes have walls that are bumpy or out of square. Gaps between moldings and walls or ceilings, or places where walls belly inward, are typical problems in trim installation. Tom Silva's approach is to make subtle modifications as he goes, filling gaps with wood strips rather than caulk. "I like to leave a nice, clean edge for the painter," he says. On a piece of scrap wood, he uses a compass to scribe a line matching the wall's curve. Then he cuts the piece on a jigsaw, applies carpenter's glue, and taps it into place. "With a light sanding and paint, the joint disappears."

repairing and replacing trim

Original wood moldings in period homes are as valuable as antique furnishings, which is why the TOH crew tries to preserve them when possible. Even aged, timeworn wood can be repaired with a variety of traditional and modern techniques or, as a last resort, replaced with authentic-looking facsimiles. The key to making repairs and filling in damaged areas is matching the texture and craftsmanship of the original moldings. "If it isn't perfect to begin with," Silva says, "you don't want to make the fill perfect. It'll stand out more than before."

filling in Moldings such as baseboard and chair rails are not just decorative elements; they are also designed to protect walls from nicks, dents, gouges, and other damage that is inevitably incurred over the years. If moldings need only spot repairs, Silva begins by scraping them clean, applying a liquid wood hardener to firm up soft or loose wood fibers, and then sanding them smooth. He cuts a disposable plastic putty knife to match the molding profile and first uses it to apply epoxy filler. When the epoxy begins to set, he shapes it with his custom-made tool and applies additional coats of filler

LEFT: Difficult-to-replace moldings can be repaired with a coat of epoxy. Note how the putty knife has been shaped to fit the profile. RIGHT: A large hole can be cut out and a "dutchman" wood patch shaped to fit. Cracks should be filled, then all surfaces sanded smooth.

as needed. A final sanding after the filler hardens leaves the molding ready for painting.

piecing in To fill small holes or replace damaged or decayed spots, Silva shapes a piece called a dutchman from wood that matches the original molding. He cuts a hole in the molding that is similar in shape but slightly smaller than the replacement, chamfers the sides of the dutchman with sandpaper to ease the fit, coats its edges with wood glue, and taps it into place. After the glue dries, seams are filled and the patch and surrounding area are sanded smooth.

Warm wood paneling accented with white trim creates a cozy cottage feel.

paneling

Richly wood-paneled interiors have long been a treasured, traditional look for offices, club rooms, and libraries. A room lined with wood from floor to ceiling—including the ceiling, in some cases—lends an air of distinction to most any home.

During the 1970s, the advent of thin, low-grade 4-by-8-foot plywood sheets with a micro-thin hardwood veneer or only a photocopy imprint of a real wood surface turned many homeowners and decorators away from paneled interiors. But when done right, wood paneling can trans-form a room into a truly warm and regal space.

Solid-wood paneling is the epit-ome of beauty for this technique. It is available in a number of profiles, including square-edge, tongue-and-groove, and beveled-edge or V-joint. Familiar standards are oak, maple, mahogany, and pine. It's also avail-able in exotic varieties ranging from blood-red African bubinga to worm-holed pecky cypress.

The materials and labor required to line an interior with solid-wood planks, or with hardwood panels framed by matching moldings, can be expensive. But if your heart is set on an intimate, beautifully appointed study or office, there are ways to reduce the expense.

One is to have ½-inch-thick hard-wood veneer plywood installed over drywall, with solid-wood strips and moldings covering the joints. Another is to fill wall areas with bookshelves made from edge-banded plywood of the same, or similar, look as the room's hardwood paneling. It's hard to tell the difference between solid-maple plank walls and cost-efficient birch plywood shelves if you have enough books to fill them.

wainscoting If full-wall paneling is more wood than you want, a good alternative is half-wall paneling, or wainscoting. This traditional wall treatment is typically made from less costly softwoods and, as a result, is often painted rather than stained. Although any wood grade, species, or profile may be used, the classic look is beadboard, originally a narrow plank with a decorative bead cut into its surface. Individual tongue-and-groove planks are available, but 4-by-8-foot sheets of plywood or MDF beadboard panels are more cost-effective, can be installed faster, and expand and contract less than solid wood.

"Wainscoting is one of the things I love adding to a house," Silva says.

tip: things to check with trim Long runs of baseboard, ceiling, and chair rail moldings should be arrow straight. Intersections should be almost invisible. Splices that telegraph through the paint or noticeable joints in stain-finished trim indicate shoddy work. Miters must meet evenly, without overlaps or gaps. Any nail holes, hammer marks, or other minor damage incurred during installation should be filled or sanded. Trim should be nailed into the wall framing at 16-inch intervals. Trim joints must be nailed at stud intersections. Good installers will drive or shoot nails through the notches, folds, and crannies of molding profiles, which helps hide the marks. Each nail is then countersunk below the molding's surface, and the hole is covered with spackling compound if the trim is to be painted, or wood-colored filler if it's to be stained.

"I use it in pantries, hallways—any area where the wall could get worn or damaged. It protects the wall and looks good at the same time."

Finished wainscoting can be any height, but where its top trim serves as a chair rail, Silva sets it 32 to 36 inches above the floor. "Start a wainscot installation where it's most visible and end it where it's least conspicuous," he says. A backing layer of ½-inch drywall is recommended in new construction to level uneven studs and provide a layer of fire resistance. If beadboard paneling is used, Silva cuts sections to height and nails them directly to the wall studs. If individual planks are used, horizontal blocking must be installed between studs in open walls, or furring strips over an existing wall, and then the planks are nailed every few inches.

Silva finishes the bottom with 1⅛-inch shoe molding, "a more traditional detail than baseboard molding," he says. For the top, he creates a cap rail by combining 1-by-2 trim, installed flat, with a simple cove or ogee molding below to support it.

This dining room is enhanced with painted beadboard wainscot and a cap rail to display the family dish collection.

floors

A dark wood threshold creates a smooth transition from carpet to a slightly higher tumbled marble floor.

Of all a home's features that are both structural and decorative, flooring has perhaps the most difficult job. It endures constant use and abuse, yet is expected to last a lifetime while keeping up appearances. For this reason, selecting flooring involves many considerations: durability, looks, maintenance requirements, cost, and ease of installation, to name a few.

Because flooring needs to perform various functions in different areas of the home, materials choices also tend to vary by room. For example, though stone and tile are popular for areas that receive heavy use and are exposed to moisture, such as an entry, these very hard materials can take a toll on your legs and back after long periods of standing. So more forgiving yet waterproof materials, such as vinyl and cork, are often chosen for kitchens, baths, and play areas. Hardwood can be used nearly anywhere, but because it requires greater maintenance and is more susceptible to moisture and damage, it is usually reserved for rooms that receive less rigorous use.

Before any type of finish flooring is installed, your flooring contractor should thoroughly inspect the substrate it will be applied over, as well as the support framing below (see page 60). The new materials should be installed on a base that is free of moisture, is in sound condition, and is flat, smooth, and strong enough to support them. A sturdy subfloor is especially important for rigid materials like ceramic tile that can't flex.

Installing a new material will affect the finished height of the floor. Wood flooring is thicker than resilient and most engineered wood flooring, tile can vary widely by type, and carpeting comes in many thicknesses. Different materials also require different substrates, some thicker than others. If you lay a new floor atop an old one, you add even more height.

If you can, try to minimize raising or lowering the new floor in relation to the floors around it. You may be able to build up the subflooring to adjust for thin materials or choose a thickness of flooring that doesn't add more height but is acceptable to you. Discuss the best ways to handle this with your contractor or flooring dealer before you buy materials.

Also consider what kind of thresholds you'll need. Thresholds smooth transitions from one flooring material to another, and make for more graceful changes in height between rooms when it's unavoidable. Wood, tile, and marble are most often used for thresholds. They are available in stock shapes and sizes or may be fabricated on site by the flooring installer. Preformed metal and plastic transition strips are also available for thin flooring materials like laminates and tile, and for installed carpeting, but they're not always things of beauty.

Though there are many kinds of flooring, for the sake of discussion they can be grouped into a few key categories: wood, resilient, tile, decorative concrete, and carpet. Following is a closer look.

wood

This traditional favorite has evolved into a spectrum of products beyond the original solid strip and plank materials of yesteryear. So-called engineered wood flooring—laminated, compressed, or reconstituted wood products topped with a thin layer of solid wood—are the fastest-growing category. Most come finished and offer good value, as well as manufacturer warranties.

solid hardwood and softwood

Wood flooring generally refers to strips, planks, or blocks of solid wood. Strip flooring is available in widths from 1½ to 3½ inches—2¼-inch is the most popular. The standard thickness is ¾ inch, but less durable ⅜- and ½-inch strips are available. Most strip flooring has tongue-and-groove edges and is nailed to the subfloor. Solid plank flooring is typically ¾ inch thick and is sold in varying widths from 3 to 9 inches, with either tongue-and-groove edges or square edges.

Strips and planks both may be blind-nailed through their tongue edges, but planks are frequently attached with screws driven through their faces and covered with wood plugs for a rustic appearance.

Oak and maple are the most common native hardwoods used for

A knotty pine floor will wear more quickly than hardwood, which makes it a good choice for more rustic settings, where a timeworn look is a plus.

floors, but many other species, such as exotic tropicals, are available.

All wood flooring is rated on the Janka hardness scale; the higher the number, the greater the resistance to denting and impact. Many hardwoods such as oak, ash, cherry, and walnut range from 1000 to around 1300. Specialty woods such as mesquite and some tropical hardwoods score well over 2000. Most

softwoods are, not surprisingly, much softer. Douglas fir flooring, a softwood not often seen in new construction today but used extensively until the 1940s, is rated at 660, and white pine falls to 380. Though softwood floors wear faster and show more distress, many homeowners choose them for just this reason—they like the appearance of the wood as it ages.

If you are installing new hardwood flooring, keep in mind that its final appearance depends not only on the wood species but also on the wood's grade, grain, and finish. A select grade of red oak, for example, is completely free of knots and is uniform in color, but it is far more expensive than a slightly lower grade, No. 1 common, which allows tiny knots and some color variation.

Select wood flooring has always been prized for its flawless appearance, but today, many homeowners prefer wood with a more dramatic, character-rich look. That makes a slightly lower grade an excellent, and economical, alternative. When renovating an older home, choose new wood flooring to match the original grade or that of the surrounding floors.

Installed prices for typical solid-wood floors range from about $8 to $11 per square foot. If you want exotic species, be prepared to pay much more. As a rule, you'll pay more for wider and thicker planks, higher wood grades, and more coats of finish.

Much of the lumber sold today is flatsawn, which is identifiable by its wide, V-shape grain lines. Flatsawn red oak is the most popular hardwood flooring in use. Cutting logs into flatsawn lumber makes the most efficient use of a tree, but flatsawn wood is more susceptible to changes in humidity than wood sliced at an angle to the grain. In hardwood flooring, this can result in cupping, splintering, and dimensional changes that open gaps as the wood dries and shrinks.

Quartersawn or riftsawn wood is cut so that the grain runs more or less at right angles to the board's face. Although it's harder to obtain and more expensive to buy, the wood is more dimensionally stable, and it has an attractive long-grain appearance. "Anytime I want a board that doesn't expand and contract too much—on decking, flooring, trim—I look for that vertical grain," Silva says.

Most solid-wood flooring must be sanded and finished after it is installed. The wood is then stained before it gets several coats of protective finish. If left

A warm mahogany floor works well with this room's red and brown color palette.

OAK

MAPLE

AMERICAN CHERRY

MAHOGANY

TEAK

BRAZILIAN CHERRY

unstained, natural tones can vary widely unless all heartwood or all of the same grade is specified.

Hardwood flooring is expensive, so it makes sense to protect it with the best finish available. Penetrating oils, waxes, and oil-based varnishes were once preferred, but synthetic varnishes, or urethanes, have improved greatly in quality and desirability. Also known as polyurethanes,

these finishes no longer have the plastic look of early products. Like varnishes, they are sold in gloss, semigloss, and satin sheens. "I like to finish floors with two or three coats of high-gloss polyurethane, followed by a coat of satin," Silva says. "High gloss gives you durability; the satin cuts down the shine and gives the grain of the floor some depth."

Oil-modified urethane is a professional-grade product that offers superior wood protection but with less subtlety and more shine than consumer-grade finishes. Though honey-colored when new, it darkens

over time, so it is not a good choice for a light, clear finish. Another option is water-based urethane, which is low in flammable solvents, has less odor, dries quickly, and does not yellow.

The life of a finish depends on many factors: use, too little or too much maintenance, and exposure to sunlight and to direct or indirect moisture. Eventually every finish, including factory-applied coatings, wears off or is damaged and the floor must be sanded and refinished.

PATCHING A FLOOR

When remodeling, you're likely to encounter areas where sections of flooring must be replaced. If an existing floor is salvageable but a few small areas are damaged, replacing sections may be a good option. Also, when walls are moved or removed during a remodeling project, sections of flooring must be filled in where the walls once stood.

Assuming that you aren't lucky enough to have a few pieces of the original material stored away from when the existing floors were installed, matching and blending

new material to the old so the patch isn't obvious can be a real challenge. If the material is relatively inexpensive, such as vinyl, you're often better off replacing the entire floor. But hardwood and other expensive materials are not so easy to completely replace.

If you can't find new material that's a very close match, one option is to steal flooring from a closet or other out-of-view spot, then replace the flooring in that area with new flooring. This way you can achieve a better match where it counts.

Replacing solid strip flooring is not a difficult job, especially with the tongues removed from a few key pieces. But here's where a bit of artistry makes a big difference in the finished look. The ends of the new strips should be staggered, just like the original flooring, and not lined up in a row. "Otherwise you'll end up with a square patch that looks like a trapdoor," Silva says. After the repair work is done, the entire floor will probably need to be sanded and refinished, which will make the patch disappear.

engineered wood For the look of wood flooring without the cost, finishing, or maintenance requirements of solid wood, there are many engineered flooring products available. About 40 percent of all floors installed today, in both new construction and remodels, are engineered wood products. They typically come factory finished with 25-year warranties and are quickly installed. Engineered wood floors often run about $4.50 to $5 per square foot for materials, but prices can range up to $15 per square foot or more. Figure another $2 per square foot for installation.

Consider adding a border strip in a contrasting color, which is easy to do with prefinished engineered wood flooring.

Laminated or plywood styles typically have a fine hardwood surface veneer atop several plies of lower-grade wood. Most are half the thickness of solid wood floors, but after installation they are almost indistinguishable from solid-wood flooring.

Keep in mind that with engineered wood products, the more plies, the more stable the floor. Three plies are minimum, five are optimum. Top veneers can range from $3/8$ inch to less than $3/32$ inch; obviously, the thicker the better. The thickness of the top veneer layer should extend at least to the tongue-and-groove joint, allowing the surface to be sanded and refinished, just like a solid-wood floor. Some engineered flooring can be sanded up to three times, while some can't be refinished at all, so check the manufacturer's fine print before you buy. Flooring finished with a urethane coating is good, but products with an additional aluminum oxide layer last longer.

Adding a border strip or custom inlay is easier with engineered wood flooring; because these products come stained and finished, all you need to do is replace one or more strips with an alternating color, or choose a different wood species with a contrasting appearance. The added cost of borders and inlays is mainly in the extra labor, but you're also paying for the skill of the installer. If you want this effect in solid, unstained strip flooring, the cost may be higher if each strip has to be finished separately from the main flooring.

Parquet provides the warmth of a wood plank floor for less money and can be repaired more easily.

parquet wood Block flooring, also called parquet, comes in squares or rectangles made from wood strips and is installed in an alternating right-angle pattern. Today, parquet is more often made of laminated rather than solid wood.

The individual squares, or tiles, of parquet are relatively easy to install, with tongue-and-groove edges that are most often glued down, though some can be blind-nailed or stapled. Because parquet squares are factory-made from many small wood pieces—often short cast-offs—they tend to be more economical than solid-wood strip or plank floors, but you can easily pay up to $20 per square foot, installed, for elegant varieties. Several wood species are available, with finishes that range from natural to stained. Like all hardwood flooring, parquet can be scratched or damaged; however, replacing a tile or two is easier than replacing a section of strip flooring.

bamboo In appearance and form, bamboo is very similar to engineered hardwood flooring, but the material is actually a form of grass. Because it is handsome and is a natural, rapidly renewable resource, it is gaining in popularity as a flooring choice. Bamboo gets its woodlike appearance from the way it's manufactured. Narrow strips are cut and bonded edge to edge or face-glued to create tongue-and-groove strips or planks. The edge-bonded boards display bamboo's characteristic joints, or nodes, while the face-joined strips have narrow, closely spaced, uniform grain lines. Both types are equally durable, with the hardness of oak and maple but with less than half the shrinkage in humid environments. Installed, bamboo flooring runs from about $3 to $7 per square foot.

Imported bamboo flooring is not manufactured to the same standards as flooring made in the United States, so check strips or planks closely before installation. Each strip should be the same, or gaps will appear in the finished floor. Also check whether the manufacturer or distributor offers a warranty or will take back unusable materials.

Bamboo is an environmentally sound choice that's as durable as hardwood.

ENGINEERED WOOD INSTALLATION

Many types of engineered wood flooring are available, and proper installation methods vary with each. The key is to be sure your installer follows the manufacturer's recommendations.

One advantage of engineered wood flooring is that it can be installed over an existing wood floor, even if the old floor is damaged, provided the old surface is in basically sound condition and is properly prepared. Patching compound is first used to fill large cracks, holes, or depressions, and then the existing floor is sanded smooth. If engineered wood is installed over strip flooring, planks must run perpendicular to the old flooring.

Many engineered floor products are designed to "float" on a thin layer of plastic foam insulation, which "makes things quieter downstairs," Silva says. These floors are not attached to the subfloor. Instead, their individual strips or planks are glued to each other, or the boards snap together or use proprietary hardware that holds them together. Once assembled, floating floors are held in place by their weight and by baseboard moldings installed around the perimeter.

resilient

Resilient flooring includes vinyl, linoleum, cork, and rubber.

vinyl One of the most popular flooring surfaces for kitchens and baths is vinyl, a modern, plastic material available in a vast range of colors and designs. Vinyl flooring is comfortable to walk on, easy to install and care for, and highly water and skid resistant. Though it is very durable, it is not impervious to scratches, cuts, burns, dents, and other damage. Low-grade vinyl is inexpensive (you get what you pay for), while high-quality vinyl can be comparable in cost to wood or ceramic tile.

Vinyl flooring is sold in sheets or tiles. Sheet vinyl comes in rolls up to 12 feet wide, so a floor that can be spanned by a single roll width is virtually watertight. Vinyl tiles are available in 12- or 18-inch squares, but because they have joints, a sealer must be applied periodically to prevent water from getting underneath. Adhesive is required to install all

VINYL

vinyl flooring, though some tiles come with their own adhesive backing. Sheet vinyl prices are generally quoted by the yard, including installation; expect to pay $6 to $10 or more per yard. Vinyl tiles are usually priced by the square foot, ranging from $1 to $2.50; installation typically runs about $1 per square foot.

Two types of vinyl flooring are available today: printed and inlaid. Printed vinyl, the least expensive, has a microscopically thin overlay pattern or veneer atop a vinyl base layer. Inlaid vinyl flooring costs more, but its patterns extend deep into the material, which results in richer, more vibrant, and longer-lasting colors and patterns.

Higher-quality vinyl is thicker by comparison and offers a superior wear layer. No-wax vinyl has the least protective coating but is sufficient for areas of light foot traffic. Urethane coatings are more resistant to scuffing and scratches, and an enhanced urethane wear layer holds up best in areas of heavy use. When buying vinyl flooring, ask for PSI (pounds per square inch) ratings, which indicate dent resistance and general toughness. Commercial vinyl flooring is by far the strongest, longest-lasting grade, but it comes in fewer patterns and its colors tend to be muted.

Installation may be done atop a previous vinyl floor, but this requires a smooth subfloor surface. Even minor bumps and dents will eventually telegraph through this flexible plastic material and, over time, conform to the contours of the substrate. Though manufacturers offer do-it-yourself kits, professional installation is recommended for sheet vinyl. Self-adhesive tiles are easy to install, but those applied with a separate adhesive are generally more reliable.

Vinyl tiles are easier to repair because they can be individually removed and replaced. Sheet goods can be repaired successfully, especially if the flooring has a pattern that will camouflage the cut lines and patch material.

> **tip: asbestos in old flooring** "Most of the vinyl and linoleum flooring made before 1985 contained asbestos, and there's no way for you to know if yours does just by looking at it," says This Old House master carpenter Norm Abram. Sanding, sawing, or scraping the old floor will send dust airborne, creating very harmful conditions. The simplest solution is to encase or cover the old material with new material, making sure the old flooring is left undisturbed. If old flooring must be removed and it is found through testing to contain asbestos, it must be removed by a certified asbestos abatement contractor.

A mix of soft browns, tans, and creams creates a bright and natural-looking linoleum floor.

from $6 to $40 per square yard installed.

Like vinyl, linoleum is easy to care for, comfortable to walk on, and resistant to moisture. But unlike vinyl's thin top layer, linoleum's colors extend completely through the material, making scratches and cuts easy to fix; simply fill in the damaged area with a mixture of wood glue and fine scrapings from a piece of scrap. Because it is also naturally resistant to bacteria, linoleum has been a traditional choice for hospitals, schools, and day-care centers; it is an excellent choice for children's rooms.

Installation is fairly easy as long as the substrate is very smooth. Linoleum floors have been known to last 30 to 40 years with proper care. If repairs are required, most can be handled by an installer who will charge about $75 an hour.

linoleum Many people think linoleum is just an old-fashioned term for vinyl. The two products may look similar, but they are worlds apart. Modern vinyl is a synthetic, purely plastic product, while linoleum is an environmentally-friendly, recyclable amalgam of wood fibers, cork, plant resins, powdered limestone, and linseed oil pressed onto a natural jute backing.

Linoleum used to have its shortcomings, such as drab colors and a tendency to curl and crack as it aged. Even so, on the whole it was a good, labor-saving material that your grandmother probably had in her kitchen and bath. It almost disappeared with the advent of vinyl flooring, but it is making a comeback today thanks to modern production methods that allow it to be manufactured in hundreds of colors ranging from sophisticatedly subtle to vibrantly modern. Depending upon the pattern and the quality of the material, linoleum ranges widely in price,

LINOLEUM

RESILIENT FLOORING INSTALLATION

From vinyl to cork, methods for installing resilient flooring products are relatively similar. As with engineered flooring, it's important to pay close attention to the manufacturer's recommendations.

Resilient tiles are usually laid out starting at a centerline that runs across the length of the room. This ensures a symmetrical pattern that finishes with equally sized tiles at opposing sides of the room. It also reduces waste. Ask for the tiles to be laid out in a dry run so you can see how they will look when installed.

With sheet goods, a single piece may cover an entire floor, but one cutting mistake can ruin the whole piece. Some installers make a paper template of the floor and use it to mark and cut the sheet. If a room is too wide for one sheet, seams should be placed away from high-traffic areas, fit tightly, and be thoroughly sealed.

After resilient flooring is installed, it must be smoothed in place with a 100-pound roller or a hand roller with plenty of elbow grease. Manufacturers recommend waiting at least 24 hours before stepping or placing furnishings on the floor to allow the adhesive to harden; otherwise, permanent dents can form.

Cork is soft underfoot and comes in a range of colors.

cork For floors that are warm to the touch and feel slightly springy underfoot, cork is hard to beat. Though strong enough for day-to-day foot traffic, cork flooring is so resilient and soft that you can drop a wineglass and it might not break.

Made from the living bark of Mediterranean cork oaks, this material is first shredded and then processed into thin square-foot tiles or thicker planks that measure 1 by 3 feet. Various looks, from light and evenly shaded to mottled and dark, are available. Cork is easily installed with a special adhesive, and it can be finished or sealed in several ways: with an old-fashioned wax and oil mixture, with brushed- or rolled-on polyurethane, or with an acrylic coating that is less durable than urethane but is easily applied by mop. Cork is more susceptible to damage than other types of flooring, but replacing tiles is easy. Installed prices range from about $5 to $10 per square foot. Experienced do-it-yourselfers can handle installation, but labor typically accounts for only about $1.50 to $2.50 per square foot of the overall cost, making a professional job within reach for most.

laminates

Laminates can do a convincing job of imitating wood, stone, and tile and are far less expensive. Prices run from $3 to $6 per square foot installed. This composite sandwich of paper, wood, and plastic offers decent durability and an incredible variety of appearances. While a uniform wood look is most popular, planks and tiles of different styles and colors can be mixed and matched in limitless patterns.

Formed into thin tongue-and-groove planks or square tiles, laminates are easily glued or snapped together to create a floor that is resistant to scratches, stains, and wear. If a section is badly scratched or damaged, it can be removed and replaced. With this in mind, it's a good idea to keep a few extra pieces stored away in case you need an exact match later.

While laminates with high- and medium-density fiberboard cores are highly water resistant when properly installed with tight-fitting seams, less costly products or poor installation can produce floors that are susceptible to damage by spills and moisture.

Laminates can be installed directly over concrete slabs or nearly any flat, smooth surface, but Tom Silva advises applying a vapor barrier over concrete first. A type of floating floor, laminates are typically installed over a thin pad of closed-cell foam plastic that both cushions the flooring and provides a moisture barrier.

rubber Rubber flooring is similar to vinyl in qualities, installation, and price, but it is used less frequently and comes in limited styles and patterns. Available in sheets or tiles, it is commonly found in commercial applications because of its high durability and resistance to moisture and damage from chemicals. Styles with raised nubs or patterns that resemble diamond-plate metal are more skid-resistant than smooth types.

LAMINATE

RUBBER

tile

Tile is one of the most water- and wear-resistant, low-maintenance flooring materials around. It is also among the most attractive and desirable, with a variety of styles, sizes, colors, and designs available. A well-installed ceramic tile floor will last a lifetime with little care, and some tile floors actually improve in character as they age while still providing good performance.

Standard tile comes in 4-, 6-, and 12-inch squares. Custom, imported, and handmade tiles may not conform to any standard at all. But with tile, differences in size and shape present a creative opportunity; skilled installers pride themselves on their artistry and ability to mix and match various shapes and designs to create attractive mosaics, classic tile "paintings," and dramatic one-of-a-kind patterns.

Tiles are rated according to their intended use. Some are made specifically for indoor or outdoor areas, while others may be installed anywhere. Heat-resistant tiles are required in or around fireplace openings and near cooking surfaces. Hardness

Ceramic tile is durable and easy to keep clean, making it the perfect choice for entryways, kitchens, and bathrooms.

ratings are critical where tiles will be subjected to weight, impact, or abrasion. Porosity, which measures how much water a tile absorbs, is an important consideration for bathroom and kitchen installations. Vitreous tile is water repellent, while nonvitreous tile is more absorbent.

Most tile made today falls into four broad categories: ceramic, porcelain, mosaic, and stone.

ceramic Made of kiln-baked clay, ceramic tiles are fairly porous, brittle, and easily broken until they are installed, after which they become a solid-surface mass that is extremely durable. Ceramic tiles are either glazed or unglazed. Glazing is a baked-on surface treatment that adds resistance to stains and water and makes colors brighter and more vibrant. Like paint, glaze comes in a range of reflective finishes: glossy, matte, and textured. Glossy tiles resist stains and are easiest to clean but can be slippery when wet. Matte and textured finishes—which are scored, sanded, or roughened in some way—also resist stains and are more slip resistant when wet. Unglazed quarry tiles

have a more rustic, unfinished appearance, and colors are generally limited to earth tones. Terra-cotta tiles are the most recognizable type. They are also resistant to water and skidding, but they absorb stains easily and must be sealed periodically.

porcelain Porcelain tiles are glazed and fired to become very hard and waterproof. They are more difficult to cut and install, but their subtle, attractive coloring and unique luster make them a popular choice.

PORCELAIN

mosaic Mosaic tiles, typically 1 to 2 inches square or hexagonal, are often assembled to create pictures or patterns. They can be made of ceramic, porcelain, glass, or stone. Mosaic tiles date back thousands of years, but today they are more often custom-ordered from manufacturers and come attached to an easy-to-install mesh backing. These tile sheets, typically measuring 12 by 18 inches, are set in adhesive and grouted like individual tiles.

Expensive mosaic tiles can be used sparingly in a decorative inlay.

TUMBLED MARBLE

POLISHED MARBLE

GRANITE

stone Tile cut from stone is a natural choice for beauty, ruggedness, and innate character. Stone tiles with slip-resistant surfaces are labeled "tumbled," "honed," or "sandblasted." However, they also soak up water and stains unless sealed. Before choosing a type, know its characteristics and pick the correct one for your installation.

Granite, one of the hardest and most expensive stones, is difficult to stain, scratch, or break, making it a premium choice for flooring and countertops. Slate is generally much less expensive, but only some varieties are impervious to water and stains. Most slate is soft, porous, and brittle and can flake, spall, or crack under impact or pressure.

Marble is a calcium-based stone with a classic, often translucent beauty that ranges from elegantly subtle to wildly variegated. Limestone and travertine are close molecular cousins and are more even in color and pattern. All of these stones are porous and will absorb stains unless sealed and cared for properly.

Stone is installed in the same way as ceramic tile. Because many stones are slightly translucent, they should be laid in white thin-set mortar instead of the usual gray, especially if the stone is light in color.

PROPER TILE INSTALLATION

Natural stone and ceramic tiles are the hardest-wearing floor materials, able to last for centuries if properly installed, but an inadequate underlayment can cause them to crack and fail. The area to be tiled should not flex when someone walks on it. For maximum stability, a concrete base is usually preferred, but the use of cement backboard screwed to a wood subfloor is acceptable if properly prepared. Tile is bedded in fresh concrete or thin-set mortar, or in one of several types of premixed adhesives.

A concrete or "mud" base is best, but it's also the most expensive and raises the height of the floor. Most tile setters are also confident in backerboard, which is screwed to a plywood subfloor. The tiles are then set in thinset mortar or adhesive directly atop the underlayment. The backerboard resists water damage and adds strength to the floor. The backerboard should be oriented at right angles to the plywood. A self-sticking anti-fracture membrane over the joints helps to prevent cracks from telegraphing through to the tile.

With any type of tile flooring, the layout must be planned to create a pleasing pattern and to minimize cutting and odd-size pieces at the floor edges. To visualize the finished installation, you can ask the installer to lay out the tiles in a dry run with plastic grout-joint spacers in-between.

Tile adhesive or thinset mortar may be used to install the tiles. Mortar should be reinforced with a latex admixture to enhance strength and resist cracking. The surface of the tiles should be consistent in height. Floor tiles are typically finished with a sanded mortar grout, which is available in different grades of coarseness and a variety of colors. The width of the grout lines affects not only the appearance but also the performance of the flooring. For example, wider lines provide more traction. With this in mind, be sure to ask your installer how the floor will be grouted before work begins.

Most grouts are porous and must be sealed after they set to prevent stains and moisture penetration. Sealers that form a surface film produce a wet look, while penetrating sealers may darken both the tile and grout.

decorative concrete

For the ultimate in simplicity, durability, and low cost, concrete floors are worth considering. On its own, concrete is not an inherently lovable surface material, but when treated, cared for, and used in the right location, this "liquid stone" offers many advantages. Consider a concrete floor for any high-traffic area, or rooms where kids or animals are likely to track in mud.

Tints may be added when the material is mixed to give the concrete a rich, deeply embedded color, or applied in dry powder or liquid form to the surface after it is poured but before it sets. Once the concrete cures, it can be easily painted or stained like wood. Concrete is not as hard as stone, and unless it is sealed, the surface will slowly wear and produce dust from foot traffic alone. Special

sealers are available, but almost any type of paint or polyurethane is suitable if the concrete is dry and clean.

Poured concrete's firm, flat, stable surface provides a perfect canvas for artistic treatments such as faux finishing. Concrete can also be stamped, embossed, scored, etched, or saw-cut to simulate other materials, such as stone, slate, tile, or even wood. Old concrete that has a deteriorating surface but is otherwise in sound condition can be restored with a thin layer of new concrete containing acrylic hardeners.

Installing an interior concrete finish floor is a challenge that calls for skilled practitioners who typically are not the same concrete contractors who pour driveways and outdoor patios. Finding an installer with excellent references and successful jobs you can inspect

may be difficult. Two resources on the Internet are the National Concrete Masonry Association at *www.ncma. org*, and *ConcreteNetwork.com*.

Typical concrete slab work can run from $5 per square foot to $10 or more per square foot installed, depending upon the situation, the installer, and the type of floor you want. Staining a simple concrete slab is at the low end of the cost spectrum; pouring a raised, specialty-finish floor is at the high end. Raised floors are particularly costly because of the support required to bear the concrete's heavy weight.

The process is also challenging because of the time needed to level the concrete before it "sets up"— which can take hours of screeding, floating, and troweling. Although concrete sets up in a few hours, it must be kept damp for several days to cure properly. Remember that concrete is unforgiving; once it cures, it's permanent.

Concrete shrinks as it hardens, so it will always crack. The trick is to control where the cracks will occur by placing control joints where cracks will be least visible.

Like any flooring material, concrete can be damaged, but cracks and chips are more easily repaired than in many other materials.

Installers create control joints in concrete floors to minimize cracks. For a unique look, these joints can be made in interesting patterns and each section stained a different color.

spiral staircases

In a class of its own is the spiral staircase. Uniquely stylish and highly space efficient, it is a common choice for lofts or other occasionally used spaces. For example, a spiral staircase can rise 15 feet in the same space that a straight staircase climbs 9 feet.

Spirals can be installed in openings as small as 5 feet in diameter, which makes them ideal for tight spaces (those used as a primary stair must be 8 feet in diameter or larger). As with conventional stairs, codes restrict their specifications. For example, a tread must be at least $7\frac{1}{2}$ inches deep, measured 12 inches out from its narrow end. The rise cannot be higher than $9\frac{1}{2}$ inches. Minimum headroom for a spiral stair, measured from the edge of each tread, is 6 feet 6 inches, and, as with other stairs, the handrail must be positioned from 34 inches to 38 inches above the nosing of the tread. Because most spiral staircases are narrow and winding, they make it very difficult to move furniture up or down and can be dangerous for people who have difficulty negotiating a steep, twisting climb. For the same reasons, consistency in tread depth and riser height is extremely important.

Custom, self-supporting spiral staircases can be built, but the most common type wind compactly around a central support pole and are available in kits. These kits are typically all metal and can be ordered to fit virtually any space. They are also cost efficient and easily installed. Accessories such as hardwood treads and handrails increase the price.

When planning a spiral staircase installation, first determine which direction you want to be facing when you enter and exit the staircase. Then factor in the total width of the well opening and add on for the handrail clearance, typically 2 inches. Spirals positioned in a corner or alcove can take full advantage of otherwise unusable space.

This industrial-style spiral staircase connects three floors in the most space-efficient way possible.

doors

Perhaps the most overlooked element in a remodel or new construction is the interior door. Because interior doors do not have to be as strong or weather resistant as exterior doors, when push comes to shove on the budget, many homeowners figure that even the most basic interior door will at least provide privacy.

But high-quality interior doors serve many other purposes. They resist the occasional hard knock, defend against the transfer of moisture, tolerate fluctuations in temperature, reduce sound transfer, and hold paint and finishes longer.

In addition, they can complement a home's décor, adding visual interest and helping to create a unified, harmonious impression from room to room. In older homes, well-crafted doors were considered as much a part of the interior décor as were moldings, wallpaper, and paint.

A solid-wood panel door with a clean coat of paint makes the entire room look great.

choosing doors

Doors come in two basic types: flush and panel.

Flush doors have featureless surfaces, making them unobtrusive in any setting. However, this style has given rise to many inexpensive hollow-core doors over the past 50 years. These doors typically have a narrow, solid-wood perimeter faced with lauan, a tropical softwood, over a core filled with cardboard honeycomb. Though serviceable, they absorb rather than retain paint and other finishes, are easily damaged, and provide little sound abatement. Higher-quality flush doors faced with birch or other hardwood veneers are stronger, feel more solid, and take finishes better.

Panel doors have flat or raised wood panels inset between stiles and rails. Glass panes may be used in place of some or all of the panels. Traditional panel doors are built like furniture, with many interlocking sections precisely fitted, glued, and doweled together. This assembly process makes them strong and warp resistant but more costly, especially if made out of hardwood.

As a less expensive alternative, the TOH crew likes medium-density fiberboard (MDF) doors, which are equally substantial and take paint well. They are less likely to bind or swell than solid wood doors, although to lessen the effects of humidity, MDF doors should be sealed on all surfaces and edges.

An MDF door can be pressure-molded to look like almost any type of panel door; it will feel more solid and heavier than hollow interior doors. Tom Silva and the TOH crew like this option even in period home renovations. Several classic panel styles are available, and even the more elaborate models cost far less than the real-wood panel doors they closely imitate.

sizes and configurations Interior doors come in many sizes. Standard types—hollow-core, flush, or panel—are $1\frac{3}{8}$ inches thick and 6 feet 8 inches tall. Taller doors may be special-ordered but are more expensive. Standard widths run from 24 inches for closets and small bathrooms up to 36 inches for handicap accessibility. Narrow passage doors are a space-saving option, but many furniture pieces cannot pass through an opening of less than 30 inches.

Interior doors are available as slabs or pre-hung. Blanks, or slabs, are doors without any jambs, hinges, knobs, or latches (called locksets). Blanks may be ordered with a hole

bored for the lockset, but they are otherwise incomplete until the carpenter installs them into jambs. Pre-hung doors come attached to a frame with hinges already mortised into the edges and with holes cut for the knob and strike plate. All new wood doors are unfinished and must be stained or painted, while MDF doors come primed and prepped for painting.

Because patience and skill are required to install jambs and properly hang a door, many contractors today prefer pre-hung doors for both new construction and remodels. If your home has usable existing jambs and you just need to replace a door, or if you have salvaged or restored doors that you want installed, have the door hung the old-fashioned way. Tom Silva loves this challenge and the craftsmanship it requires. "You just have to take your time and remember a few basic principles," he says.

smooth operation Every door, whether pre-hung or assembled on site, should open and close easily and

shut with a solid-sounding thunk. The gap between door and jamb must be a consistent $\frac{1}{8}$ to $\frac{1}{4}$ inch all around. If the door rattles when closed, the strike does not engage, or it's difficult to turn the doorknob when it is latched, the strike plate or stop molding usually needs adjusting.

Tom Silva hangs a door after trimming it to fit the opening, screwing on hinges, and installing the lockset.

A properly hung door will not swing open or closed by itself, touch the floor or saddle, or drag on carpeting. Lightweight hollow-core doors need only two hinges, but more substantial panel or MDF doors may require three to prevent warping or binding.

bifolds and sliders Closet doors that slide or open accordion-style save space in bedrooms, hallways, and laundry rooms. Louvered bifolds provide ventilation for closet interiors; flush, panel, and mirrored styles are also available in a range of sizes. Track-type hardware is needed for these doors and is sold separately. Some doors are suspended from overhead tracks, while others require both a top and a bottom track.

pocket doors Another type of space-saving door, requiring no swing room at all, is the pocket door, which discreetly slides into a gap in the wall. Pocket doors, frequently found in homes built before the past half-century, are regaining popularity.

Hardware kits are available for installing these "disappearing" doors in a remodel or new construction, but planning is essential. The door track is built into the wall framing, so adequate clearance must be provided to the left or right of the door opening (or both sides for double pocket doors).

Pocket doors can give out over time if the hardware deteriorates. In some cases, repairs require that a surrounding wall be torn open. "Often a screw falls out or the door comes off the track," Silva explains. If the doors are in generally good shape but the original operating mechanism can't be

With a mirror on one side and six panels on the other, this pocket door is both stylish and efficient.

saved, then new, improved hardware usually can be adapted to the old doors. Modern pocket-door hardware consists of nylon-wheeled trucks that glide smoothly in overhead aluminum tracks, providing reliable support for even the heaviest doors. A pulley mechanism is available for double doors so that both move in unison when one or the other is opened.

Installing a new pocket-door frame requires enough wall space for the entire frame and track unit, which is roughly twice the width of the door and 4 to 6 inches taller. No wiring, pipes, or ducts can be routed through

A "barn door" that slides on an overhead track saves space and complements the décor of the rooms in this comfortable, country-style home.

this space. If the pocket is to be positioned in a load-bearing wall, a header properly engineered to span the space must be installed.

Once the opening is framed, the aluminum track is cut to length and attached across the top of the opening. Pocket frames are compact, allowing a standard-size door to slide in and out of a finished wall approximately the same thickness as a typical interior wall made with 2-by-4 studs and $\frac{1}{2}$-inch drywall. After the door is hung from the track, drywall or other interior surfacing is attached to the frame in the usual way. Some door kits require a guide groove routed into the door bottom to prevent the door from swinging.

hinges and locks

In older homes, interior doors often have mortise latches or box locks, both of which require a key. Mortise latches are fitted into the door's edge; box locks are attached to the inside face of the door. Both have springs and other parts subject to wear over time. A locksmith can sometimes repair or rebuild these locks, and modern replacements are available through woodworking catalogs for restoration projects.

Whether or not they include locks, doorknobs and latches are called locksets. Interior passage locks are generally nonlocking, but privacy locks, such as for bathrooms, generally have a button or lever lock.

Today, door hardware is typically made of brass-plated base metal. This plating can wear off doorknobs and other parts that receive repeated use, and hinges can rust through in moisture-rich atmospheres like bathrooms. Higher-priced alternatives are solid brass, nickel, and brushed stainless steel. Though they cost more, they stand up better to years of use and often look noticeably richer than plated hardware.

SALVAGING OLD DOORS

Though you can choose from many styles of new doors when updating your home, it's hard to equal the character and style of older doors. Instead of buying new ones, you may be able to restore your existing doors. If yours are beyond repair, search salvage yards for doors that will fit your doorways.

Interior doors that are simply run down or caked with paint are begging to be restored. This involves removing each door and its hardware, then stripping and refinishing the door and stripping or replacing the hardware. You can strip the hardware parts yourself by letting them soak in a bucket of paint stripper, or you can drop them off at a metal plating shop for a new coat of brass, nickel, or chrome.

Stripping the door is more involved—and a lot messier. Paint stripper is applied in repeated coats between scraping and sanding sessions. If three or four days sounds like more than you want to spend on this project, look up "Furniture Stripping" in your telephone book and simply drop off your doors (and hardware, if you wish). Depending on the business, you may still be required to sand, patch, seal, and stain or paint the doors.

This four-panel door was brought back to life with a custom-blended red mahogany and cherry stain after twelve coats of paint were removed. Though salvaging a door is often more expensive than buying a new one, preserving the character and beauty of the past is well worth the cost.

fireplaces

When it comes to creating a sense of warmth, comfort, and ambiance, nothing compares to a fireplace. Whether in a new master suite, a family room addition, or a living room remodel, a fireplace is sure to become the center of attention.

Many older homes have traditional masonry wood-burning fireplaces that are wonderful to look at, whether dormant with logs stacked neatly inside or alive with a crackling fire. But older traditional fireplaces are likely to drain more heat from a room than they produce unless they have been improved over the years—and they require increasing amounts of attention as they age. If you have an existing traditional fireplace, consider some of the repairs and improvements that follow. If you plan to install a new fireplace, turn to page 121 for information on factory-built models.

traditional fireplaces

Traditional fireplaces are actually very simple in design and operation. A firebox, built of ordinary brick or concrete block, is lined with special heat-resistant tile or firebrick. The firebox angles upward and culminates in a smoke shelf, which juts forward to trap the rising smoke inside a smoke chamber above.

Natural convection draws the smoke up into the chimney and out of the house. An operable metal door, called a damper, is built at the front edge of the smoke shelf to close off the chimney when the fireplace is not in use. Chimneys are lined with a sectional clay pipe, or flue, stacked from the smoke chamber to the chimney top.

When remodeling a room, don't forget to give the fireplace a face-lift. New stone facing and a refinished mantel make this fireplace a focal point in the living room.

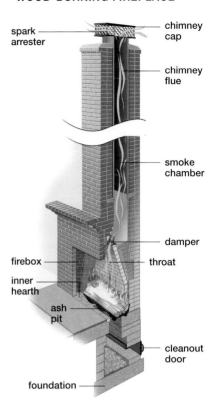

spark arrester · chimney cap · chimney flue · smoke chamber · damper · throat · firebox · inner hearth · ash pit · cleanout door · foundation

fireplace repairs

Despite a fireplace's straightforward construction, the skill of the mason or builder determines how well it draws and how efficiently it burns fuel. If your fireplace has become smoky and drafty, it can usually be fixed by a professional.

Sooty mantels indicate that a fireplace isn't burning right, and loose or crumbling mortar joints and ill-fitting dampers are signs that it could be hazardous. Experienced chimney sweeps are trained to spot these and other flaws. It's best to have a wood-burning fireplace inspected and cleaned by a licensed professional once a year if it is used regularly.

Some masons also specialize in fireplace construction and repair. If your fireplace is old or you're uncertain when it was last inspected, a pro can check it from hearth to chimney top and tell you whether the structure needs repointing (repair of the mortar joints), the firebrick needs replacing, or the flue needs to be lined or relined.

Very old fireplaces may not have an inner flue, which is a red flag because smoke and sparks can penetrate through to the house's structure. Contractors can use any of several methods to reline a flue; talk about the various options and your expectations before work begins.

RUMFORD REVIVAL

Occasionally, what is old becomes new again. Such is the case with Rumford-style fireplaces, an eighteenth-century invention that seemed headed for the dustbin of history until new environmental standards brought about its revival. The unique Rumford, it seems, is one of the only traditional brick-and-mortar fireplaces to reduce smoke and particulates to acceptable levels.

Invented in 1796 by a somewhat eccentric American known as Count Rumford, these fireplaces may be odd-looking by current standards, but they are undeniably effective. With a firebox only 12 inches deep—

very shallow compared with modern fireplaces—and with sidewalls splayed at a wide 135 degrees, the original design looks as though it could not contain even a small fire and would spew smoke instead of heat. But looks can be deceiving. A properly constructed Rumford "minimizes heat loss and emissions while at the same time radiating heat to the room," says Paul Tiegs, an emissions-control expert who has tested Rumford fireplaces for This Old House.

Warming up to the Rumford's unusual appearance is just the first hurdle. A Rumford must be crafted to exacting specifications or it won't work properly, and builders need to be experts in its design and construction. One reason for its high efficiency is a curved front, or breast, that directs room air into a narrow throat. The throat works like a carburetor, effectively shooting smoke and hot gases straight up into the smoke chamber.

How good are Rumfords? This Old House master carpenter Norm Abram installed one in his own home, and he remains an enthusiastic supporter. "It gets used in my house all winter long," he says.

Glass fireplace doors can save on home energy bills by minimizing the loss of room heat (or air conditioning) up the chimney.

hearth improvements

A number of improvements are helpful for giving new life to old fireplaces. Glass fireplace doors, for example, are now required for new fireplaces by home energy codes in many areas to prevent loss of heat and cold up the chimney. If you have an existing fireplace without doors, installing them will keep cold air out and warm air in the room, saving on energy costs. When you make a fire, doors also contain sparks.

Another product that prevents heat loss and cold-air intrusion is a temporary inflatable or custom-fitted flue sealer. Like insulation in your walls, it provides a layer between you and outdoor temperatures. To check

the effectiveness of your damper, set it in the closed position, then light a candle in the fireplace and blow it out. If the smoke rushes upward, your fireplace is an energy loser even when the damper is closed. After installing a flue sealer, hang a tag on your fireplace to remind you to remove the sealer before lighting your next fire.

Chimney pots, chimney-top dampers, and flue-mounted fans can improve the way a fireplace draws smoke up and out. A chimney pot is simply an extension that adds space between the flue top and the roof to increase the air draft.

It's easier to install a top damper (operated by a pull-chain) than to replace a built-in damper that has broken. Electric fans and wind-powered ventilators may be installed at the chimney top to create a stronger draft, pulling smoke up from the fireplace.

If your goal is to enhance the heat radiated into the room, firebacks (below) are an old and time-honored solution. Most modern fireplaces are lined with light-colored firebrick used to keep the heat inside the hearth. A fireback—consisting of a heavy iron plate that stands in the back of the firebox—absorbs heat and reflects it back into the room. Ornate, antique firebacks are much in demand; re-creations of popular styles from past eras are more affordable.

Sometimes, installing a fireplace insert is the best way to improve an inefficient fireplace. Inserts are essentially built-in, high-efficiency cast-iron stoves manufactured to fit into the fireplace opening, providing a somewhat smaller firebox inside the hearth. Inserts have no flue of their own; they exhaust directly into the fireplace chimney or a new liner in the existing chimney. The original firebox space behind and around the insert is filled with lightweight concrete, the insert's front is sealed against the old hearth, and the unit is securely bolted in place.

factory-built fireplaces

Among all new fire-places installed today, factory-built units are by far the fastest-growing option. Manufactured fireplaces offer many benefits, from low cost to easy installation to high-efficiency operation. Most units are made of steel. Some models include fans that blow air—heated in a plenum separated from the fire—into the room or through ducts to other rooms for additional space heating.

options Manufactured fireplaces may be fueled by wood, gas, or electricity. The fuel the unit burns and the heat expelled through its combustion gases determine the type of flue needed.

Conventional wood and high-output gas fires require a double-wall chimney pipe that goes up and out the roof. Most fireplaces that burn natural gas or propane instead of wood burn so efficiently that they can be vented directly out through a wall (no tall flue is required). With advances in artificial log technology, many of the newer gas fireplaces offer very realistic-looking fires. These are an excellent option for remodels because they burn cleanly

(minimizing environmental concerns), start at the flip of a switch or remote control, and eliminate the need to stock firewood. Installing a gas line to a new or existing fireplace is a simple task for a plumber.

Somewhat less realistic looking and less satisfying than direct-vent styles are vent-free gas fireplaces, which are completely sealed and produce a much

An insert can make an old fireplace more efficient, forcing warm air into the room rather than letting it escape through the chimney.

For easy installation, consider a gas log prefab with ready-made surround and hearth.

smaller flame. Because even efficient combustion produces some carbon monoxide, these have sensors to monitor this dangerous by-product and to automatically shut off the gas if the room's oxygen drops to a dangerously low level.

Electric fireplaces are also an option, though they are the least realistic. These simply plug in (or are hard-wired) to the electrical system and require no venting. Most provide warmth like an electric heater and mimic the appearance of a fire—some more successfully than others.

flues are well insulated, Silva also insulates the exterior walls behind them. "You want the heat from the fireplace to stay in the house," he says. He also covers the wall and chase with a vapor barrier and ⅝-inch fire-rated drywall as an extra, inexpensive precaution.

Like kitchen stoves, manufactured fireplaces do not require additional fireproofing or special framing unless they are exceptionally large or heavy. Once the unit is positioned, all that's left is to install the flue, which is stacked in sections that lock together. The chimney chase and fireplace surround can be completed afterward in any interior finish the homeowner wants, including lightweight brick or stone facing for an authentic look.

the stone alternative Other manufactured fireplaces include units made of manufactured or natural stone.

One type uses blocks fabricated with pumice and heat-resistant refractory cement. These units look and feel like stone but weigh two-thirds less than masonry units of a similar size. The blocks stack together quickly, cutting installation time from weeks to days. "It's a breakthrough product for anyone who appreciates the value of solid masonry construc-

installation basics Manufactured fireplaces are designed to be built in, and are often referred to as zero-clearance (requiring only ½ inch of spacing from wall framing materials). Once a unit is installed and trimmed out, it's hard to tell that it wasn't part of the home's original construction.

Tom Silva likes the flexibility of these units. "As long as I can run the chimney up or out, I can position the

firebox anywhere in the room," he says. "That's the beauty of it." Working with a helper, he can get the entire installation done in less than one day.

The first step is to position the fireplace and cut a hole in the roof. Then he builds the chimney framing, or chase, for the stacked, double-wall flue pipe (when working with a wood-burning model). Though manufactured fireplaces and their in-wall

tip: fireplace maintenance Creosote is a black, tarlike residue produced by burning wood. When it builds up inside chimney walls, it can pose a serious fire hazard. Before the first fire of the season, have your chimney inspected and swept if necessary. This is also a good way to make sure no critters have taken up residence inside. Also check that the damper operates easily, locks securely, and closes tightly. If you or the chimney sweep notices any signs of damage, have a mason inspect the chimney inside and out and make repairs right away.

tion," says builder Jason Yowell, who installed one in the TOH project home built in Atlanta.

Another option is imported quarried European soapstone hearths. Sold as kits, these units are dense, heavy, precisely cut and polished solid rock. Their biggest advantage is heat retention. Once they warm from the fires within, they radiate a long-lasting, gentle heat.

trimming out

As the hearth of the home, every fireplace, new or old, deserves an attractive surround. The fireplace is often the first thing you see as you come into a room, so it's important to put some effort into making it a deserving focal point.

Fire codes are specific about safety setbacks for decorative materials and the different types of fireplaces. Materials that may be used near or

against the hearth typically include brick, tile, fieldstone, and cut or quarried stone. If ceramic tiles are used close to a fire, they must be of the proper type that can withstand heat. Even noncombustible materials placed at floor level in front of a hearth are required to have a cement backerboard or other fire-resistant material installed below them. At a specified distance around the hearth,

wood and other combustible materials can be used.

Prefabricated mantels and surrounds are readily available in every conceivable size and style. Wood remains popular, but mantels also may be ordered in composite materials, metal, and natural or faux stone.

A newly refurbished wood mantel and limestone tiles gave this wood-burning fireplace a face-lift.

kitchens

BLEND THE SCIENCE OF FUNCTION AND THE ART OF DESIGN TO CREATE YOUR IDEAL KITCHEN

THOUGH THE KITCHEN WAS ONCE A UTILITARIAN SPACE used solely for cooking, today it's the heart of the home, often also serving as office, study hall, playroom, and central command post for the entire household. Its dimensions have grown to accommodate new roles, and modern kitchens are also expected to look stunning.

If your kitchen is outdated, remodeling it can dramatically transform your house, the way you live in it, and the value of your property, since an updated kitchen tops the list of improvements that buyers seek. But renovating a kitchen presents countless design challenges and involves sub-contractors from every trade. Even when things go smoothly, there are weeks of dust and disruption. And with the average kitchen remodel costing $20,000—and many exceeding $50,000—it's imperative to get everything right the first time.

That's what this chapter will help you do. It covers every aspect of kitchen remodeling, from floor plans to appliances. It also provides guide-lines the TOH crew has developed over 25 years of renovating kitchens. The goal is to help you find the best solutions for your house, your taste, your family's lifestyle, and your budget.

kitchen planning

It's often said that planning is the most important part of a home improvement project, and this is never truer than for a kitchen remodel. Because the kitchen is such an active, complex, multipurpose area, a remodel demands a great deal of forethought.

Though a kitchen remodel may be at the top of your wish list, it shouldn't necessarily be first on your to-do list. Kitchen remodels are very expensive and disruptive, and in some neighborhoods, you risk investing more in the project than you will gain in value if you sell your home. If you plan to stay in your house for only a short time, or you just want your kitchen to have a fresh look, your best option may be to reface the cabinets, replace worn-out countertops, or simply paint the walls.

If you do decide to remodel, make sure you'll be creating your new kitchen in a sound structure. The TOH crew recommends updating your house from the ground up, starting with the systems that make your kitchen function (see Chapter 3 for information on your home's systems). It's much more difficult and costly to replace plumbing, heating, and wiring after a renovation, and a failing system that's left in place can seriously compromise the new kitchen you've worked so hard to create. "We see people putting in new sinks and cabinets, then six months later pulling the walls apart again to put in new plumbing because the old pipes sprang a leak," says This Old House plumbing and heating expert Richard Trethewey. Even if the systems are not worn out, Trethewey likes to update them whenever a remodel calls for opening a wall.

possibilities

A kitchen remodel can cost under $10,000 for a simple face-lift to tens of thousands or more for a major remake. The scope of your project should depend not only on your budget but on how you plan to use your new kitchen. If you don't particularly like to cook, a simple kitchen may serve you better than a culinary cathedral with 12-foot ceilings and a restaurant-style range. On the other hand, if your family includes an avid chef or two, a spacious, well-scaled kitchen with all the trimmings will pay you back in pleasure and convenience.

This luxurious remodeled kitchen features an island that can seat five, custom cabinets with carved-wood detailing, and a stainless-steel range.

major remodels If your existing kitchen is cramped, the configuration is awkward, or natural light is lacking, a major remodel might be the only solution. Though a major remodel is expensive, it's often a better investment than a minor upgrade if you intend to stay in the home more than a few years. An ambitious renovation allows you to create a carefully designed, solidly constructed space exactly suited to your needs; the chances are good that it will endure for as long as you remain in your house. While you may redecorate or update it as the years go by, your kitchen will continue to function efficiently and meet your needs.

If you want just a little more elbowroom, you may be able to get it by bumping out along one wall (see pages 18–19). A bump-out, typically 3 to 5 feet wide, can give you enough room for an eating area or island, and it offers the opportunity to add windows that will bring in more light.

Opening up the wall over the kitchen sink allows for a view of an enclosed porch. While no square footage was added, the kitchen feels bigger and brighter.

A more affordable alternative is to add kitchen space without changing your house's footprint. Non-load-bearing walls can be removed relatively easily, and even load-bearing walls can be replaced by beams and other structural support. You can annex a little-used adjacent room to create a spacious area for cooking and eating, or combine your kitchen, family, and dining rooms into a great room.

Even if you're happy with the size of your existing kitchen, you may have other goals that warrant a major remodel. Structural changes such as moving doors, adding windows, altering the ceiling, and changing the floor plan in a way that involves reconfiguring plumbing and wiring are major changes. Even new cabinets—which typically account for close to half the cost of a major kitchen remodel—will place you in that category.

makeovers If you're satisfied with the basic size and layout of your

kitchen, you can focus on simple improvements that won't break the bank. For an average cost of about $6,000 to $15,000, a minor kitchen remodel typically includes new paint or wall covering, additional lighting, countertops, flooring, repainting or refacing cabinetry, plus one or two new appliances.

A minor remodel can make a dramatic difference in the way the room looks and functions. For example, a well-planned lighting scheme can utterly transform a space that is drab or difficult to work in, and any budget can accommodate handsome hardware that will bring a touch of class to refurbished cabinets. Replacing old appliances with new ones can cost relatively little if you look for updated models without all the bells and whistles.

However, don't settle for a makeover if your priority is a kitchen design that will last a lifetime. If your budget is limited, consider remaking your kitchen in stages. Begin by solving the problems that demand structural and mechanical solutions, and then plan to add finishes and new appliances when you can. In the meantime, make creative use of inexpensive materials such as off-the-shelf ceramic tiles, paint, and plastic laminates.

Adding colorful ceramic tile to countertops and the backsplash is a relatively inexpensive way to give your kitchen a fresh face.

the design process

tip: removing a wall To find out whether you can easily remove an interior wall to expand your kitchen, call your local building department and request that a building inspector come by and check it out. "It's one of the most effective and least expensive ways to find out whether your walls are load bearing," says This Old House master carpenter Norm Abram.

Designing a kitchen renovation can take as much time and attention as the construction phase. A well-planned design is particularly crucial in a major remodel, in which costs are high and even small errors can become daily annoyances. Detailed planning will save you significant costs down the road. For example, if it costs a dollar to plan your kitchen well on the drawing, it will cost $10 to make a change if your cabinet-maker has already begun, and it will cost $100 to make a change if you don't catch a problem until the crew is on the job site.

If you're just beginning to think about remodeling your kitchen, give yourself at least a few months to come up with a suitable design. You can begin the process on your own, but the TOH crew strongly recommends hiring an architect or kitchen designer to finalize the plans. Though this will add a bit to the cost of your project, it's less expensive than wasting your money on a kitchen that ends up being unworkable or unsuitable (see pages 29–34 for information about hiring and working with professionals).

cultivating ideas

The best way to start designing your new kitchen is to evaluate the one you have. Identify what works for you and what doesn't, and note which features you like and which you dislike. Perhaps the location of the sink causes traffic jams or the color of the countertop makes you queasy. List everything you find unsatisfactory, and write down solutions as they occur to you. Analyzing your existing kitchen's inadequacies in this way will help you determine what features you want and need in your remodel.

Your next task is to visualize your ideal kitchen. Imagine all the changes you would make if you had an unlimited budget. In your mind, knock down walls, raise the roof, even move the entire room to a different part of the house. The point is to open yourself up to possibilities that you might not otherwise consider.

Exposed-beam ceilings open up this long, narrow kitchen, while a functional island that seats four makes double use of the space.

Having a small kitchen allows you the luxury of using more expensive materials, such as these copper wall panels.

Often an idea that seems outlandish turns out to be quite feasible.

While you're conceptualizing your dream kitchen, look out for design ideas and features that appeal to you. Visit showrooms, attend a home show, or take a neighborhood home tour. Study remodels that your friends have done, and ask them what they would have done differently, if anything. Make a design notebook filled with magazine and catalog pictures of kitchen features that you like. Note whether you're consistently attracted to certain colors, materials, or decorating motifs. Collecting these images will help you clarify your priorities and convey your preferences to your designer.

Once you've spent some time fantasizing, focus on practical details. To ensure your kitchen will work for you and your family, consider how it will be used and by whom. Will you need extra workstations for multiple chefs? Will you need special accommodations for a child, a disabled person, or someone who's very tall or very short? Do you want a place for

guests to congregate, an area where the kids can do homework, a pantry for bulk purchases, a pastry counter? Take an inventory of your fantasy kitchen to see whether it includes everything your family needs. You may find that some crucial features have been omitted while others that appeared to be attractive no longer make the cut.

When considering decorating styles and materials, be honest with yourself about your habits and housekeeping tendencies. If you're a clutter collector, you may find it difficult to maintain the sleek, ultra-clean look of a contemporary kitchen; a less formal country décor will be more forgiving. Also keep in mind how much wear and tear your kitchen needs to be able to take. Pale hues and scratch-prone surfaces may be perfect for fastidious cooks and elegant parties, but a heavily trafficked family kitchen requires materials that are durable and easy to clean.

Remember to include special features in your remodel that suit your needs. If you are an avid baker, consider a slide-out marble slab for making breads and pastries.

SITING YOUR KITCHEN

In new construction, the TOH crew has had great success with southeast-facing kitchens, which catch the rising sun and remain cheerfully bright even in winter. Which orientation is best for your kitchen depends on where you live. A southern exposure generally offers the best light but may generate too much heat in a Sunbelt kitchen. A west-facing kitchen may get too much afternoon sun in Florida, but it may be just right in Maine.

While it is not practical in most kitchen remodels to change location, you can improve the room's present position. Observe how the sun hits the room at various times of the day and year to choose ideal spots for skylights. Gain a better view by repositioning windows. Resituate your kitchen's exterior door so that you can easily carry groceries from car to countertop. In colder climates, you may want a buffer area to keep out cold air; this mudroom can also provide a landing zone for wet coats and muddy shoes. If your kitchen has too many interior doorways, eliminate one to control traffic and create more wall space. Or open the wall around it to improve traffic flow and sight lines to the rest of the house.

universal and accessible kitchen design

During the past two decades, kitchen design has moved away from the "one size fits all" model to a more flexible approach. Now the emphasis is on making the kitchen adapt to the user rather than the other way around. This concept grew from the principles of universal design, a set of standards for creating barrier-free environments for disabled people.

A raised dishwasher (foreground) lets you load and unload dishes without bending down. It also provides a higher countertop with a storage drawer below.

Today, universal design doesn't have to mean lowering every counter to wheelchair height; it can mean lowering one section of counter and raising another so a grandmother and her young grandson can both help prepare dinner. The concept has worked so well that the National Kitchen and

Bath Association recently revised its design guidelines to incorporate concepts borrowed from universal design.

Versatility is the key to creating a kitchen that will work for people of any age, stature, or physical ability. For example, universal design calls for a knee space under a sink or a cooktop to make those areas wheelchair accessible, but with the simple addition of a stool, an able-bodied person can use the space to sit and work. When not in use, a knee space can be hidden behind cabinet doors that slide into pockets. If it won't be needed in the foreseeable future, a knee space can serve as a storage area with the addition of removable doors and shelves (a knee space also requires a finished surface on all sides of the cabinet, as well as flooring underneath).

Accessibility, the foundation of universal design, depends on kitchen features placed at the right height for everyone who will use them. Adding variety to your kitchen plan is the best way to achieve this. One of the simplest things you can do is to set counters at different heights. The National Kitchen and Bath Association recommends including some countertops that are 28 to 32 inches high for seated or shorter users and for use as a chopping or

baking center. A countertop 42 to 45 inches high is suitable for taller users and works well as a snack bar.

You needn't add a slew of custom-sized counters. A cutting board on top of an open drawer equipped with heavy-duty slides can serve as a lowered work surface, and a butcher block on top of a standard 36-inch-high counter will create a raised work surface. It's easiest to reach shelves that are no lower than the waist and no higher than the shoulders, but many kitchens offer no storage in that zone. If possible, use pantry cabinets for storage. Or add shallow shelves under wall cabinets where seated people or short people (including kids) can reach them.

Many universal design features offer advantages for people of all abilities. Replacing cabinet knobs with wide pulls will make them easier for everyone to open. Installing full-extension slides on drawers and pullout shelves makes it possible to access heavy and hard-to-reach items. A single-lever faucet is simpler for all members of the household to operate. Large drawers in the base cabinets

tip: counter height

To determine the right height for your counter, stand in your most comfortable working stance at a low surface, then stack up books or boards until you can rest your palms on the surface with a slight break in your elbows. The ideal height for food preparation is 2 to 3 inches below your flexed elbows.

sink/cleanup center The main sink/cleanup center should be conveniently located for the cook but also accessible to other household members who want to wash up or get a drink of water. Because so much time is spent at the sink, designers often place it first and lay out the rest of the work triangle from there. The sink is best placed at the center of the cook's work path, between the refrigerator and the range or cooktop. For maximum efficiency, allow 36 inches on the cooktop side and 24 inches on the refrigerator side. This will give you a staging area for dirty dishes and a drying area for clean ones.

The dishwasher should be within 36 inches of one end of the sink. Which side of the sink depends on the route dishes will take from table to dishwasher, and perhaps also on whether you're right- or left-handed. More than one person at a time should be able to reach into the dishwasher.

Other items that should be close to the sink are cleaning supplies, cutlery, and waste and recycling bins. Cutlery is best stored just outside the work triangle so that it's possible to set the table without disturbing the cook. Rather than placing the garbage container directly under the sink, put it a step or two away so that the person washing dishes won't have to move aside whenever someone wants to dispose of something. Do the same with any recycling bins.

The dishwasher should be placed within 36 inches of the edge of the sink so you don't have to shuttle dripping dishes to another area of the kitchen.

Include as much countertop space as possible between the sink and range, as this is the primary food-prep area. Keep cooking utensils close by.

The area around this range includes a cooking sink, which has a double boiler/steamer insert designed for pasta, potatoes, or anything else that requires a pot of boiling water.

cooking center The cooking center should be the most protected area of the work triangle because of the risk of having lots of activity around hot pots. The cooktop or range should be in a traffic-free location near the sink to make it easier to fill and drain pots. Optimally, the cooktop should be on an exterior wall so a ventilation system that vents directly through the wall can be installed (see pages 150–151). Allow for plenty of counter space—the TOH crew recommends 16 to 18 inches—on either side of the range or cooktop and be sure each side has some provision for hot pans coming off it. You'll also need a 21- to 30-inch overhead clearance so cooks can see and access rear burners and the ventilation system can work efficiently.

The oven, which gets less use and needs less tending than the cooktop, can be placed outside the primary work triangle. Typically, a wall oven is placed at the end of a cabinet run. It needs at least 15 inches of countertop beside it. If the oven door doesn't open into a traffic area, the countertop can be opposite but no more than 48 inches away.

The microwave oven can also be placed outside the kitchen triangle so that it won't create traffic jams in the main work area. Because it's often used for heating snacks or leftovers that have required cold storage, the microwave should be near the refrigerator. Allow 15 inches of landing space above, below, or adjacent to the microwave.

other centers A run of countertop at least 3 feet long between the sink and the range or refrigerator will serve as the primary area for preparing food. If two people will cook at the same time, you may want to include a supplementary preparation center consisting of an additional work surface and a second sink. If it's contiguous with the primary preparation area, the total work surface should be at least 72 inches long. Choose a deep single-bowl sink and equip it with a garbage disposal so you won't have to carry vegetable peelings and such across the room. If you have the space, you may also want a baking center, designed especially for kneading bread and rolling out dough, though the countertop should be lower—30 to 33 inches.

islands and peninsulas
Because it will become the focal point of the kitchen, a built-in center island must be designed with great care.

An island can serve as a secondary work center. This one has a prep sink in addition to plenty of space for chopping and assembling.

If you want a center island, first consider what functions it needs to serve. The TOH crew feels that an island works best as a versatile stand-in for the old-fashioned kitchen table—a place to prepare food and serve informal meals and snacks. Though islands are often equipped with sinks, dishwashers, cooktops, and barbecue grills, the TOH crew prefers to place such features on the perimeter of the room. A sink requires about 5 feet of surrounding counter space for staging and drying dishes, which leaves very little surface area on the island for food preparation. For similar reasons, the TOH crew advises against island-mounted cooktops and grills. In addition to accumulating grease, smoke, and mess, these appliances are difficult to ventilate well.

The best kitchen layouts for an island are one-wall, L-shaped, and U-shaped plans (see pages 132–133). The island should not block the work triangle, and doors on island cabinets and appliances should be able to freely swing open. Floor space should allow for a 42- to 48-inch clearance between the island and the counters; the upper part of the range when more than one cook must be accommodated. A smaller aisle will be cramped, and a larger one will make it difficult to pivot between the island and other work zones. If people will sit at the island, you'll need a larger aisle—from 54 to 60 inches wide—plus at least a 12-inch overhang on the island's surface to accommodate stools.

The island can be the same height as other countertops, or it can be higher or lower depending on its purpose and the people who will use it most. You can also have more than one counter height. For example, a 36-inch-high primary surface for food prep, and a 42-inch-high breakfast bar for eating on bar stools.

For food preparation, the island's surface must be at least 36 inches long (72 inches if two cooks will work side by side). If your island is 6 feet or longer, consider rounding the corners to cut down on bruised hips and to facilitate traffic flow. You can also select an L or U shape instead of a rectangle. An angular island works well in an open-kitchen plan, where it separates the kitchen from the social area without blocking it off. Though such designs cost more to build, they typically offer more storage space and more room for amenities such as a wine rack or warming oven.

A peninsula presents many of the same design issues as an island. In some open-kitchen plans, a peninsula is the only possible location for a sink or cooktop. If this is your case, some simple measures can make the best of the situation. To hide clutter on the work side of the peninsula, put the sink or cooktop behind a 4- to 6-inch-high ledge that divides it from the seating or social area. If the peninsula is to be used as a cooking center, think carefully about ventilation. An overhead hood will do the best job, but it's a prominent design feature and must be carefully chosen and placed so that it doesn't obstruct your view or destroy the openness of your floor plan. Because they are exposed on all sides and are a decorative element, they are also expensive. A downdraft cooktop is less obtrusive, but invest in a high-quality model that will ventilate properly even in the presence of cross-drafts (see pages 150–151).

A peninsula is all that separates this dining area from the kitchen, creating a continuity between the spaces that encourages gathering.

tip: round tables If you want a table in your kitchen, consider a round one. It takes up less space than a rectangular table yet it can seat more people. A round shape also facilitates conversation, since everyone can easily talk to people seated across the table as well as those on either side.

additional areas

Unless your kitchen is quite small, your remodeling plan will probably call for at least one specialized area in addition to the primary work zones. Here are a few to consider.

dining area If you want your kitchen to be a true family gathering place, it should allow for cooking and eating in the same space. A dining area can be a separate breakfast room, a table in the middle of the kitchen, or a section of an island or peninsula. If you choose an island as an informal dining table, allow for adequate aisle space (see page 137) and an overhang to comfortably accommodate sitters' knees. If you want a kitchen table, allow at least 2½ feet of clearance on all sides for chairs. A dining area can double as a food preparation area when counter space is limited, and it will also encourage people to congregate in the kitchen.

sitting area A sitting area adjacent to the kitchen work space is ideal if you like to socialize while cooking. A sitting area, like a dining area, will allow guests to gather in and around the kitchen. However, before you decide to open your kitchen to a sitting area, make sure that you have strategies for dealing with the noise, odors, and visual clutter that are bound to invade both spaces. To mitigate these problems, you can upgrade your ventilation system and purchase top-quality, quiet appliances that can be customized to blend with your cabinetry.

Because the kitchen is often where the family congregates, it makes sense to create an adjacent sitting area. In this room, kids can relax on the large sectional or sit on the chairs at the island and still be part of the kitchen activity.

This open kitchen features desk space and two dining areas, creating a truly multifunctional core.

desk/work area A desk/work area can be a place to pay bills, store cookbooks, open mail, plan menus, and do homework. Add a computer with Internet access, however, and you'll draw the crowds. The best solution is to locate an office area outside the work triangle, but design it to blend with the kitchen using matching cabinetry and counters.

entertainment You may want to combine a seating area with a home theater system, or simply add shelves for a television and stereo, as you're choosing cabinetry. Keep in mind that your electronic gear will have to stand up to the heat and humidity generated in the adjoining kitchen. Some models made especially for the kitchen come with magnetized remote controls that stick to the refrigerator, or sealed controls that will survive being doused with coffee. Some newer refrigerator models are also available with television screens built into the door—a space saver if you're trying to conserve counter space—but a small shelf or wall-mounted TV is probably better for more continuous viewing.

A television in the kitchen allows you to catch the morning news over a cup of coffee, cook while watching a cooking show, and keep the kids entertained while you're preparing a meal.

putting your plan on paper

Though it's best to have a professional design your new kitchen, you may want to come up with a few plans of your own first. Having grappled with the problems your project presents, you'll be able to evaluate the solutions your designer comes up with, and you'll know better which ones are likely to work for you. If your kitchen is going to keep its current size and shape, check into design services offered—often for free—by major home improvement centers. You may even find that you can use one of your own designs. If you do, you should still have a designer look over your plans so you don't make errors or miss opportunities.

Working on graph paper, draw a base map of your existing kitchen, penciling in walls, doors, and windows in their current locations. Cut out pieces of paper or cardboard to scale (typically ¼ or ½ inch equals 1 foot) to represent the refrigerator, sink, and cooktop, and begin arranging them into a work triangle that meets your needs. Then add cabinets, tables, islands, and other major features. When you have an arrangement you like, place a sheet of tracing paper over the graph paper and draw the floor plan in bold lines. If you prefer to work on a computer, you can use kitchen design software.

As you work on your floor plan, different configurations may occur to you. Draw each variation on tracing paper and assign it a number. Try to come up with

The smaller your space, the more planning is needed to tailor every square inch to your needs, such as an integrated wine cubby and a lazy Susan inside the corner cabinet.

several alternatives, including some that explore more radical possibilities such as relocating walls and windows. On TOH projects, kitchen remodels generally begin with a number of floor plans. Each option is scrutinized, and the final plan is often a synthesis of several plans.

Once you've decided on a floor plan, you may want to make a scale model to help you visualize how the room will look when you're standing in it. To do this, draw each kitchen wall in scale, this time showing a front view of cabinets, appliances, and other large features. Glue each drawing to cardboard backing and then tape these walls together to form a miniature room. To get a ground-level view of your kitchen, place the model at eye level and look into it from the side.

You can also do a full-scale mock-up of your kitchen. It takes just a few hours to set up a life-size representation of your floor plan using materials you have on hand (see Tip on opposite page), or you can ask your contractor to do this for you.

For TOH's Manchester House renovation, This Old House general contractor Tom Silva mocked up the kitchen in full scale on the floor using plywood and tables to represent counters, cabinets, and other major items. This gave the owners a better sense of the space and led to a few significant revisions, including a shortened cooking island. It also helped Silva to think about structural implications, plumbing and electrical locations, and requirements for the appliances. Silva estimates that his mock-up represented about $250 worth of work—a low price for preventing big mistakes in design. Considering how quickly you can run through tens of thousands of dollars on a kitchen remodel, spending a couple of hundred on a mock-up in the planning stages is an excellent investment.

STANDARD KITCHEN DIMENSIONS

In a well-planned kitchen, doors have room to swing freely, people have room to enter and exit easily, and countertops are at a height that's comfortable for the cook. The illustration at right shows industry standards for clearances. These are appropriate for most people and most kitchens, but they can be altered to fit specific circumstances or individual cooks (see pages 130–131).

There should be at least 42 inches between an island and a countertop, sink, refrigerator, or range; 48 inches if two people will cook at the same time. Allow at least 36 inches between an island and a traffic corridor. Twenty inches in front of an open dishwasher door will allow enough room for loading and unloading. Keep the edge of a table or eating counter at least 36 inches from a wall or other object, or 65 inches if the area behind the table is a walkway. Counter-height seating for an eat-in area should allow a space 24 inches wide by 19 inches deep for every diner.

Standard heights, recommended for an average-size adult with no physical challenges: The highest shelf in a wall cabinet should be 72 inches high. Electrical outlets and switches should be 15 to 48 inches from the ground. Countertops are typically 36 inches. The standard is 36 to 42 inches for an eating counter. Stools for an eating counter should be 12 inches lower than the countertop, allowing at least 9 inches of leg space.

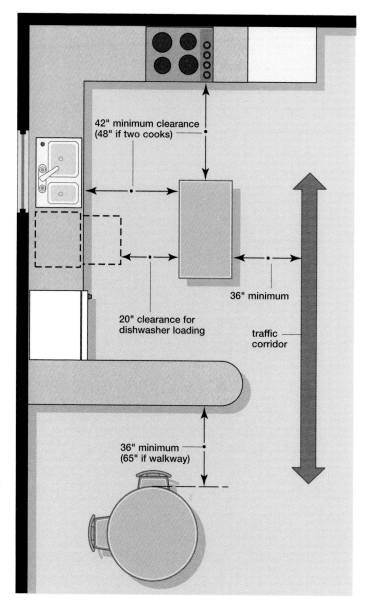

42" minimum clearance (48" if two cooks)

20" clearance for dishwasher loading

36" minimum

traffic corridor

36" minimum (65" if walkway)

creating a budget and controlling costs

The key to controlling the price of a kitchen renovation is developing a plan that focuses on essential elements and solves problems in the simplest ways possible. A sound and efficient design saves money both now and later because it's easier to maintain and upgrade.

The TOH crew firmly believes in having a professional design your kitchen (see pages 144–145), but there are ways to save money during this phase. If you decide to hire an architect, you may be able to keep expenses down by looking for a small firm rather than a larger office with a big reputation. Some architects will allow you to reduce your bill by doing your own research for appliances, sinks, etc. If you have your plans drawn by a kitchen designer affiliated with a particular store, you can often have the design fee credited toward the price of goods. For a simple job, you may be happy using a cabinet shop or carpenter who will charge much less than you would pay an architect.

To price your project, present your design to a few contractors you're considering and ask for bids. Make sure that your plans are as detailed as possible so that the figures you're given are accurate and you can make a fair comparison. When the bids come in, add at least 10 percent (for smaller projects) or up to 30 percent

To cut the cost of a kitchen remodel, opt for stock cabinetry instead of custom.

(for major remodels) to the bottom line for cost overruns or changes. "If you have $50,000 to spend, see if you can get your project done for $40,000," Silva says. With that cushion, "you'll be prepared for surprises, and be much, much happier for it."

Don't attempt to cut corners by simply hiring the contractor who charges the least. "The real problems come when homeowners try to get a bargain," Trethewey says. "If you choose your contractor simply by taking the lowest bid, you become a co-conspirator when the project never gets finished or when you hate the way it turns out." He suggests throwing out the low bid and taking the middle or even the high one. As Norm Abram points out, you need someone who's reliable and dependable if you hope to set a budget and stick to it. "Hire a reliable contractor who will work for a fixed contract price," he advises (see page 34).

If all the bids you get exceed what you can afford, you can make signifi-

cant cuts to the total by economizing on major design elements. Since cabinetry can account for nearly half of the total bill, you'll realize a significant reduction if you choose stock cabinets instead of custom-built ones—and even more by refacing or painting the cabinets you have. Substituting low-cost materials such as vinyl and laminate for expensive ones such as wood and stone can also be a major money saver. Alternatively, you can complete your project in phases. Sometimes people live with a plywood floor for several months until they can afford their flooring of choice.

While careful planning is the most important cost-containment measure, you'll need to be disciplined during the construction process as well. "Avoid making changes and adding projects once the work has begun," Abram says. "Nothing wrecks budgets faster than sentences beginning: 'While we're at it, why don't we…'"

The TOH crew strongly recommends working with designers and contractors when you are remodeling a kitchen.

BUILDING A SAFER KITCHEN

The kitchen has just about every hazard you can find in a home, from sharp implements and hot surfaces to combustion gases and appliances that grind and cut. The dangers are magnified because people tend to congregate at the riskiest time: when meals are being prepared. Consequently, it's crucial to keep safety in mind when you are planning a kitchen remodel. As you are designing your kitchen, incorporate safety solutions into your layout.

■ You'll need a clear pathway for carrying hot food to the dining area and enough clearance for cabinet, oven, and dishwasher doors to swing open without blocking the traffic area (see page 141). For convenience as well as safety, locate the range outside the kitchen hubbub and away from flammable items such as window coverings. Allow adequate space for heat-proof landing areas next to the cooktop, microwave, and oven (see page 136).

■ Be sure your plan includes plenty of electrical outlets (at least one every 4 feet along countertops, except next to the sink) so you won't ever have to use an extension cord. All outlets must be protected by ground fault circuit interrupters (see page 148).

■ Proper lighting is often viewed as a cosmetic issue, but in the kitchen it's a safety consideration as well. Sufficient ambient light can help prevent bumps and falls, while task lighting in work areas enhances safety when chopping with sharp knives or at a hot stove. If glare is a problem, you can control it with dimmer switches or window coverings.

■ Wall cabinets should be firmly anchored to wall studs, and only light items should be stored on shelves that are above your head. Poisonous chemicals and dangerous objects require storage that's locked or otherwise inaccessible to children.

■ Also make safety a priority when selecting appliances if your household includes children. Choose a batch-feed disposal that won't operate unless it's closed with a lid; if you really prefer a switch-operated model, put the switch where children can't reach it. Look for a trash compactor that requires a key, and a dishwasher that's difficult for small hands to open. If you choose a dishwasher that heats the water it uses, you can turn your water heater below 120 degrees, making all your faucets safer (see page 211).

■ Controls for your cooktop or range should be at the front or side of the appliance, not in between burners. For added safety, consider a model that also has staggered burners. If you like the look and capability of a commercial range, choose one that has been modified for home use; some true commercial ranges can get extremely hot to the touch. When installing a gas range, be especially careful to select a ventilation hood that can remove dangerous combustion gases from the room (see pages 150–151 for more on ventilation). Any home with gas-powered appliances should be equipped with carbon monoxide detectors, and every kitchen should have a smoke detector nearby (install it between the kitchen and living or dining area). A class A-B-C fire extinguisher should be mounted between the kitchen and an exit.

■ Spilled food and soapy dishwater can make the kitchen floor slippery, so choose skid-resistant flooring if your household includes people who are unsteady on their feet. Softer materials such as resilient flooring are more forgiving in the event of a fall and are less likely to shatter a dropped glass.

■ To make countertops safer, have them built with rolled edges and rounded corners. Finally, look for cabinet pulls that have no sharp edges.

working with professionals

For a project as complicated as a major kitchen remodel, Norm Abram advises homeowners to hire an architect or a kitchen designer. Architects are trained in all phases of design and project management, and they are qualified to make calculations for structural changes. They're also trained to give you something interesting in terms of light, space, and shape. As a result, their services are particularly valuable if your plan includes major structural changes or an addition. "You don't want the addition to destroy the proportions of the house, which could actually devalue the property," Abram says.

Kitchen designers bring a different set of skills to the table. Because they specialize in kitchens, they are very familiar with the full range of products on the market and how to put them together for an attractive and efficient kitchen.

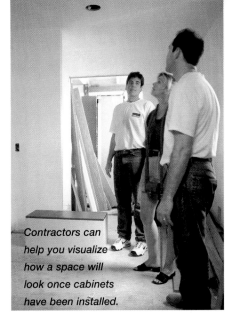

Contractors can help you visualize how a space will look once cabinets have been installed.

You can find a kitchen designer at a kitchen showroom or through the National Kitchen and Bath Association (NKBA), a 40-year-old not-for-profit trade organization dedicated to promoting professionalism and ethical business practices among its members. You may want to look for someone who has received the NKBA's Certified Kitchen Designer (CKD) credential, which is based on written examinations and extensive industry experience. Designers who work for a kitchen showroom are usually paid a set fee (generally a few

hundred dollars) that can be credited toward the price of goods you purchase. Those who aren't affiliated with a showroom charge either a flat fee or an hourly rate ranging from $25 to $100 (see pages 29–34 for more information on hiring architects and designers).

If your project is relatively simple and you know exactly what you want, you may be able to have a cabinet shop that specializes in kitchens draw up a design. Look at examples of its construction as well as its design work. The shop will recommend subcontractors and may even agree to supervise the project.

A general contractor's role is to organize and supervise construction. You can save as much as 20 percent of your project cost by acting as your own general contractor, but don't test your skills on a kitchen renovation unless you have building experience, organizational abilities, and plenty of time. If you do decide to take on the job, your greatest challenge will be hiring and scheduling subcontractors. Sequencing the many trades needed for a kitchen remodel can be mind-boggling, and "subs" may give low priority to an amateur contractor offering one-time-only employment (see page 35 for more information on being your own contractor).

Tom Silva and Norm Abram carefully salvage this old marble backsplash from a kitchen that's about to be completely remodeled.

A good contractor installs all elements of a kitchen with precision, ensuring that the work follows building codes and will pass inspections.

As always, it's wise to get bids from a number of contractors. And for a kitchen remodel, it's particularly important that you have complete and detailed specifications for your project, since kitchen fixtures, materials, and appliances vary so widely in quality and cost. The same admonition applies when you're drawing up a contract for a kitchen renovation. If you don't specify what you want, the contractor will probably include a fixed dollar amount known as an "allowance," which may end up being insufficient. As Norm Abram says, a contract with many allowances is a weak one, and that goes double when it comes to remodeling a kitchen.

Your written agreement should include a specific payment schedule, and as construction proceeds, you should make sure the contract terms are being met. "If you have to pay for things in advance, such as custom cabinets, ask to see receipts as proof

that they've actually been ordered," Silva says, "and ask for a regular accounting of costs so you know where you stand." Since a kitchen renovation requires many subcontractors, your contract should also have a waiver of subcontractor liens to protect you if your general contractor fails to pay the plumber, the electrician, the tile setter, or anyone else who provided services or materials for your job (see page 34 for more information about what your legal agreement should include).

building codes and inspections

Unless you're merely replacing existing appliances and surfaces in your kitchen, you'll need a permit from your local building department to begin your remodel. A permit is particularly important in a complicated kitchen renovation, since it ensures that your contractor is following your

plans to the letter. Prepare yourself for frequent visits from the inspector. There are many types of work to be approved in a kitchen remodel, and some (such as plumbing and electrical work) require multiple inspections. Your contractor can obtain building permits, schedule inspections, and deal with inspectors. If you act as your own general contractor, these responsibilities will fall to you.

Kitchen renovations that include bump-outs or additions are subject to zoning laws that dictate whether and how much a house can be expanded. If you intend to enlarge your kitchen, find out about local zoning restrictions before you even begin planning your project.

Don't try to skirt building codes or save money on permit fees when you're renovating a kitchen. Local codes reflect good building practices for your area, and they're your best guarantee that your kitchen will be safe, sound, and built to last. "Get inspections—from structural to insulation, rough plumbing, electrical, and wallboard—before finishes are put on," Silva says. "In some parts of the country, this is required before an occupancy permit is issued, but it's in your best interest to make sure all sign-offs are done." (See pages 36–37 for more on codes and permits.)

surviving a kitchen remodel

No construction project tops a kitchen renovation for inconvenience. Even a bathroom remodel is less onerous. While most houses have an extra bathroom that can be used during construction, few have a spare kitchen. In addition to dealing with noise, dust, and other typical remodeling annoyances, you'll need to find strategies for feeding your family.

A major renovation will put your kitchen out of commission for at least two months—often more. You'll probably eat a lot of restaurant meals, but you'll still have to establish a temporary kitchen somewhere in your house. The gear for your kitchen "camp" can be as simple as a refrigerator, a hot plate, and a microwave.

If you expect your remodel to drag on to the point where take-out food loses its allure and gets expensive, you may want to relocate your range (or buy a cheap used one) and have an electrician establish a temporary power supply. The same can be done with a gas range and a bottle of propane. You can even install some of your old cabinets and countertops. Just be sure that even any temporary work is done by licensed plumbers and electricians for safety's sake.

When deciding where to put your alternate kitchen, look for a spot with water close by. Kitchenless homeowners have been known to decamp to the laundry room, the basement, or even a spare bathroom. If you can postpone remodeling until summer, outdoor cooking can eliminate the need for a stove.

Plan the progress of your remodel carefully so the work will go quickly and smoothly. Don't start construction until your local building department gives your project the go-ahead. Order custom-made items such as cabinets, windows, and stone countertops well ahead of time, and have all crucial materials on site before any work begins. If you plan to act as your own general contractor, carefully sequence the various trades. Many of your subcontractors will have to make multiple visits, so check their availability well in advance, and be persistent in pressing them to show up when they are needed.

One family set up a temporary kitchen in their laundry room. They installed their old range and cabinets, a deep sink for cleanup and food preparation, and used two small cabinets above the washer and dryer to store food and dishes.

kitchen systems

A new kitchen places tremendous demands on all the systems of a house. If you're altering your kitchen's floor plan, chances are you'll need to tap into or reconfigure your plumbing, wiring, heating, and ventilation. Even if your floor plan will remain the same, upgrading your systems should be a priority (see Chapter 3 for a general discussion of house systems).

When installing new systems, try to think about future needs as well as current ones. If you anticipate wanting a second dishwasher or a home entertainment system a few years from now, it's best to put in the plumbing and wiring while the walls are open.

plumbing

How expensive it will be to relocate a sink or add a wet bar depends on how far the new fixture will be from your home's main soil stack. "If the new sink is within, say, 5 feet of the old one, there shouldn't be a problem," Trethewey says. "Your plumber can run the pipes horizontally behind the new cabinets or, if he must, within them." Much farther than that will require putting in a new vent—an expensive procedure that may involve opening walls all the way to the roof. In some areas, an island-mounted sink can be "wet-vented" using an oversized branch drain as both drain and vent. Check with your local building department to find out whether this is permissible where you live.

Though you can save money by keeping your existing plumbing, it doesn't pay to do so if you'll be stuck with an unworkable floor plan, so you may be better off economizing elsewhere. One option is to have your plumber run rough plumbing for accessory fixtures you'd like to have but can't afford now. The pipes can be capped off, and later you can easily have that vegetable sink or ice maker installed.

If you're having problems with low water pressure in your kitchen, you'll have to add this item to your budget. The cure is to upsize or replace the supply pipes from your water main to your faucets. "There's no point in trying to save money by tolerating inadequate water pressure," Trethewey says. "You want to make sure that you'll have a system that will give good service for a long time."

Kitchen plumbing is tightly regulated by local and state codes that cover both water and gas systems. To ensure that your plumbing systems are properly installed, an inspector will visit your job site when pipes are placed and when the entire installation is complete. Installation should include shutoff valves for every sink and appliance. Gas appliances should have a nearby code-approved gas cock (valve) with a blade handle for easy shutoff in an emergency.

It doesn't make sense to remodel a kitchen's floor plan without updating the plumbing systems as well. Strong water pressure and convenient, up-to-date fixtures make food preparation and cleaning much easier.

electrical

Unless your house was built in the past decade or so, you'll almost certainly have to upgrade its electrical system to accommodate your new kitchen. You'll need new circuits to support the number of appliances, switches, and outlets commonly found in a modern kitchen (the typical makeover requires three to five new circuits). If you have an older house with a 60-amp service panel, you'll also have to step up to a 100- or 200-amp service panel to support any major improvements.

The National Electrical Code prescribes specific requirements for electrical circuits serving a kitchen. For example, there must be two 20-amp circuits for countertop appliances, a designated 50-amp, 220-volt circuit for the range, and a separate 20-amp circuit for kitchen appliances such as the refrigerator, microwave, or garbage disposer. An electrical contractor can tell you how many circuits you'll need and what capacity they should be.

To determine exactly what your electrical needs are, make a complete list of all the electrical devices you want in your kitchen, including telephone, cable television, sound system, security system, and high-speed Internet connection. Carefully consider where everything should be placed, as the design of your kitchen's electrical system will substantially affect how the room looks and func-

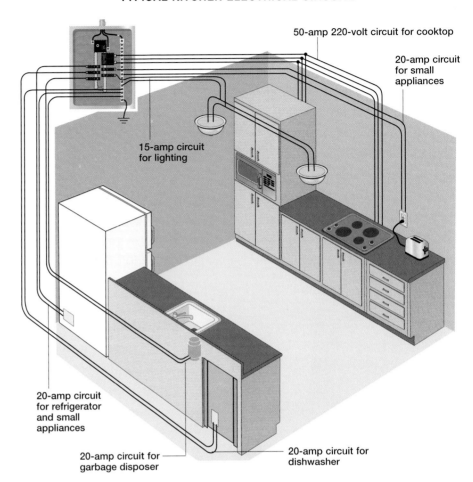

TYPICAL KITCHEN ELECTRICAL CIRCUITS

50-amp 220-volt circuit for cooktop

20-amp circuit for small appliances

15-amp circuit for lighting

20-amp circuit for refrigerator and small appliances

20-amp circuit for garbage disposer

20-amp circuit for dishwasher

tions. For an extensive remodel, your electrician will work from an electrical plan supplied by your architect or designer. Such a plan shows where outlets and switches should be and specifies what fixtures you want.

Electricians tend to specialize, so look for one who does renovation work rather than just new houses or electrical repairs. A remodeling specialist will be well qualified to judge how much electrical capacity you'll need and will have experience performing renovation-specific tasks such as snaking wires through finished walls. If your project requires

a complete electrical makeover, including a service upgrade, expect to spend about 10 percent of the total budget on this.

If you're just beginning to update your electrical system, the kitchen is a great place to start. Norm Abram suggests running new wiring to heavy-load appliances and to any outlet within 6 feet of a sink. Countertop outlets must be protected by a GFCI device—either a GFCI circuit breaker at the electrical panel or a GFCI receptacle placed in first position (upstream) along the circuit of outlets.

heating

Over the years, the TOH crew has found that kitchens demand more heating capacity per square foot than any other room in the house except the bath. At the same time, the kitchen is probably the most difficult room to heat since there's little wall or floor space for vents, baseboard units, or radiators.

If you're building a house, you can choose any of the heating systems described in Chapter 3. If you're renovating, your options for warming the kitchen will probably be limited by the heating system you already have. However, adapting your heating plan to serve your new kitchen will almost always save you money.

Forced hot air, the most common kind of heating system in the United States, can often be extended to serve a renovated kitchen. If your home has a forced-air system that's in good condition, you will need to have new ductwork added and one or more registers installed in the kitchen. It's best to have registers placed in the floor and near windows. However, for homes built on a slab, the new ducting will have to be run between floors or in the attic.

There are several types of systems that use hot water to provide warmth. If your kitchen has old-fashioned cast-iron radiators, you can replace them with modern versions that take up less wall space. Several European companies now make slim, attractive radiators available in a variety of configurations that work well in a kitchen and essentially become part of the wall. For example, you can get vertical units that fit next to a pantry cabinet. If your home has a fin-tube baseboard heating system, your plumber can often extend it.

Another option is to install a kickspace heating unit that fits into the void below base cabinets. Kickspace heaters, which blow air across coils that circulate water heated by the water heater, produce plenty of heat without taking up wall space. However, some homeowners find them too noisy and drafty.

Richard Trethewey has used hot-water radiant floor heating in several kitchen remodels, with excellent results (see page 72). Radiant heat is ideal for kitchens because it maintains a constant temperature and requires no wall or floor space. Its chief disadvantage is cost—nearly double that of a standard fin-tube system. It can also be hard to find an experienced installer, and it's the most difficult system to retrofit. However, you can equip a finished floor with radiant heat by putting the tubing under the subfloor—if you have access to a basement or crawl space— or you can lay it between the subfloor and the finished floor.

Since there's little available wall space in a kitchen, consider putting a forced-air register or kickspace heating unit in the void below the cabinets.

ventilation

In a typical household, kitchen activities produce about 3.3 pounds of moisture every day, not to mention odors, smoke, grease, and combustion gases. If these various unwanted by-products aren't removed, they can damage your house, threaten your health, and spill into adjacent living areas. For all of these reasons, the TOH crew considers good ventilation as indispensable as heating, plumbing, and electricity.

To be effective, a kitchen ventilation system must be ducted to expel steam and smoke outdoors. There are two general types of ducted systems: hood and downdraft. Both types use a fan to suck dirty air from the cooktop and transport it away from the house through the wall, roof, or eaves. Though you can save money

by installing a so-called ductless kitchen ventilation unit, Richard Trethewey doesn't recommend this option. Rather than ventilating the kitchen, these devices merely pull air through a filter and send it back into the room without removing water vapor or noxious gases. Compared with ducted systems, they're also not very effective at removing grease, smoke, and odors.

Hood-type ventilation systems work because warm air naturally rises toward the overhead fan, aided by its drawing power. To capture rising air and steam, the hood should be as broad and deep as possible—at least as large as the cooktop.

The height at which the hood is mounted will also influence its performance; 21 to 30 inches above the cooking surface is optimum (unless

you have commercial-type equipment, in which case the hood should be installed 30 to 36 inches above the cooktop). The best place to put a cooktop-hood combination is along a wall, where crosscurrents won't interfere with ventilation. A hood mounted above an island or peninsula will perform adequately when placed at the proper height, but it may obstruct your view across the kitchen. You can raise it higher than 30 inches from the cooktop as long as you install a more powerful fan. However, it will still be less effective than if it were set at the standard height. Plus, the larger fan will also draw in and expel a great deal of clean air, which you've paid to heat or cool.

Though second best, a downdraft system is unobtrusive, and it's often the best compromise if you're installing your cooktop on an island or peninsula. These systems pull air downward and through ductwork beneath the floor or along the cabinet kickspace. This arrangement makes a downdraft unit more expensive to install. Like hood-type systems, downdraft units work best against a wall. You can mitigate the crosscurrent problem of a downdraft system in the middle of the room by having a lip built around the cooktop. But because it works against warm air's tendency to rise, a downdraft system functions most effectively when cooking is done in low pans; tall pots will simply send vapor into the kitchen.

The result you get from any type of ventilation system depends in part on the size of its vent fan or blower. To calculate the minimum fan capacity your system should have in CFMs (cubic feet per minute), multiply the linear footage of your cooktop by 40 if you have a wall-mounted hood. If the hood is mounted above an island or peninsula, multiply by 50. Keep in mind that these are minimum values that will vary depending on what kind of cooking you do. Cooking that generates more steam or smoke will require a vent fan with a higher airflow rate.

The Home Ventilating Institute, a trade group that tests and certifies ventilation products, recommends stronger ventilation—at least 100 CFM for wall-mounted hoods and 150 CFM for island-mounted hoods. If you mount the fan at the opposite end of the ductwork from where the air is collected to cut down on noise, you'll need up to 400 CFM for a wall unit and 600 CFM for an island cooktop. Downdraft systems and commercial ranges require even more fan power. If your new kitchen has a commercial range or will require a complicated downdraft system, consult an HVAC contractor.

Unless ductwork is carefully planned and installed, even the best

ventilation unit won't do its job properly. A duct run should be no longer than 30 feet to keep air moving—the shorter, the better. Try to avoid turns in the ductwork (every elbow will add the equivalent of 5 feet to the run of your duct), and never downsize it in the middle of a run. Such interruptions restrict airflow and provide a place for grease and particles to collect. Choose smooth-sided galvanized or stainless-steel ducting rather than the flexible kind, which has spiral ribs that grab dirt and inhibit air movement. If you're

installing a downdraft system, it might require longer ductwork runs and more turns. Be sure the manufacturer's restrictions on installation are followed carefully.

For powerful, nearly silent ventilation, consider an in-line system that serves the entire house. With these, ducting runs from bathrooms and the kitchen vent hood to a remote fan that exhausts to the outside. Though expensive, these whole-house systems are highly effective and especially long-lived.

ANATOMY OF A HOOD VENT

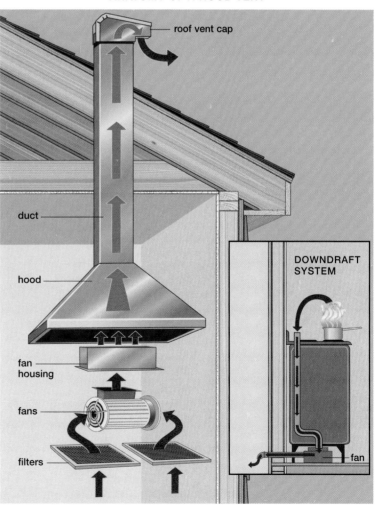

defining a style

Once you've settled on a floor plan, it's time to decide on a decorating scheme. This stage is not just about window treatments and paint color; it will affect just about every decision you make, from choosing appliances to selecting baseboard and casing profiles.

If you've gone through the pre-design process described earlier in this chapter, you probably already have some ideas about how you'd like your kitchen to look. Now think about how the kitchen you have in mind will blend with the rest of your home. Tom Silva believes that the best design—for both resale value and aesthetics—is one that stays reasonably faithful to the period in which the house was built. If your house has a definable architectural style—Greek Revival, Craftsman, or Spanish Colonial, for example—the décor you choose for your kitchen should capture that spirit.

If your home doesn't have a distinct style, you'll have more options, which actually makes decisions harder. In some cases, the space you're working with may suggest a particular decorating scheme. For instance, a small kitchen may beg for the sleek, unbroken lines of a contemporary décor in order to seem more spacious. Or a large space may seem more intimate if designed with the cheerful clutter of a country scheme.

The style you choose may also affect how much your kitchen costs and how easy it is to maintain. A formal, traditional décor featuring crown molding and solid-wood cabinetry will be harder on the checkbook than a country-style scheme with open shelving and painted cabinets. A rustic-looking kitchen will be easier to keep up than a sleek, modern one full of highly reflective surfaces.

Last but certainly not least, keep your lifestyle in mind. For example, users with physical challenges may have difficulty operating in a minimalist kitchen where cooking paraphernalia is placed behind doors. On the other hand, it may be the perfect setup for a family with small children.

successful design elements

No matter what décor you choose, your kitchen plan should be fine-tuned through basic principles of good design. The goal is to combine the various elements of your plan into a harmonious whole, using shapes, colors, and textures for an effect that's balanced and visually pleasing.

An artistic tile backsplash is the focal point of this Craftsman-style kitchen. Together with the custom cabinets and iron knobs and pulls, the kitchen makes a grand design statement.

stone

Natural stone such as granite, marble, and limestone makes a durable, heat-proof, water-resistant countertop that's very easy to clean (though it can get cold when placed near windows or on an outside wall). Few materials look as elegant—or cost as much. Stone-slab countertop prices range from $120 to $200 per linear foot installed.

A stone counter is generally made from a ¾-inch-thick slab that's fabricated to fit a specific kitchen. Fabricators usually won't handle a slab larger than 9 feet long; if your countertop is longer, it will have a seam. The stone can be set directly atop base cabinets and affixed with silicone or epoxy, or it may rest on a plywood substrate. Do-it-yourself installation is out of the question except in the case of slate, which can be tackled by a homeowner with advanced skills and a diamond-tipped circular saw blade.

Granite slabs make beautiful and durable countertops, though stone does require yearly maintenance.

To save money, buy directly from a stone yard where you can choose your own slab. For an even better price, go to a large stone fabricator that handles big jobs such as facing office buildings. You may find a remnant that will fit your kitchen.

Though nearly indestructible, stone can chip around the edges of a sink. Oil, alcohol, and acid will stain or etch marble and limestone and damage their finish. Granite is more impervious, as long as it's polished, but dark varieties show smudges and lighter varieties can stain. The best way to improve stone's stain resistance is to apply a penetrating sealer, also known as an impregnator. To determine whether your countertop is susceptible to staining, place a drop of water on the surface. If the area under the drop becomes dark within five minutes, the stone is porous and should be sealed. Sealing should be repeated at least every year.

If you want the natural look of stone without the high price, consider stone tiles, which start at around $22 per linear foot for the material.

You can have a real stone countertop for 80 percent less if you choose tiles instead of a slab.

Precision-cut granite and marble tiles can be installed with tight grout lines to mimic the look of a slab. You may have to pay a fabricator to shape pieces for the edge and backsplash.

quartz

If upkeep rather than price is your concern, consider man-made stone. Though it costs roughly the same as the real thing, man-made stone takes abuse gracefully, requires no special care, and never needs sealing. A composite of mostly ground-up natural quartz mixed with polymers and epoxy, this highly durable material offers many more colors and patterns than stone, and slabs are consistent in appearance. It is heat, stain, and scratch resistant. Slabs are typically 52 or 53 inches by 118 inches and ¾ to 1⅛ inches thick.

Countertop-grade ceramic tile that is installed properly can last for decades, though grout lines make it harder to clean than a smooth surface.

ceramic tile

Ceramic tile comes in an endless array of styles that can be mixed and matched for a custom look. Tile is durable, heat resistant, and, if installed correctly, water resistant. There's a price for every budget, from $5 per linear foot to more than $50 per tile.

Tile is installed on a solid, water-resistant underlayment—typically plywood topped with cement backerboard. Some installers still use a thick bed of Portland cement (called a "mud job" or mortar bed) atop a base of exterior-grade plywood, a traditional practice that works extremely well when properly executed. Beware of an installer who attempts to save time and money by using only a thin layer of mastic adhesive on a plywood base. This method is unacceptable for a countertop installation, since water can reach the plywood substrate and cause tiles to come loose.

Labor rates for setting tile vary by region as well as by the complexity of the job. The range is from $5 to $17 per linear foot for materials and installation, but prices are higher in some markets. Choose your installer carefully, for the quality of installation will determine whether or not your countertop lasts for decades.

Choose tile that is rated for countertops. Look for matte glazes and subdued hues; brilliant colors and high-gloss surfaces will show scratches. If you want handmade tiles, keep in mind that their irregular surfaces can be hard to clean. Small tiles will also make cleanup more difficult. For easier maintenance, choose larger tiles so you'll have fewer grout lines. Epoxy grout is best for countertop applications. It costs about three times as much as other types but is strong, flexible, and resistant to stains and mildew.

Ceramic tile countertops are most often edged in a matching or contrasting color of the same tile used on the surface. You can buy an edge manufactured for this purpose or build up an edge with bullnose tile. A wood edge looks handsome, but it will expand and contract at a different rate than the tile and grout, eventually producing a crack or gap that will catch dirt. Metal edging, such as aluminum, brass, or stainless steel, will maintain tighter contact.

A tile countertop may require some adjustments in your daily routine. Even epoxy grout can be hard to keep clean, and tile's hard, irregular surface can chip plates and glasses if they're set down carelessly. Most ceramic tile is long-lasting, but foods, acids and household chemicals can damage certain glazes. Ask about maintenance before you buy.

wood

Wood has long been considered the perfect surface for chopping and preparing food, but many people select wood countertops simply for their elegant, warm appearance. Wood is easily installed, kind to dishes, and if damaged can be sanded and refinished. For less than half the cost of stone (about $60 per linear foot), it can add a lot of class to the kitchen. However, it's not good around water and is best enjoyed by a careful housekeeper.

A wood countertop can serve as a giant cutting board or a purely decorative surface, depending on what type of wood you use and how it's finished. Maple and other closed-grained hardwoods are the most suitable for cutting-board use. Oak, ash, hickory or other open-grained woods can harbor germs and decaying food particles. If the counter is sold as a manufactured product, you may want to look for the seal of the National Sanitation Foundation to be sure that the counter meets industry standards for sanitation.

If your countertop will be used as a cutting surface, it must be treated with several coats of an inert, non-toxic oil, but never a hard finish like alkyd varnish or polyurethane. Raw tung oil is recommended because it leaves the countertop dry to the touch. You can also use raw almond oil, walnut oil, or mineral oil. Avoid vegetable or cooking oils, which will turn rancid. Whichever oil you choose, think of it as a continuing treatment rather than a finish. Tung oil should be applied monthly, other oils as often as daily, depending on your standards for its appearance.

You can use any type of wood for a kitchen counter that won't be used for food preparation. Your selection should be properly dried and fabricated by someone who knows the characteristics of the species. Decorative counters can be finished with oil or with a sealant such as urethane or varnish.

Richard Trethewey cautions against installing a wood countertop around a sink, as it will leave the wood vulnerable to warping, discoloration, and mildew. "Standing water can make that counter look like a curved hockey stick," Trethewey says. Nor will wood satisfy the need for a heat-resistant counter material in the cooking area. If you love the look and functionality of wood, your best option may be to combine it with other materials.

A wood countertop should be properly sealed with a water-resistant finish to avoid mildew, warping, and discoloration.

stainless steel and other metals

Stainless steel is nonporous and heat resistant, and it holds up extremely well in wet areas. It's easy to clean and sanitize, and it's impervious to most kitchen insults. Stainless steel itself is relatively affordable—about $40 per linear foot—but fabrication can be expensive because it requires a specialist. Be sure to get two or three bids.

Most stainless-steel counters installed in residential kitchens are designed by an architect and custom-built by a fabricator. When you're ordering, specify the thickest stainless steel you can afford; 16-gauge is minimum, and a lower gauge—which is thicker—is better. Choose a chromium-nickel blend with a matte or satin finish for easy care. Be sure it's installed over a ¾-inch plywood substrate for support and to deaden noise.

A stainless-steel countertop requires almost no maintenance, unless you can't live with water spots (in which case you must be vigilant about wiping up). Scratches are inevitable, but most people find them inoffensive. Stainless steel is perfect for creating an integral sink, which will simplify cleanup considerably. However, don't chop food on a stainless-steel countertop, or you'll damage both the counter and the knife.

You can save money on a stainless-steel countertop by using flat sheeting with a wood edge detail. This combination looks attractive and cuts fabrication costs. You might also consider a metal-faced laminate, a thin sheet of metal applied to a substrate in the same fashion as plastic laminate. Available through fabricators and home centers, metal laminate runs $12 to $16 per linear foot; fabrication and installation will add $16 to $18 per linear foot.

Concrete countertops are extremely durable and can be customized in any color, shape, and texture.

A copper countertop is both unique and beautiful, but it's expensive and needs regular polishing.

At the other end of the price spectrum are specialty metals such as copper and zinc. These make beautiful countertops, but they cost around $300 per linear foot, uninstalled, and they are definitely high-maintenance finishes. Softer than stainless steel, they dent and scratch readily, and they can be damaged by a number of substances commonly found in the kitchen. To keep their original appearance, they must be polished regularly.

concrete

Concrete is virtually indestructible, and it can be colored, shaped, and decorated to fit any décor. When properly sealed, it makes a stain-resistant, easy-to-clean surface. Prices start at $135 per linear foot installed.

Concrete countertops are custom-made, either off-site or in your kitchen. You can have precast slabs delivered to your house, complete with holes for your sink and faucet. If you want a seamless slab, you can have the countertop poured in place and troweled, tinted, and textured on the spot. In either case, be sure that the slab has adequate support; you may need to beef up cabinet supports to hold it.

Concrete countertops are labor intensive and require a great deal of skill, so make sure you find a fabricator with lots of experience. A properly finished concrete counter will have a shiny surface. To achieve this, the installer should trowel the concrete, let it set, and repeat the process several times. "Every time you trowel wet cement, you work up the finer and finer sediment in it, which fills in all the little voids," Silva explains. "The more you trowel it, the 'creamier' the material becomes and the shinier your countertop will be."

Concrete is very hard on kitchen utensils, so you won't be able to chop food on the countertop. Keeping the surface sealed is crucial if you want to avoid stains. If you're not sure a concrete countertop is right for your kitchen you may want to consider another option, because few countertops are more permanent than cast-in-place concrete.

backsplashes

Because a backsplash has a big visual impact but requires very little material, it is a great place to splurge on decorative flourishes you really love. There are no real rules for choosing a backsplash. The only requirement is that it be easy to clean and durable enough to withstand splatters and repeated scrubbings.

Because a backsplash bridges the counter and cabinets, choose a material and color that will work with those elements. The most obvious option is to make the countertop and backsplash from the same material, but using a mix of materials can give the kitchen a distinctive look.

Any countertop material makes a suitable backsplash. Ceramic tile is popular for its sheer variety in color, shape, and size. Tile backsplashes can include a mural: Mass-produced versions may cost as little as $45 for a six-tile pattern, but you can spend thousands of dollars for an original hand-painted design. When installing a ceramic or stone tile backsplash, check horizontal grout lines to make sure they align with wall cabinets and countertops.

A backsplash can be the perfect place to put an exotic material that's too expensive or high maintenance for an entire countertop installation. For example, a skilled metal worker can fabricate a backsplash out of virtually any specialty metal on the market (such as copper, zinc, brass, or nickel) and provide a range of surface textures (including hammered, ribbed, and even quilted).

LEFT: Ceramic tile backsplashes are available in customized designs. BELOW: Brick-shaped tiles with a crackle finish have a refined look.

Large slate tiles give texture to the wall and, when sealed, they wipe down easily.

The standard height for a minimum backsplash is 4 inches, but you can choose any dimensions you like. A backsplash that runs all the way up to the bottom of the wall cabinets gives the room a finished quality and adds protection.

The least expensive solution is to have no backsplash at all. A high-quality semigloss latex paint or a scrubbable wallpaper (over water-resistant drywall) will do until your budget or creative streak recovers.

flooring

The kitchen floor gets more use and abuse than any other floor in the house. Ideally, it should be durable, easy to care for, skid resistant, and comfortable to stand on. And because it's also a very conspicuous design element, it should be attractive. Any of the flooring materials mentioned in Chapter 4 (pages 96–108) can be installed in a kitchen. To choose one, you'll need to weigh a number of factors, including cost, maintenance, longevity, and looks.

sheet vinyl Sheet vinyl is by far the most popular kitchen flooring, and not just because of its budget-friendly price. Vinyl is particularly suited to kitchen installations because it's a warm, nonslip surface that's simple to maintain and easy on the legs. However, the limited colors and often dominant patterns they come in can be a drawback. There is also an unavoidable seam when sheet vinyl is installed in a large kitchen. Choose a product that comes in 12-foot widths, and be sure the seam is properly sealed so it doesn't attract food and dirt. Also take special care when installing appliances, for even if they are equipped with casters, like a refrigerator, they will leave permanent marks.

Vinyl comes in a huge array of patterns and is soft both on the feet and the pocketbook.

other resilient products Other types of resilient flooring offer many of the same advantages as vinyl. Linoleum, a natural product that once covered miles of American kitchen floors, now comes in a wide range of styles and colors. Linoleum is less vulnerable to nicks and dents than vinyl because it's colored all the way through, but it requires occasional waxing and must be installed by someone who knows the product.

Rubber flooring is soft, quiet, stain resistant, and highly durable. It can be a good choice for a contemporary kitchen that gets heavy use. For the ultimate in comfort, check out cork tiles, which are as durable as vinyl and even softer underfoot.

wood Wood makes a beautiful, comfortable kitchen floor, though it's a risk in any wet room such as a kitchen, and it's less practical for an area that gets a lot of wear and tear. As long as the wood is protected by a sturdy finish such as a polyurethane, small spills can be wiped up. A flooding dishwasher, on the other hand, can ruin a solid-wood floor. A better choice is prefinished engineered wood flooring laid as a floating floor. Not only is the factory-applied finish very durable, but the flooring's construction—whether laminated or MDF—makes it far less likely to warp.

If you want a wood floor in your kitchen, a wood floating floor with a factory-applied finish is safer around water.

Ceramic tiles stand up well to water in the kitchen but can be hard underfoot.

ceramic tile A properly installed tile floor offers several advantages for kitchen use: It is attractive, low maintenance, water resistant, and offers superior durability. However, it has a hard surface that will shatter dropped glassware and cause feet to ache. Shiny tiles are generally too slippery in the kitchen; look for matte finishes or choose small tiles (the extra grout lines will provide more traction). A tile floor needs frequent sweeping and damp-mopping so that it won't scratch, and grout lines will darken no matter how often you clean. Unglazed quarry and terra cotta tiles look beautiful in the kitchen, but they must be thoroughly sealed for kitchen use, and even then they will stain and darken with age. A tile floor is also cold and will make it difficult to keep the kitchen cozy. Consider installing radiant floor heating (see page 149), which works very well under tile.

stone Natural stone makes a beautiful kitchen floor. Some types, notably granite and slate, are durable enough to withstand the extra punishment they'll take in a kitchen. Others, such as marble, will scratch and show wear. Most types are porous, and if installed in the kitchen, they will collect stains (again, the exceptions are granite, which is not porous, and

RIGHT: Mosaic stone tiles can be used on an entire kitchen floor or just along the edge. BELOW: Stone is a durable and beautiful choice for kitchen flooring, but it needs to be sealed to resist stains.

slate, which is reasonably stain resistant). Sealing the floor—an absolute must when you're installing stone in the kitchen—will help. Stone comes with either a polished or a honed surface. Honed finishes are better in this case because they're less slippery. Like ceramic tile, stone is hard on the legs, and it's cold underfoot unless backed by radiant heating. However, cleanup of stone entails little more than a swabbing with a wet mop.

kitchen fixtures

Sinks, faucets, lighting, and appliances are the finishing touches in your newly remodeled kitchen. Be sure to buy high-quality items that will last. Remember, the quality of each fixture is just as important as its appearance.

the kitchen sink

In a typical household, up to 50 percent of kitchen time is spent at the sink. Because it receives so much use, the sink must be well made, easy to care for, and configured to suit your needs and habits. In addition, the sink you choose should complement the rest of your kitchen.

You'll discover a wide variety of shapes and sizes when shopping for a kitchen sink. Two factors should influence your decision: your work habits and the size of your kitchen counter.

Kitchen sinks come with one, two, or three bowls. You'll want more than one bowl if you intend to use one side for food preparation. Single- and double-bowl sinks are typically the same size (33 inches long and 10 inches deep, though double-bowl models can be found in lengths up to 39 inches). A single bowl is less confining and may be all you need, especially if you're planning a separate food preparation area with a second, smaller sink. A double-bowl sink can be divided in half, or it can combine a large bowl with a smaller one that's used for tasks such as cleaning vegetables. Triple-bowl behemoths, which can be up to 46 inches long, generally have the food-prep sink in the middle. It is often equipped with a garbage disposal and sometimes a fitted cutting board.

installation choices Most sinks are made to sit inside a cutout in the countertop. Typically these are self-rimming, meaning that they have a lip that overlaps the counter. Self-rimming sinks are the cheapest, and they work well with any countertop material. However, crumbs get caught where the rim meets the countertop, and it's impossible to sweep water or debris directly into the sink.

Undermounted sinks are fastened to the underside of the counter with metal clips. They cost more than self-rimming versions, but they look sleek, and their low profile makes for easy cleanup.

Integral-bowl sinks are molded into a countertop of the same material, forming a seamless one-piece unit. Integral bowls eliminate the possibility of water collecting around the sink rim and damaging the countertop, and they're a cinch to keep clean. Their only drawback is that they tend to be shallow, which can cause water to splash out of the bowl when the faucet is running at full strength.

sink materials

Kitchen sinks are made from a variety of materials, each with its own distinctive look and set of qualities. Here is a brief overview.

enameled cast iron The most popular material is enameled cast iron, which is handsome, sturdy, quiet, and easiest to clean. Available in a variety of glossy colors, cast iron adapts well to any décor. Though durable, it can chip if it's struck by

This cobalt blue enameled cast-iron sink features a built-in cutting board in the prep sink and a rack to dry dishes in the larger bowl.

a heavy object such as a frying pan. Enameled steel, a lower-quality lookalike, costs much less but is much noisier, and the steel will flex under pressure, weakening the bond with its enamel coating.

A deep stainless-steel sink provides restaurant-quality durability in the home.

stainless steel Stainless-steel sinks can take a beating, resist stains, and stand up to abrasive cleansers—just a few of the reasons they're found in restaurants everywhere. Good sinks are made from at least 18-gauge stainless steel; 12- and 16-gauge versions are significantly better (the lower the number, the thicker the metal). Twenty-two-gauge is too flimsy. Chromium-nickel blends are the only real stainless sinks (others will stain). The best contain more nickel, which gives the sink a richer luster, a warmer color, and more resistance to spots, stains, and scratches. Running water can make a drumming sound on stainless steel; a thicker gauge and undercoating will help.

solid surface A solid-surface sink is usually an integral bowl that's molded right into the countertop, though self-rimming and undermount versions are available.

Decorative options include inlays, borders, and contrasting colors. Integral sinks can be ordered with built-in drain boards. Solid-surface sinks are quite durable, and they can be repaired if damaged.

composites A number of different sink materials can be classified as composites. Acrylic and fiberglass are not durable enough for kitchen use, but newer composites with high quartz content are light, flexible, and tough. They resemble enamel but resist chipping and are easier to maintain. Composite can be expensive, and color choices are somewhat limited.

vitreous china Vitreous china sinks, once confined to the bathroom, have begun to show up in the kitchen. They are usually highly ornamental, often hand-painted, and meant to provide a decorative accent. Though scratch resistant and easy to clean,

A richly detailed vitreous china sink is a great addition to a country, Mediterranean, or Spanish-style kitchen.

Solid-surface sinks that are built into the countertop are easy to keep clean and come in a wide variety of configurations.

vitreous china is prone to chipping, which means you'll need to be extra careful when wielding pots and pans.

specialty metals Specialty materials such as brass and copper look striking, but they require vigilant maintenance. They should be polished often and wiped dry after each use to prevent tarnishing. Given the amount of upkeep necessary, these materials are usually best reserved for a secondary sink such as at a wet bar.

This smooth copper bowl is a beautiful but high-maintenance choice, best for seldom-used sinks.

faucets

A high-quality faucet is a necessity in the kitchen, where the water gets turned on and off thousands of times a year. "What matters most is what the faucet is built of on the inside rather than what it looks like on the outside," Trethewey says. There is only one option that will provide the kind of durability and reliability you need in a kitchen faucet: "In every case, you should choose solid-brass workings because they hold up," Trethewey says. "Anything else, especially plastic, will deteriorate quickly." When you're shopping for a faucet, pick it up. The heavier, the better. Look for the words "all-brass body" on the box.

To avoid maintenance headaches, buy a washerless faucet. If your budget will allow, spend a little more for one that uses ceramic disc valves to regulate the flow and temperature of the water. "These valves can last forever," Trethewey says. Ceramic disc faucets are drip-free, and they provide a smooth, easy-to-control water flow.

The most practical style of faucet for a kitchen is a single-lever model that can be adjusted with one hand. Centerset faucets, which combine a spout and handles on a single base unit, are less expensive, but they can be more difficult to operate with greasy or soapy hands. For an ornate or traditional look, you may want a widespread (or spread-set) faucet, with separately mounted spout and handles that sit directly on the sink or countertop. A widespread faucet typically costs about twice as much as a comparable centerset model.

Make sure the model you choose matches any pre-drilled holes on your sink or that it has a cover plate that will allow it to adapt. Also consider what accessories you may want, such as a water filter, a soap dispenser, or an instant hot-water dispenser (see page 179). A standard centerset faucet with a separate sprayer requires four sink-mounting holes, which may leave no room for the extras you have in mind. If there are too few holes on your sink rim, you may want a faucet with a combination pullout sprayer and faucet head.

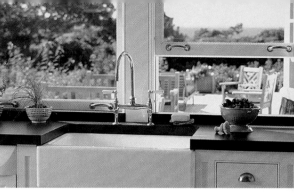

A tall spigot allows plenty of space to wash a sinkful of dishes.

Choose a spout design that suits your sink and kitchen equipment. For example, the combination of a tall, curved spigot and a deep sink will make it easier to fill and wash big pots. In any case, you should be able to swing the spigot without causing too much splashing.

Polished chrome is the most popular kitchen-faucet finish, thanks to its durability and versatile good looks. Other common finishes include brushed chrome, polished and antique brass, and powder-coated enamel, which comes in a wide range of colors. Satin finishes are easiest to maintain because their muted tones hide water spots, scratches, and fingerprints. If you want a polished brass faucet, a factory-applied clear coat will keep it maintenance-free.

Prices for kitchen faucets range from $100 to $600. Price is a good indicator of quality, and you can expect to spend at least $100 for a ceramic-disc faucet with solid-brass workings. Stick with reputable name-brand products; others are often poorly made, and it's difficult to get replacement parts. Ask a plumber if you have questions about reliability or maintenance.

TOP LEFT: This widespread faucet has a more elegant look than centersets, which combine spout and handles on a single platform. BOTTOM LEFT: A single-lever faucet is easiest to use and can have a sleek, sophisticated appearance.

lighting

In the kitchen, lighting is as important for safety as it is for aesthetics. More than in most other rooms, it's crucial to have multiple sources for adequate, even illumination without shadows or glare. Your plan should include ambient lighting for the entire room, task lighting for work surfaces, and accent or mood lighting that is primarily decorative.

You'll probably be living with most kitchen light fixtures for a long time because they are expensive and built in, so plan with care. It's best to err on the side of too many rather than too few fixtures; dimmer switches allow you to control brightness levels.

planning your lighting Begin with the work surfaces that will need illumination. At a minimum, you'll want task lighting for the sink, cooktop, and food preparation areas. Task-lighting fixtures should be placed so that your body won't cast

shadows over the work area when you're standing there. One of the best places to install task lighting is on the underside of wall cabinets (the cabinets should have a lip at the bottom to help hide the fixture from view). You may also want task lighting over the table or eating counter.

Ambient light usually comes from ceiling fixtures—recessed, surface, or pendant. Ambient lighting need not be too bright; in fact, a small kitchen may need only a single fixture—as long as you have good task lighting. To avoid harsh light and shadows, ambient lighting fixtures should be diffused with a cover or directed to bounce off a wall or ceiling. Task and decorative lighting can often double as ambient lighting. For example, decorative cove lighting placed on top of a wall cabinet or behind a soffit will create gentle ambient light that shines up at the ceiling, also making the room seem larger.

Decorative lighting can be used to highlight beautiful objects and archi-

Look for a hood with lights built in so you can easily see into deep pots on the stove.

tectural features, to set a mood and enhance the kitchen's overall atmosphere, or even to improve safety, as in the case of toekick lighting that defines the perimeter of the kitchen in the dark. Accent lighting often requires a designated fixture—for instance, a strip light placed inside a glass-front kitchen cabinet to display a collection of crystal or china. Creating mood lighting is often just a matter of adding dimmer switches to ambient- and task-lighting fixtures.

For a project as complicated as a kitchen remodel, electricians generally prefer to work from a lighting plan that details the placement of fixtures and switches, so make sure your architect or designer provides one. Keep the plan as simple as you can. Place switches and controls close to the areas they will illuminate, and try to put no more than two switches together in any one place.

This large space utilizes recessed lights for overall illumination, pendants hanging over the island for task lighting, and under-cabinet fluorescent lights that serve the same purpose.

light fixtures

Most light fixtures fall into four distinct categories: recessed, track, surface-mounted, and pendant.

recessed Recessed fixtures are set into the space between ceiling joists, which makes them unobtrusive enough to be compatible with nearly any décor. Recessed lighting is directed downward, so you'll need more fixtures than you would with other types of ceiling-mounted lighting. For even, shadow-free illumination, space fixtures no more than 4 feet apart.

Recessed fixtures do many jobs well. Installed over a work surface, they can supply task lighting, and there will be enough light spillage to provide ambient lighting also. Equipped with dimmers, recessed fixtures can also create mood lighting.

However, high-quality recessed fixtures are expensive. You'll pay $90 or more per unit, and you'll need a dozen or more for a large kitchen. Don't try to save money on the trim, which is usually purchased separately from the canister. The cheapest trims lack a baffle to diffuse the light, so they create glare and cast shadows. Also, if you live in a warm climate, keep in mind that recessed lights give off a great deal of heat.

track Track lighting offers many of the same advantages as recessed lighting, along with ample flexibility. You can add, remove, or relocate individual lights, using some for ambient lighting and others for task lighting. However, track lighting is conspicuous, can give the room a cluttered look, and is not appropriate for all décors. It also requires more maintenance than recessed lighting because the light heads must be cleaned periodically to remove kitchen grease and dust. And while their flexibility is

Track lighting now comes in a variety of artistic designs.

great in theory, many people never bother to move the light heads around.

Despite these drawbacks, track lighting is an excellent choice if you don't want to disturb your kitchen ceiling or you have a limited budget. Although the cost of high-quality track lighting is similar to that of recessed fixtures, it's often possible to feed electricity to the track from an existing ceiling box, which will save on the price of running new wire in finished areas.

surface-mounted A surface fixture mounted to the ceiling supplies lots of ambient light. Indeed, there was a time when the typical kitchen had just one surface fixture for the entire room. Though not as popular as they once were, surface fixtures are still the least expensive option, and they can still be used to good effect. In a small kitchen, a single surface light in the center of the ceiling will work just fine. In a bigger kitchen, a large fluorescent fixture can flood the room with enough light for both ambient and task lighting, or you can install several smaller incandescent fixtures around the room.

Two rows of track lighting are all that's needed to illuminate this small kitchen.

pendant Pendant fixtures are suspended from the ceiling by a cord or conduit, typically over nontraffic zones such as islands. They can provide either task lighting or general illumination, and they can be dimmed for mood lighting. The diffuser that covers the bulb will determine function as well as style. A pendant with a metal globe will direct light straight downward on a particular area, while a glass globe will provide ambient as well as task lighting. Pendant fixtures should be hung high enough so that they don't obstruct your view: about 36 inches above a countertop or 30 inches above a table.

dimmers

Dimmers provide the kind of flexibility that particularly benefits a kitchen. They're available for almost any fixture, including fluorescent lights that are specified as "dimmable," and low-voltage halogen lights, which require dimmers designated for low-voltage use. You can choose from touch-pad, slide, knob, or toggle controls; pick one that's simple to adjust, and be sure you can easily tell what levels of lighting the controls are set to provide.

Dimmers for incandescent light fixtures are relatively inexpensive—as little as $15— and they pay for themselves by reducing electricity consumption. They can also extend the life of bulbs; it's been estimated that dimming an incandescent bulb 25 percent can triple its life span. Fluorescent bulbs, however, are more difficult and expensive to dim than incandescent types, and dimming actually shortens their life span.

bulbs

Incandescent bulbs emit a familiar, warm-toned light that's flattering to any kitchen décor. They're inexpen-

sive, but they must be replaced often, produce heat, and use more electricity than other types of bulbs. Low-voltage versions, which are more expensive, can provide attractive mood and accent lighting.

Halogen bulbs produce a whiter, brighter light that can bring out truer colors in everything from food to flooring. They're more expensive than incandescent bulbs, but they last longer. The most common types are used in recessed fixtures, though they are also found in some surface fixtures and wall sconces. Because they generate a lot of heat, they can be used only in halogen fixtures.

Fluorescent lighting offers bright illumination for less than one-fourth the electricity of incandescents and halogens. The traditional type of fluorescent bulb, and still the most common, is "cool white," which when used in a kitchen will make the cook appear ghoulish and the food unappealing. Fortunately, fluorescent bulbs are now available in a wide spectrum of hues that create much more natural light. Fluorescent bulbs are produced in an array of shapes suitable for recessed, pendant, and under-cabinet fixtures. They're ideal for hard-to-reach fixtures because they seldom need replacing.

choosing appliances

Considering that you'll probably be living with your kitchen appliances for a decade or more, it's worth finding room in your budget for high-quality brand-name products that will look beautiful and perform well for a long, long time—ideally until you renovate again.

Choosing appliances was once a matter of deciding what color to buy (and quite often the choices were white and almond). But today, the ever expanding universe of household appliances includes space-saving, multi-tasking, high-tech products that perform more effectively than ever before. Commercial-grade ranges provide restaurant-quality precision and power. High-speed ovens can roast a chicken to perfection in 25 minutes. Super-quiet dishwashers can operate unobtrusively while people carry on a conversation at the kitchen table. Refrigerator-range hybrids can keep dinner ingredients chilled all day and have them cooked by the time you get home from work.

But buying the best appliances doesn't mean paying top dollar for fancy gadgetry. It means finding sturdy, serviceable products with features your family will truly find useful. If you're trying to save money, check out midline offerings from a top manufacturer. You'll get everything you really need, without a bunch of unnecessary extras.

Measure your kitchen before you shop for appliances so you'll know how much space is available. Check clearances as well so you don't buy a refrigerator that's too tall or an oven that's going to become an obstacle when its door is open. If people with physical limitations will be using the kitchen, consider what appliances will be easiest for them to operate, and look for locking devices and other safety features if you have children (see pages 130–131 for more about universal kitchen design, and page 143 for tips on kitchen safety). Finally, check the informational stickers that tell you how much energy and water an appliance will use. Even basic versions of most new appliances are more energy efficient than older models.

ranges

A standard range, with burners on top and an oven below, provides a homey, traditional touch and is more affordable than separate cooking components. Ranges come in three varieties: electric, gas-fired, and dual-fuel varieties that combine an electric oven with gas burners. Standard-size ranges are 30 inches wide, but you can get them as narrow as 21 inches and as wide as 48 inches—or even wider if you're buying a commercial-type range.

Freestanding ranges, as their name implies, can stand anywhere. Slide-in types are made to fit between cabinets and so have no side panels. Drop-in models are also installed between cabinets, but they're made to rest on a wood platform, and their integral rims cover the gap between range and countertop so food won't fall in.

All-in-one ranges offer the same features as separate cooktops and ovens (see pages 176–177),

The high cost of a large commercial-type range may be worth it for people who spend a great deal of time cooking.

Look for ranges with special features, such as this indoor grill and dedicated wok burner, which can be converted to accommodate large pots.

including self-cleaning mechanisms, smooth-top electric burners, and electronic touch controls. A basic gas or electric range that sells for $400 to $800 often, but not always, includes a self-cleaning oven. Midrange models selling for $900 to $1,500 may include a convection feature that circulates hot air with a fan to reduce cooking times. Top-of-the-line dual-fuel ranges, which cost from $1,500 to $4,000, offer the best of both worlds: gas burners (generally considered superior for stovetop cooking) and an electric oven (which provides the most accurate and consistent temperatures for baking and roasting). These high-priced models may include extras such as a bread-rising or browning feature.

Serious cooks may want to consider a commercial gas range with more burners, increased power, and extra-roomy ovens. But true professional ranges are off-limits. They're

not insulated like residential units, so they get hot enough to cause burns and require clearances of an inch or more to combustible surfaces. They're also hard to clean and can weigh as much as half a ton, which means beefing up your kitchen floor joists. To top it all off, many cities and towns now forbid them for residential use.

A better option for most people is a residential-commercial range that has been adapted for home use. Developed over the past decade or so, they offer most of the advantages of restaurant ranges with few of the disadvantages. They have high-output 15,000- to 18,000-BTU burners (nearly twice the power of a standard range) and large ovens, but they're better insulated and are scaled to residential proportions so they don't protrude into the room. They also offer amenities such as electric burner ignition and self-cleaning ovens— options not available on a true commercial range. Prices start at $2,000 to $2,500 for an entry-level 30-inch unit, but a 48-inch dual-fuel, two-oven version with convection cooking sells for around $9,000. If you're shopping for commercially adapted ranges, look for sealed burners, porcelain-coated cast-iron grates, and an anti-tipping device that helps to keep these heavy units level and stable.

WARMING DRAWERS

Used in restaurants for many years, warming drawers have recently become popular for residential use. Measuring 24 to 30 inches wide, these devices contain an electric heating element that keeps food warm without cooking it. A temperature control adjusts the heat from 90 to 250 degrees; the lower setting can serve as a plate warmer, while the high setting keeps soups and sauces hot. Some models have humidity control to keep food from drying out. Most have one or more racks, so you can stack plated meals or keep several foods warm at once. You can also purchase a trim kit so your warming drawer front will blend with your cabinets. Warming drawers cost nearly as much as conventional ovens: from $500 to $1,400.

cooktops

A separate cooktop offers more flexibility than a traditional range. You can put it on a countertop, set it in an island, or mount it on a shelf so someone in a wheelchair can use it. You can choose any type of burners you like, regardless of whether your oven uses gas or electricity. With no oven underneath, there's room to store cooking utensils conveniently close at hand. A cooktop offers plenty of design possibilities as well, since its thin profile blends with any decorating scheme.

Standard gas and electric cooktops are built into the countertop in the same fashion as a drop-in sink. They come in a standard 30-inch width with four burners, or 36-inch or wider with five, six, or more burners. Commercial-residential units have as many as eight burners, each with twice the BTU output of a standard cooktop burner (see page 175 for more about commercial units). Modular versions let you replace burners with specialized accessories such as grills, griddles, and woks.

Natural gas is the fuel of choice for the cooktop because the burner flame is visible, heats up quickly, and is instantly adjustable. Burners on a conventional gas cooktop generate about 9,000 BTUs, but you may want a model that has burners with different BTU ratings. It's useful to have at least one high-powered burner (12,000 to 18,000 BTUs) that will

boil water faster or provide enough heat for a wok. A low-heat burner with a simmer setting will eliminate the need for a double boiler or a heat diffuser. When shopping for any type of gas cooktop, look for easy-to-clean sealed burners. If you choose a commercial model, be aware that it will need to be installed on a base of tile, brick or other noncombustible material.

Electric burners have traditionally been considered second best because they take longer than gas burners to heat up and cool down, though many newer models include fast-starting coils. Old-fashioned electric coils are the least costly electric burners available and are one of the fastest to heat. They work with all kinds of cooking pots and transfer their heat fairly well. The burners on smooth-top electric cooktops are similar to traditional coils, but they have a ceramic glass surface that disperses heat and makes for easier cleaning. Smooth tops have been significantly improved; once slow to heat, they now respond quickly, and glass surfaces now resist yellowing and

This low-profile electric cooktop has five dedicated burners, and the smooth ceramic surface is easy to keep clean.

scratching. Some cooktops use quick-heating halogen bulbs in place of coils underneath ceramic glass. Halogen burners are more energy efficient than coils, but they're expensive, and the bulbs need replacing every eight years or so.

Gas and electric cooktops are comparably priced, at $500 to $1,500, though you can get a bottom-of-the-line electric for as little as $150. Commercial-type cooktops sell for $1,300 to $4,000.

This gas cooktop is inset nearly flush with the surrounding granite countertop. Heavy pots can slide from one area of the continuous grill to another without being lifted.

ovens

Because they can be installed at any height that's comfortable for the cook, wall ovens combine back-saving ergonomics with easy access to what you're cooking. They also simplify the process of designing a kitchen that works. Liberated from the frequently used cooktop, a wall oven can be placed in its ideal location on the outskirts of the kitchen triangle. Streamlined and unobtrusive, it can adapt to any décor.

Like cooktops, wall ovens can be powered by either gas or electricity. Electric ovens have several advantages over gas models, including more even heat and a better self-cleaning feature (though recent advances have narrowed the gap). Because most cooks prefer them, electric wall ovens are easier to find. No matter what fuels the oven, you'll have a choice of cooking methods. Radiant heat, used in conventional ovens, is by far the most common. Convection ovens use a high-speed fan that circulates heated air to cook food faster. They're excellent for turning out juicy roasts and delicate baked goods, and even if you load the racks heavily or put the enchilada casserole in with the pie, the food will cook evenly and without transfer of flavors. Many models combine radiant and convection heat in one unit so you can switch back and forth depending on what you're cooking. Some have a microwave cooking option as well.

Unless you enjoy scrubbing the oven walls, you'll want a self-cleaning option. This function, which burns away food deposits with intense heat, is superior to continuous cleaning, a steady but not very effective process that is supposed to combat grease and other deposits using a chemically treated textured coating. A dark interior will make your oven look cleaner because it shows less baked-on grime. If you use a broiler, choose an oven that has one with at least 3,000 watts of cooking power. Also look for racks that pull all the way out and lock in place for safe, easy access. Other features you may want to consider include warming shelves, a variable-speed broiler, a rotisserie, and an attached meat thermometer.

Built-in ovens are sized to fit standard 24-inch-deep cabinets. The most common width is 27 inches, though you can get 30-inch models as well as space-efficient 24-inch-wide units. Be sure to check the interior as well as the exterior dimensions. Some units are too small inside to hold a typical roaster or cookie sheet. Conventional ovens are usually available as either single or double units.

Double ovens can be installed one above the other or side by side. Expect to pay from $750 to $1,900 for a single wall oven and $1,200 to $4,000 for a double.

If you have the space, double ovens allow you to cook the main course and dessert at different temperatures at the same time.

microwaves

Microwave ovens are not really ovens at all. They use high-frequency radio waves instead of heat, so foods cook quickly but don't brown. Standard models offer 1.5 cubic feet of cooking space and 1,000 watts of power, but power and performance can vary considerably. As a rule, a more powerful microwave is more useful.

Microwaves can simply sit on the counter, but because they're bulky, it's best to include a place for one in your kitchen design. You'll need to provide cabinet space (many models are designed to be built into cabinetry) and an electrical outlet (a microwave oven should be placed on its own circuit). If possible, mount the microwave so its bottom is 24 to 48 inches off the floor; this will allow kids and shorter adults to reach it. One way to do this is to place the microwave right under the countertop so that hot dishes have a nearby landing area. Models that include a vent and are intended to be installed above the range can be space-savers, but you'll still need a separate hood vent as they alone do an inadequate job of ventilating the kitchen.

Microwaves can be placed almost anywhere, including underneath top cabinets, which frees up valuable counter space.

Locate the microwave where you'll use it most. If you use it to heat snacks and leftovers, place it near the refrigerator. If you use it for preparing meals, you may prefer it in the cooking area. You might even consider putting a small unit next to the refrigerator and a larger one in a bank of wall ovens. Your cooking habits should also determine what features you choose. Microwaves are available with extras such as rotisseries, temperature probes, and electronic sensors that automatically calculate cooking time and power levels. But if you use the microwave only for popping popcorn, a more basic model will better suit your needs. You can get a small microwave for as little as $40. A full-size brand-name model will cost at least $100 to $150, and with a bundle of extra features the price can rise to $600.

speed cookers

Much faster than a convection oven is a new hybrid that combines microwaves and radiant heat to cook foods in a fraction of the usual time. These speed cookers brown foods like a standard oven. Meat, baked goods, and other items that look pale when cooked in a microwave come out crisp and golden in record time—as little as 25 minutes for a roasted chicken, 15 minutes for lasagna, 10 minutes for baked potatoes, and 3 or 4 minutes for cookies. In addition to being fast, they're energy efficient. There's no need for preheating, and with shorter cook times, they use about 25 percent less power than a conventional oven.

A few speed-cook ovens are as large as a standard-size oven, with a 4.1-cubic-foot capacity. Others have about the same interior space as a microwave. Smaller models are adequate for preparing a family meal, but they definitely cannot handle an elaborate dinner party. The most

Get dinner on the table in record time with a speed cooker. They're fast and energy efficient, and they come in a variety of sizes.

diminutive can accept nothing larger than an 8-by-11 pan. Speed-cook ovens come in different configurations. Most are installed as single or double wall ovens, with or without a lower convection oven. One model is meant to replace a standard 30-inch range, and it comes as an electric slide-in with a smooth ceramic cooktop. All models offer the ultimate in programmability. Some have preset cooking times for 100 or more standard recipes, so you can press a pad and call up a combination of microwave and radiant heating tailored to a particular dish.

Speed cookers also require a dedicated 240-volt line, which means you will have to spring for electrical work unless you're replacing an existing electric oven. The intense heat these devices generate can cause a lot of splattering, though smooth stainless-steel or enamel interior surfaces and self-cleaning cycles help minimize cleanup. And the built-in convection or vent fans are somewhat noisy. Ask for a demonstration before you buy. Most speed cookers are relatively new, so it may be difficult to find sales clerks or repair technicians who are knowledgeable about the product.

There are some jobs a speed cooker simply can't do. For example, it's not possible to cook slowly braised dishes or to keep food warm. Consequently, you'll probably want a conventional oven as well. Speed cookers aren't cheap at $1,300 to $5,000, but cooks who are on duty every night may find it a reasonable price to pay for getting dinner on the table in a hurry.

kitchen fans and ventilators

Kitchen ventilation principles are discussed on pages 150–151; here we take a closer look at the types of ventilation appliances available for kitchens.

A vent hood can be either wall-mounted or suspended from the ceiling. Wall-mounted hoods are usually installed underneath a short cupboard that conceals the exhaust duct. The most basic wall-mounted units start at about $50. In the $200 to $400 range are hoods equipped with multiple lights, timers, and easy-clean surfaces. A stainless-steel pro-style hood with a deeper canopy can run $1,000 or more but is very effective and provides an interesting focal point for your kitchen design. Be sure to choose a hood that's at least as deep and wide as your cooktop.

If you'd like the hood to be less obtrusive, there are a number of low-profile options. A slide-out vent has a shallow canopy that remains concealed in the bottom of a wall cabinet until you pull it toward you. You can even get a vent that's styled to resemble a wall cabinet. When you need it, you pull the "cabinet" toward you, and when you're finished cooking, you push it back against the wall.

INSTANT HOT-WATER DISPENSERS

A hot-water dispenser delivers water at 190 degrees Fahrenheit on the spot so you can make tea, instant soups, and drip coffee without waiting for a kettle to

boil. Water is stored in a small heater under the sink and is dispensed through a spout mounted on the sink or countertop. The tank typically holds $1/3$ to $1/2$ gallon of water, and it can deliver 60 cups of steaming water per hour. The higher its wattage, the more quickly it can heat another load of water after the tank has been emptied. Though the instant-delivery system never shuts off, it uses very little energy.

Hoods placed over an island deserve special attention. They can be finished to match the walls or covered in anything from tile to glass.

A hood hanging over an island will definitely be visible, since freestanding ventilation devices are typically quite large. However, you can find a wide range of stylish, sculptural models that will actually enhance your kitchen's décor. A custom or semicustom vent hood trimmed with tile, wood panels, or stainless steel costs $800 to $2,000. Some custom hoods are effectively art pieces, with canopies made of glass, brass, or copper—and art-gallery price tags to match.

Most vent hoods come equipped with a fan-speed control and a light. As you move up in price, look for high-quality halogen lighting, dishwasher-safe grease filters, and sensors that automatically turn the fan on and off as the air above the cooktop heats up and cools down. Even the most basic model you're considering should have a grease filter that fits snugly into the hood and lifts out easily for cleaning.

A fan's strength to exhaust moisture and cooking odors is rated by CFM (cubic feet per minute). A kitchen vent-hood fan should be rated at a bare minimum of 100 CFM. You'll find many are rated at 350 CFM, and downdraft ventilators average about 600 CFM. When sizing a vent hood for a residential cooktop, figure you'll need at least 40 CFM per linear foot of cooktop. In other words, for a 48-inch cooktop, you'll want a fan rated at 160 CFM at the least. However, avoid the temptation to install an oversized ventilation unit, as it will waste energy unnecessarily and create drafts.

If you opt for a downdraft system, you can choose from two configurations. Some types have a vent that rises from the back of the cooktop and retracts when not in use. This setup does a good job of ventilating the rear burners but performs less adequately for the front. Other types have a vent in the center of the cooktop, flanked by the burners. These systems work well when you're cooking on a skillet or a griddle, but they're not as effective at ventilating steam from tall pots. The air-intake grill and grease traps will need frequent cleaning, so make sure they're easy to remove.

A downdraft feature will add a few hundred dollars to the price of a new range or cooktop, but you'll save the price of a vent hood. Cooktops that include downdraft ventilation at the rear start at about $900. Separate downdraft units retrofitted to existing cooktops start at about $600. Downdraft systems will also require extra ductwork, which makes them more expensive to install.

Though you get much better results from a more powerful fan, that has always meant more noise. Manufacturers have conquered this problem to some extent. A few years ago, most ventilation systems operated at 8 sones or more. Now some kitchen fans run at a little more than 4 sones. High-quality equipment and short ductwork will help keep noise down too. Another option is to locate the blower on an outside wall at the end of the duct run. However, exterior-mounted fans need extra power, and they must be weatherproof, so you'll pay more for such a system.

Retractable downdraft vents slide down when not in use, but these smaller vents are not as powerful nor effective as standard overhead units.

refrigerators

You can hardly go wrong replacing an old refrigerator. Even the most basic new models are quieter, easier to clean, and more energy efficient than their predecessors. But there are so many options available that choosing a refrigerator can be confusing. To make sure you'll be happy with your selection, look for a refrigerator that fits your kitchen plan, your budget, and the way you cook and shop.

The first thing to think about is how big a refrigerator you'll need. As a rule, you should have at least 10 cubic feet of refrigerator space for two people, and 1½ feet more for each additional member of the household. Two cubic feet per person is the rule for a freezer compartment. However, you may want a smaller refrigerator if you go to the market every day, or a larger one if you're a bulk shopper. Keep in mind that the organization of interior space is just as important as the amount. Adjustable shelves help maximize storage space, while fixed compartments may allow less room for groceries.

You'll also need to consider how your refrigerator should be configured. An old-fashioned top-freezer unit makes it difficult to reach the lowest part of the refrigerator. A side-by-side is more convenient, but it may be too narrow for storing a frozen pizza or a Thanksgiving turkey. On the other hand, storage space isn't the only consideration. Though a unit with a bottom freezer can accommodate more bulky items, you may still want a side-by-side because you feel you can't live without optional features such as a through-the-door ice dispenser or a pass-through refreshment compartment. Side-by-sides also have a narrower door swing, which may be a necessity if you have a small kitchen.

Another important decision is whether you want a freestanding, built-in, or under-counter unit.

Side-by-side freestanding refrigerators can hold a large amount of food, have a narrow door swing for small kitchens, and offer an integrated ice dispenser.

GARBAGE DISPOSALS

Choose a garbage disposal with a sturdy motor—at least ½ horsepower. A less powerful one will clog easily and will need replacing after a few years. High-quality models have stainless-steel interior parts, an anti-jam feature, and plenty of insulation to keep noise down. The fatter the unit is, the quieter it's likely to be. A good garbage disposal costs anywhere from $80 to $250; anything cheaper is not worth buying.

There are two types of disposals: continuous and batch-feed. Continuous-feed models are activated by a wall switch. Batch-feed models start up when you turn the lid. Batch-feed types are quieter and safer, because they can't be run unless the lid is in place. The mechanism also prevents silverware from falling into the running disposal. However, they're less convenient (you can't simply drop food in and flick a switch), and they come with fewer options.

A disposal should have its own 120-volt electrical circuit. The connection can be either plug-in or hard-wired, though some communities require hardwired. Check your local code before you do anything—some building codes prohibit the use of disposals, while others require them.

freestanding The familiar freestanding type is the most popular and affordable style of refrigerator. They measure from 27 to 32 inches deep, which means they stand out as much as 8 inches from typical 24-inch-deep base cabinets. Freestanding refrigerators are available in side-by-side, top-freezer and bottom-freezer configurations, typically with a maximum storage capacity of 25 cubic feet. The newest models even offer split doors for the top refrigerator section and a single freezer compartment below. Top-mount styles are the least expensive, and they come in a wide array of sizes that can accommodate hard-to-fit spaces. Bottom-freezer models make it easier to reach the refrigerator, which gets more use. They also have a longer life expectancy, according to the Association of Home Appliance Manufacturers: about 17 years, as opposed to 14 for a side-by-side or top mount. Single-door freestanding models with a small freezer cubicle inside the refrigerator are the longest-lived, but they're satisfactory only if you really don't need a freezer.

If you don't like your refrigerator protruding into the room, you may want to consider a cabinet-depth freestanding version that sits nearly flush with the cabinet plane. Shaving the depth of the refrigerator does reduce storage capacity; the biggest model you'll find in this category is about 20 cubic feet. Cabinet-depth refrigerators sell for $1,300 to $2,000—about twice as much as conventional units. You can achieve a similar look by buying a standard refrigerator and placing it in a recess or by building your base cabinets extra deep so they'll be flush with the refrigerator. Then you can face the refrigerator with custom-made panels to match the rest of your kitchen.

Built-in refrigerators blend into the surrounding cabinetry for a clean, uncluttered look.

built-in High-priced, high-style built-in refrigerators are 24 inches deep and designed to be permanently installed in a run of cabinets. They generally come with unfinished doors into which your cabinetmaker can insert a panel, but stainless-steel and glass doors are also popular. Like freestanding units, built-ins are available in side-by-side and top- and bottom-mount freezer configurations. You can get almost any size, from a 24-inch-wide unit with 15 cubic feet of storage to a 72-inch giant with 48 cubic feet of storage. Built-ins are quiet, with well-organized, easy-to-reach interiors. Because they have top-mounted compressors, they don't have dust-gathering ventilation gaps. This combination of convenience and good looks comes at a price of around $4,000 or more.

under-counter Under-counter refrigerators make it possible to store chilled food wherever you're going to need it—in an auxiliary food-preparation area or butler's pantry, for example. Standard under-counter refrigerators, traditionally used in small kitchens or entertainment areas, look like shortened versions of their larger cousins. New, slimmer models are 24 inches deep, so they can be unobtrusively inserted into a cabinet run and concealed behind cabinet panels. These low-profile built-ins can be equipped with freezer and wine-cooling compartments, and some models have slide-out drawers. Under-counter refrigerators aren't equipped to handle all the storage needs of an average household, since most provide just 3 to 6 cubic feet. Multiple under-counter refrigerators are a possibility, but only if you're working with a generous budget. A typical unit costs $500 to $600, but some models sell for $1,000 or more. Don't make the mistake of buying a low-cost dorm-style refrigerator. They have an average life span of about five years.

If you don't need the capacity of a full-size refrigerator, under-counter refrigerator drawers may be the perfect solution in a cramped kitchen or as a smaller, second cold-storage area.

features Refrigerators now come with a host of features. Look for glass shelves, which are much easier to clean than coated-wire ones. You may also need a reversible door to make your refrigerator open away from the counter. If you're buying a bottom-mount freezer unit, spend a bit more for an easy-access roll-out bin instead of a conventional freezer door. A freezer section that can be chilled to zero degrees Fahrenheit will keep food fresher than one that's cooled to 15 degrees—the lowest temperature that some freezers can maintain.

You may also want to add a few other conveniences. Many refrigerators have interior shelves that slide, racks that hold soda cans or wine bottles, and wide door shelves for storing gallon jugs. Door-mounted ice and water dispensers have long been a popular option in side-by-side refrigerators, and now they can be equipped to filter water before it becomes ice cubes or a cold drink (don't forget that an ice maker will require a water line). A pass-through refreshment center allows you to get at frequently used items without opening the refrigerator door. For the die-hard gadget lover, there are even refrigerators that include an Internet connection for recipe swapping, as well as a television, sound system, and digital camera.

Any refrigerator you buy will be more energy efficient than the one you're replacing. In fact, a new refrigerator may pay for itself in energy savings: A 20-year-old model costs about $150 a year to run, whereas current models cost about $35. All refrigerators carry stickers comparing their electricity consumption to that of other refrigerators in their class.

Wine enthusiasts appreciate the precise cooling temperature of an under-counter refrigerator for wine only.

When looking at these energy-guide stickers, be sure the models you're comparing have similar features. Some add-ons, such as a self-defrost mechanism or an automatic ice maker, use extra electricity.

dishwashers

If you haven't bought a dishwasher in several years, you're in for a pleasant surprise. Today's models clean the dirtiest dishes with no prerinsing and no spotting. They hold more dishes than ever before, and they consume less water and energy. The best units can be programmed to handle crystal with care or scrub encrusted pots and pans. But the greatest improvement in recent years has been noise reduction. You can now buy a dishwasher that's so quiet you'll barely know it's running.

Standard dishwashers are the same size they've been for decades: 24 inches deep, 24 inches wide, and 34 inches high. A few compact units and European imports come as narrow as 18 inches. Exterior finishes include enameled steel, stainless steel, and black glass. Most models offer a replaceable front panel in a wide range of colors, and upper-end ones can be outfitted with a customized panel to match your cabinetry.

Getting dishes clean is a breeze for most dishwashers—even basic machines that cost around $350. As a rule, the more places inside the dishwasher that water sprays from, the cleaner the dishes get. Mid-range models spray dishes from five or six directions (manufacturers term this wash levels). If you also want quiet operation, flexible loading, designer styling, hidden controls, and efficient use of water and energy, prepare to pay $800 to $1,500. Top-of-the-line

models, and now some in the middle of the range, are lined with guaranteed-for-life stainless steel rather than plastic (a very durable liner in its own right, and a big improvement over enameled steel liners).

Since most models do a good job of getting dishes clean, the most important thing to look for is soundproofing. In today's open-plan kitchens, a quiet dishwasher is almost a necessity. Fortunately, improved sound insulation, vibration absorbers and low-noise pumps now make it possible to create a nearly silent machine. In most cases, price is a good indicator of noise level, since more expensive models usually have better insulation.

Extra-hot water is another feature that's worth looking for. Older dishwashers used water directly from the home's hot-water supply, which meant that dishes wouldn't get clean if the supply ran out or the water heater was set too low. Today many dishwashers have a temperature boost feature that heats the water to 140 degrees Fahrenheit before the

cycle begins (this allows you to turn your home's water heater down to 120 degrees, which is safer and more energy efficient). Some models have a sanitize option that heats water to 155 degrees for sterilizing baby bottles and "steam-cleaning" the grease from pots and pans.

Also consider the machine's loading flexibility. Features like folding tines and adjustable top racks and even third racks give you more ways to position dishes so they all get clean. Some dishwashers can be equipped with special inserts that hold wine goblets or oddly shaped items. Cup clips hold glasses securely, and an odds-and-ends basket accommodates small objects that don't fit anywhere else. For easier loading and unloading, dishwashers can also be raised above the counter (see pages 130–131).

If you have the space, two dishwashers may be better than one. Consider doubling up if you have a large family, keep kosher, or do a lot of entertaining.

Most dishwashers eliminate the need to rinse dishes before loading. Some have a self-cleaning filter with a hard-food disposer—a small built-in garbage disposal that grinds and flushes away food residue. Without it, any food particles left on plates will accumulate at the bottom of the dishwasher and you'll need to empty the filter manually (some European brands don't have self-cleaning filters, but emptying the filter is easy and needs to be done only every few weeks).

Dishwasher controls are more user friendly than ever. Most dishwashers have electronic touch pads, though manual controls are still available. For a seamless look, many models have controls on the top edge of the door rather than on the face. There's even a time-delay setting that allows you to load the dishwasher and set it to run when nobody is around to hear. Many dishwashers also have specialty cycles, such as a china wash, that protect fragile items or save water when you're cleaning a lightly soiled load.

Dishwashers continue to improve at conserving energy and water. Today's models use about half as

Two-drawer dishwashers have separate control panels, which means you can wash heavily soiled pots in one drawer and delicate crystal in the other. They also minimize the detergent, water, and energy needed to run larger units.

much electricity as earlier versions did. Many models use a scant 5 gallons of water per load—about half as much as is needed for washing dishes by hand. The biggest water waste occurs when people prewash their dishes, which modern machines have rendered unnecessary. Prerinsing also makes little or no difference in the dishwasher's cleaning performance.

water filters

If you're worried about the quality of your drinking water, or it simply tastes bad, you may want an under-sink water filter. Your first step should be to have your tap water laboratory-tested. If you discover a problem, you can choose an appropriate filtration system based on the test results. Your plumber or local water supplier can advise you about your options.

If you're concerned mainly about the taste and smell of your water, an inexpensive carbon filter system will remove chlorine and sulfur, the two most common culprits. It can also remove many different chemical compounds and bacteria. Even if your water is fine,

you may want to install such a device. "It's cheap insurance to install a granulated activated-carbon filter for your sources of cooking and drinking water," Trethewey says. The filter will need to be replaced periodically.

A bulkier, more expensive reverse-osmosis system will remove virtually all impurities down to a microscopic level. Because these systems consume 6 gallons of water for every gallon of filtered water they produce, reverse-osmosis units should be used only for limited point-of-use applications. Distillation filtration units, which boil and condense the water from your tap, achieve similar results and similar output.

It's especially important to make sure that your water doesn't contain heavy metals such as lead, cadmium, or mercury. Lead is of particular concern because it can cause illness and brain damage, particularly in children. The plumbing pipes in your house may contain lead-based solder if they were installed before the early 1980s. You can alleviate most of the danger by running your tap for 30 seconds to flush standing water out of the pipes. If you test your tap water and it is seriously contaminated with heavy metals, you may need to install a filtration system with an ion-exchange resin filter made to trap them.

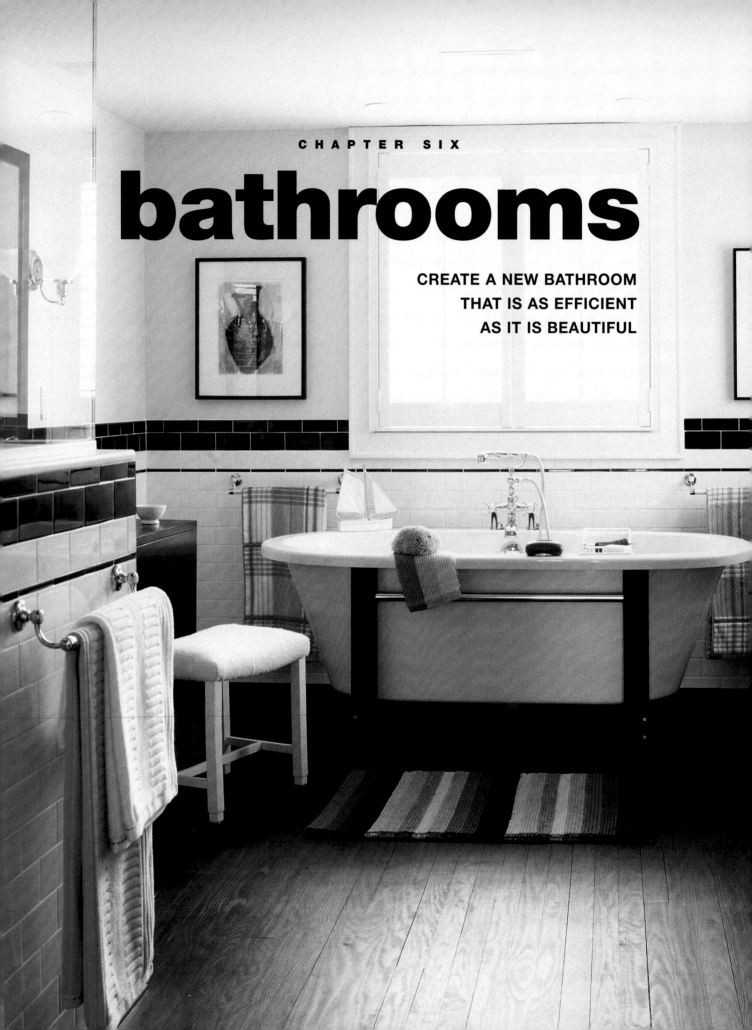

CHAPTER SIX

bathrooms

**CREATE A NEW BATHROOM
THAT IS AS EFFICIENT
AS IT IS BEAUTIFUL**

MOST HOUSES BUILT MORE THAN TWENTY YEARS AGO have bathrooms that were meant to be strictly utilitarian. "You'd put in a sink, a toilet, a tub, then call it a day," says This Old House plumbing and heating expert Richard Trethewey. Clearly, times have changed. The modern bathroom has become stylish, efficient, and comfortable, if not downright luxurious. That's why updating or building a new bathroom is one of today's most popular home projects. A bathroom remodel or addition can offer a high return on dollars spent and add immeasurably to your comfort and enjoyment.

A proper bathroom renovation presents unique challenges. Because heat, moisture, and heavy use make the bathroom especially vulnerable to deterioration and structural damage, high-quality materials and exacting craftsmanship are imperative. And because some bathroom materials are both expensive and virtually permanent, a carefully designed plan is critical.

Anticipating the decisions you'll need to make and the challenges you may encounter is key. In this chapter, you'll find practical advice to guide you, from planning and designing to streamlining the construction process.

bathroom planning

The old adage that beauty is only skin deep goes double when it comes to a bathroom renovation. Well before you begin your remodel, you should evaluate the plumbing and other systems that make your bathroom function (see Chapter 3 for more about your home's systems). If they're outmoded, updating them is a priority. "Always work on the systems before you have fun with the finishes," says This Old House general contractor Tom Silva. "The heating, the wiring, the stuff behind the walls—those are by far the most important, and the smartest place to put your money."

In keeping with that philosophy, the TOH crew likes to begin a bathroom renovation by stripping everything down to the wall studs and subfloor. "That's the only way you can get in and really see what needs to be replaced," Silva says. With the structure in plain view, you can seal leaks, repair rotted structural supports, and replace outdated plumbing and wiring. Richard Trethewey recommends upgrading your systems even if they're not on their last legs, simply because you have easy access to them when you're remodeling. Above all, take the opportunity to add proper mechanical ventilation so your hard work won't be destroyed by rot, mildew, and other moisture-related problems (for more about ventilation, see pages 200–201).

In this family bathroom remodel, no walls were moved but much-needed square footage was added. Shelves fit between wall studs, a pocket door replaces a swinging one, and a boomerang-shaped vanity makes the most of the small, odd-shaped space.

Just about anything is possible when it comes to remodeling, but not everything is worth the time or money. So before you begin planning your bathroom remodel in earnest, get a rough idea of what your project is going to entail.

Remodeling an existing bathroom can be a simple job or an enormous undertaking. If you want to make structural changes such as moving a bearing wall or altering a ceiling, you're probably looking at a complex and costly project. Reconfiguring the plumbing to accommodate a new

tag of $40,000 or more. The job will be easiest and less costly if you can put your new bathroom near existing water supply lines, drain lines, and vent stack. If you put it above an existing bathroom, you can probably run the new pipes up the same wall where the existing ones are.

If you're adding on, local ordinances will prohibit you from building too close to your property line. Even if you're working within your home's footprint, building codes apply, and permits will be needed. You may want to hire a designer or architect to help you create a bathroom that's safe, legal, and appropriate for your house (see page 197).

LEFT: This 1885 bathroom underwent a complete remodel involving expensive structural changes. The homeowners preserved its original style by using marble floors and vanities that look like period furniture.

floor plan can also turn a run-of-the-mill remodel into a real challenge, as can putting in a steam shower, oversize whirlpool, or soaking tub, all of which may require structural reinforcement or dedicated utilities. The easiest, most economical bathroom makeover is one that leaves fixtures and plumbing in their existing positions (see page 196 for advice on controlling costs).

If you plan to install a completely new and expanded luxury bathroom, expect major construction, a small army of subcontractors, and a price

Even a minor remodel can make a big difference. A marble counter with hammered steel sink, antique mirrors, and accessories add style to an otherwise ordinary space.

what type of bathroom?

The best way to begin developing a bathroom plan is to clarify what you want and need. Do you want a place to bathe the kids, a luxurious adult retreat, or a stylish half-bath where guests can freshen up? When you know exactly how the room will be used, you will have a better basis for developing a design that works. As you're deciding what features your bathroom should include, focus on the specific needs and preferences of the people who will use it.

master baths No longer just a washroom attached to the bedroom, the master bath now features luxurious amenities, from sitting areas and entertainment centers to fireplaces and panoramic views. The once ubiquitous boxy white bathtub has been replaced with a whirlpool or soaking tub, and the shower may feature water-massage jets for a soothing spa experience. "This is not just a room where you take a bath or a shower and run," says architect Robert A.M. Stern, who

Today's master baths are much larger and more luxurious than those built a generation ago. Here, a marble floor, oversized tub, and separate sink and dressing areas create an ideal adult retreat.

designed the TOH Magazine Dream House. "It's a room in which to relax, where all kinds of activities can take place, from reading books to making phone calls."

To accommodate all these extras, the master bath has grown to proportions that would have seemed gargantuan a generation ago. The TOH Dream House master bath (shown at left) includes a 16-by-10-foot area just for the whirlpool tub and dressing table. In such a large bathroom, the layout is very important. Stern emphasizes efficiency and livability. Though he uses the tub as a focal point, he believes that a separate shower stall is essential for quick wash-ups on busy mornings. Two sinks are a must, he adds, and they should be separated by at least 3 feet "so that you don't bump elbows." The mirror should be comfortably oversized. "The bigger the mirror is, the better, particularly if two people are going to be jockeying to use it," Stern says. For privacy, the toilet is in an alcove.

If your house was built for a bygone era, you may have difficulty finding enough space for an elaborate master bath. It may be possible to annex a closet, a landing, or a small bedroom, but be aware that older homes often lack adequate support for modern fixtures such as oversize whirlpools and soaking tubs. Unless you're building an addition, you may need to have a contractor reinforce

A small but bright and airy shared bath features double sinks, two mirrors, and a separate room for the toilet and tub so that one person can bathe while another uses the sink.

the floors and supporting structure. If you want to keep things simple or you can't find the room to expand, consider skipping the oversized tub and substituting a roomy shower or a smaller, lightweight whirlpool.

shared baths If your bathroom will serve more than one person at a time, it should offer each user a little personal space. The key is to compartmentalize fixtures rather than to arrange them around the perimeter of an open room. A typical configuration isolates the toilet and shower from the sink and grooming area. Ideally, the toilet should be concealed in a separate "water closet," but a low wall or even a decorative screen can provide a measure of privacy.

To effectively accommodate multiple users, a shared bathroom should

have two sinks, as well as a personal storage area for everyone. Whether you install a dual-sink vanity or separate pedestal sinks, each grooming station should have a mirror, an electrical outlet, and adequate lighting. You can enhance the privacy of shared spaces by installing an opaque shower door and concealing the tub behind a translucent pocket door, a freestanding screen, or a ceiling-mounted curtain.

Because a shared bathroom is often built between bedrooms, it's important to consider acoustics. At the TOH Magazine Dream House, Stern used bedroom closets to buffer bathroom sounds and added acoustical insulation in the walls. Without such measures, he says, "the flushing sound in the middle of the night can drive people bonkers."

children's baths A shared bath that will be used mostly by children has to be kid friendly, low maintenance, and, above all, safe. It should also be easy to update as the kids grow older and their needs, tastes, and sizes change.

Though bright colors and bold designs add an important element

of fun, a bathroom with real child appeal is one that's easy for kids to use. Try to situate the bath in a convenient location; if possible, place it between two children's bedrooms and install a door on each side. Put shelves, towel bars, and clothes hooks within easy reach, and create a color-coded storage area for each child.

A bathroom for children should feature kid-height towel bars, a step stool to reach the sink, and slip-resistant flooring.

Consider pullout faucets and shower nozzles for tearless hair washing. If you're installing a tub-shower combo, enclose it with a shower curtain rather than glass doors; you'll have more room to assist small bathers and you can install a sliding door when the children get older.

For safety, choose slip-resistant flooring, skid-proof rugs, and a tub with a textured bottom (or put in a textured rubber shower mat). Be sure that all shower faucets have scald-free valves (see page 211). All glass shower doors should have tempered safety glass. A countertop with rounded edges will help prevent cuts and bruises.

powder rooms A two-fixture (toilet and sink) bathroom in a public area of the house, the powder room is also known as a half-bath. Because it is small yet conspicuous, it should be carefully planned.

A powder room should be private, so the door should not open into a public area such as the living room

or kitchen. Ideally, it should be off of a hallway. If you're remodeling a powder room that's poorly placed, see if you can reconfigure access to the room. If you can't, it may be better to start over in a new spot (see tips below on finding space).

Designers consider 4½ by 5 feet to be minimum dimensions for a half-bath, but at this size, your options for arranging fixtures will be very limited. A pocket door can increase the number of layout possibilities while adding usable space to the room. Consider buying a compact sink and/or toilet made especially for small bathrooms.

A powder room's diminutive size makes it the perfect place to splurge on marble flooring or hand-painted tiles, since you'll be buying materials in small quantities. Because it's used infrequently, it's also the ideal place to use less practical decorative finishes such as copper and glass. Soft, indirect lighting and a generously proportioned mirror will add an elegant touch and make the room appear larger.

FINDING SPACE FOR A POWDER ROOM

Though powder rooms tend to be tiny, finding space to add one can be difficult. Tom Silva likes to use the space beneath a staircase, as long as the stairs do not have a basement staircase beneath them. The challenge is to create enough headroom beneath the stairs for people to stand comfortably. Sometimes the solution is to rearrange the floor joists to create a step down into the room, though this is expensive. Another option is to cut into the overhead stringers and add steel braces to hold the staircase up. Silva used this technique on one TOH project to create a powder room in a minuscule 15-square-foot space where the ceiling height below the stairs was a mere 6 feet. He built a curved ceiling and gained a precious 6½ inches of headroom. "It's a sweet way to make up for the lack of space," he says, "and the curved ceiling looks pretty nice too."

UNIVERSAL AND ACCESSIBLE BATHROOM DESIGN

The classic bathroom layout creates barriers for many people, especially those who are disabled, ill, injured, elderly, or very young. The goal of universal design is to make the bathroom usable by anyone. Even if no one in your family currently requires special accommodations, it makes sense to design your new bathroom so it will meet both the current and future needs of everyone in the household. Some features you may want to include:

■ An anti-scald thermostat valve, which maintains the shower water at a constant temperature (see page 211).

■ Single-lever, wing-blade, or motion-sensing faucets for people who have limited hand strength or who need a free hand to lean on a walker or cane.

■ Grab bars for people who are unsteady on their feet. If you decide that grab bars are not necessary now, place plywood or wood-blocking reinforcement in the walls during construction so bars can be installed later. Also reinforce towel bars, soap dishes, and any other protrusions that might be used to break a fall; they should be fastened securely enough to hold at least 250 pounds.

■ A mirror that extends down to the backsplash so that children and seated adults can see it when using the sink.

■ An adjustable shower-head for people of different heights. A handheld showerhead is convenient for cleaning young children and makes it possible to avoid wetting a bandage, cast, hairdo, or anything else that should remain dry.

■ Pocket doors instead of hinged ones. They save space, and they're easier for someone in a wheelchair to open. If you install hinged doors, make sure they swing out rather than into the room.

■ Shatterproof materials and slip-resistant flooring.

If someone in a wheelchair will use the bathroom regularly, create a barrier-free space using accessible-design principles. Accessible design conforms to standards established by the Americans with Disabilities Act (ADA), which prescribes specific heights, clearances, and room dimensions to accommodate people in wheelchairs. Openings and doorways must be at least 32 inches wide, and inside the room there should be a clear area at least 5 feet in diameter. The shower should be curbless, and the toilet 18 inches high with extended flush handles. The sink must have enough legroom below it for a seated person, and pipes under the sink should be insulated to prevent burns. Handles, switches, and regularly used storage areas should be no higher than 48 inches from the floor. You'll need more floor space for an accessible-design bath than you would for a conventional one.

When designing an accessible bath in a small space, leave the shower area open to the room so that the whole bathroom floor functions as a wheelchair-accessible shower pan. For extra waterproofing, install a vinyl membrane beneath the subfloor and run it 12 inches up the walls. Choose small ceramic floor tiles for extra traction.

layouts

Once you've chosen features and fixtures, think carefully about their placement. Layout dramatically affects how well the room will work.

To develop a floor plan, it helps to have a scale drawing of the space (shown at right). Include the length of each wall and the distance between doorways and windows. If you're remodeling, show existing fixtures, electrical outlets, and plumbing. Then make scale cutouts of fixtures and cabinets. By moving the cutouts around on this base map, you can visualize different possibilities. Try to use an attractive feature such as a graceful tub or vanity as a design centerpiece positioned so that it's the first thing you'll notice upon entering the room. If you have only a few options for arranging the fixtures, place the largest feature first and then the smaller ones.

When placing the tub or shower, allow plenty of space for bathers to

tip: hiding the toilet

Relocating the toilet in order to provide more privacy can be expensive, especially if you must move the toilet's closet flange (drain) or reconnect to the vent stack. Try turning the toilet 90 degrees and hiding it with a half-wall to accomplish the same result without extensive plumbing alterations.

SAMPLE SCALE DRAWING

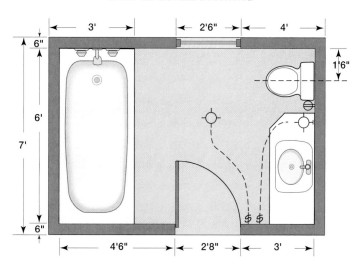

get in and out and for the door to swing open. The long dimension of the tub should be set perpendicular to the floor joists (or blocking and floor-framing modifications should be made to support it properly). Put the sink in a spot that's easily accessible but out of the traffic pattern. For privacy, place the toilet in the least visible position—preferably on the same wall as the door—so that it won't become a focal point. Don't forget storage areas such as closets, built-in shelving, or wall niches.

Building codes in your area may specify heights and clearances for fixtures. Even if there are few legal requirements, leave enough room at the front and sides of each fixture for easy access and cleaning. You'll need at least 30 inches in front of the sink, 36 inches between double sinks, and 30 inches in front of a bathtub or stall shower. The toilet requires a space measuring at least 30 inches wide

with 36 inches' clearance in front of the bowl (about 5 feet overall from the wall). Be aware that if a window is placed near the shower or tub, codes may require that it be glazed with safety glass.

Remember that relocating plumbing is expensive. If cost is a major concern, try to come up with a satisfactory floor plan that uses your existing plumbing locations. If you're building an addition, you can save money by placing all the plumbing along one wall.

STANDARD CLEARANCES

DOUBLE SINKS

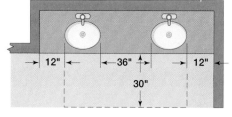

SHOWER

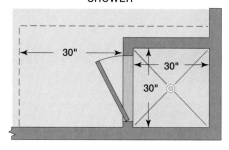

TOILET OR BIDET

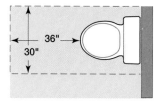

budgeting and controlling costs

Because all of the major building trades are involved in a bathroom remodel, sprucing up even a small bath tends to be expensive, especially if you choose anything but the most basic fixtures and materials. Moreover, bathroom remodels are famously unpredictable: Pulling down wall tiles or changing out old plumbing often reveals structural and mechanical problems. For bathrooms, Tom Silva advises homeowners to set a budget for the project and then add 25 to 30 percent to cover any unpleasant surprises.

For a simple bathroom remodel, materials and labor each account for about half the expense. So you can figure a ballpark price by totaling the cost of supplies and fixtures you anticipate buying and then doubling that number. If your goals exceed your budget, revisit your floor plan to see whether you can minimize structural or plumbing changes. Instead of expanding the room, see if you can gain floor space by using a pocket door and/or scaling down fixtures. Rather than reconfiguring an awkward wall, make it functional by installing storage shelves or corner bath appliances. Skip the skylight and opt for a less expensive solar tube, or substitute a glass-block partition for a solid one so light can flow through the room. If you're adding a bathroom, you can save by choosing a location near the existing main vent stack (see pages 66–67).

You can also save significantly by revising your plans for major elements. New cabinetry can account for as much as one-third of the cost of materials and fixtures in a typical bathroom remodel, so you'll save a bundle if you choose stock cabinets instead of custom-built ones. Substituting low-cost flooring materials such as vinyl and laminate for expensive ones can also save a lot of money. Hanging on to an old-fashioned pedestal sink or claw-foot tub can benefit your decorating scheme as well as your bottom line. "People often rip out old tubs because they're slightly blemished," Trethewey says, "but it's not easy to find an affordable bathtub with the look and size of a period tub." A fixture that has seen better days can be professionally refinished for $350 to $500—a fraction of the $1,200 to $5,000 you would pay to have a new cast-iron tub installed. If you truly need new fixtures, try altering your wish list. A custom-designed sink or a sculpted one-piece toilet can cost up to ten times as much as a basic version.

Some of the best tricks for rejuvenating a bathroom can cost very little. A fresh color scheme, new lighting, updated faucets, and inventive cabinet pulls can make a big difference in the way you feel about your morning shower. See pages 38–44 for more information on controlling costs.

This 1919 tub was professionally refinished in less than a day, saving the homeowners time and money and allowing them to salvage some of the historic charm of their home.

A great way to stretch your remodeling dollars is to take advantage of every inch of usable space. Here, Tom Silva prepares the area beneath the stairs for a powder room.

plumber, the electrician, the tile setter, and anyone else who provided services or materials for your job (see page 34 for more information about what your contract should include).

building codes and inspections

You'll need a permit from your local building department if your remodel calls for changes to your home's structure or plumbing and electrical systems. A permit ensures that an inspector will scrutinize every phase of construction; new plumbing and wiring often require multiple inspections at various stages. As onerous as this may seem, remember that the inspector's job is to protect you by verifying that your project adheres to safety standards and building codes.

Even if your budget is tight, don't be tempted to save money by skipping permits, especially if you're adding a bathroom. Not only will you forfeit the extra measure of safety that the inspection process provides, but a clandestine remodel can become a real problem in the future. If building officials discover that you've done the work without a permit, you may be required to dismantle the entire bathroom. And if you sell your house, a smart buyer will demand proof that the work was done under permits.

working with professionals

Because remodeling a bathroom is an involved undertaking, you may want to call in a professional. Information in Chapter 2 will help you choose a specialist whose skills match your needs. If you're planning an addition or a major renovation, you may want to hire an architect, but if your project is confined largely to the bath, a bathroom designer can draw up a plan and tell you about all the latest products.

A detailed written contract is particularly important when you're remodeling a bathroom, because fixtures, fittings, and materials vary so widely in quality and cost. Be sure your contract specifies the precise products and materials you want so that you don't find out in the middle of construction that your contractor's attractive bid included $35 faucets and a prefabricated shower unit if that's not what you intended. Since a bathroom renovation almost always requires multiple subcontractors, you'll also need a waiver of subcontractor liens to protect you if your general contractor fails to pay the

managing your project

There's no doubt about it, a bathroom renovation can be inconvenient, to say the least. In addition to noise and dust, there will be plumbing and electrical shutoffs and decommissioned showers and toilets. Bathroom remodels also tend to uncover the kinds of structural and systemic problems that can lay waste to a construction schedule. "You might think the project will take only a few weeks and then discover that you're without a bathroom for a few months," Silva says. The best idea is to prepare for such trials before you begin.

First figure out what bathing facilities your family will use during the remodel. The solution is obvious if your house has another bathroom, "but keep in mind that you could still have a major traffic jam in the morning while everyone's getting ready for school and work," Silva says. If you don't want workers using your spare bathroom, or if you don't have one, your contractor can arrange for a portable toilet to be brought to the work site. Silva cautions against using a neighbor's bathroom, since the imposition can strain an otherwise friendly relationship.

Above all, make sure that materials are on site before any work begins. "A bathroom renovation can grind to a halt if the contractor is waiting for, say, a shipment of custom-made tiles from Italy that never seems to arrive," Silva says. Also keep in mind that it can be tricky to schedule the number of subcontractors you'll need for a bath remodel, since the size of the room may not accommodate more than one worker at a time.

BUILDING A SAFER BATHROOM

Because a high percentage of home accidents occur in the bathroom, safety should be of paramount concern in every phase of your remodel.

Your layout should allow enough space for people to exit the tub or shower with ease. Create a second access to the room so someone can enter in an emergency, or at least provide a way to unlock the door from the outside. Include plenty of electrical outlets so you won't need an extension cord in a wet area. Place outlets a safe distance from any water source, and make sure they're properly grounded and protected by a ground-fault circuit interrupter (GFCI), circuit breaker, or receptacle, shown at right. Set aside a secured area for storage of potentially dangerous implements, toxic chemicals, and medicines.

Select slip-resistant flooring and nonskid rugs. Small ceramic tiles provide more traction than large ones. Some slip-resistant surfaces, such as vinyl and linoleum, can also soften the impact of a fall. Choose scald-proof valves for all faucets. Anchor cabinets firmly to wall studs, and add plywood or wood-blocking reinforcement behind the wall wherever you attach a protruding object such as a towel bar; these objects are frequently used to break a fall. Position all wall-mounted accessories above eye level.

Remodeling a bathroom in itself can be dangerous. Because the bathroom can be damp, make sure only double-insulated or grounded power tools are used and are plugged into an outlet protected by a ground-fault circuit interrupter.

bathroom systems

A grasp of basic plumbing, electrical, and heating and cooling principles will help you plan your bathroom remodel. Following is a brief discussion of each system in regard to the bathroom (see Chapter 3 for more information).

plumbing

Two main components make up any plumbing system: water supply and the drain, waste, and vent (DWV) system. Building codes often require a 1-inch-diameter supply line from the street to the house for new construction. For multiple bathrooms, a 1-inch line must run all the way to the water heater. If you own an older home, there's a good chance that your main supply line is smaller, so you may not have optimal water pressure if you increase the number and size of fixtures. If you have several bathrooms or want a luxury fixture, you may have to put in a new supply line.

Extending water supply lines is usually straightforward but expensive. Creating a new drain and vent stack is also a big job. To keep your bathroom remodel simple, try to place fixtures within a few feet of your home's main vent stack. Your local building code will specify the maximum distance that fixtures may be placed from the vent lines.

electrical

The modern bathroom uses a good deal of power. If you have an older house with small-capacity electrical service (less than 100 amps), you may need an upgrade to accommodate the latest amenities. Consult an electrician especially if you plan to install a power-hungry whirlpool, steam generator, or sauna. Electrical space heating also creates high demand. Make sure your plans conform to local electrical codes regarding the placement of outlets, appliance switches, and light fixtures, and get the proper permits from your local building department before starting construction. It's the law, and you will benefit from having your work checked both at the rough-in stage and when it's complete.

If your electrical system has not been upgraded for 20 years or more, you probably need to install ground-fault circuit interrupters. Required by code in bathrooms, they prevent accidental shock or electrocution.

Some municipalities allow homeowners to do their own electrical work, but for a bathroom remodel it's best to hire a professional. "The last thing you want to do is to make a serious wiring mistake in your home—particularly a wet room like the bath—trying to do a job yourself," Silva says. "Get an electrician, and get it done right."

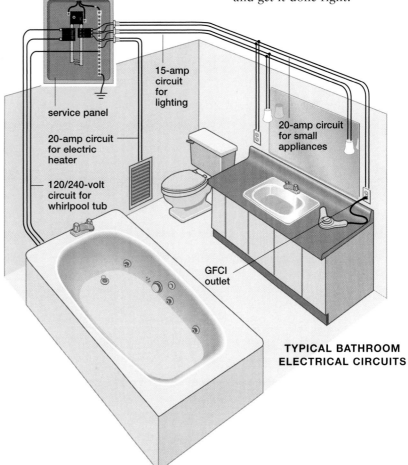

service panel

15-amp circuit for lighting

20-amp circuit for electric heater

120/240-volt circuit for whirlpool tub

20-amp circuit for small appliances

GFCI outlet

TYPICAL BATHROOM ELECTRICAL CIRCUITS

heating

"Make sure you have plenty of heat," Silva says. If you want to link your bathroom to your forced-air central heating system, you'll need to extend the supply and return air ducts that connect with your furnace—a costly job that requires professional know-how. Auxiliary heating is less expensive to install and often works well in a small space such as a bathroom. A wall- or ceiling-mounted heater will provide plenty of heat (a gas heater must be vented to the outside). Radiant floor heating is another option, and one that the TOH crew enthusiastically endorses. "Adding radiant floor heat to a bathroom is probably the single best investment in comfort you could ever make," Trethewey says.

You can use radiant floor heat to warm the entire room, or "just to chase the chill off the tile," as Trethewey puts it. For true space heating, especially in cold climates, a system that carries hot water through a series of tubes underneath the floor is most

Radiant heat is a great way to warm up a chilly bathroom tile floor. This electric system's coils are covered with mortar and standard tiles, creating a floor so thin that even the toilet won't have to be raised.

effective and energy efficient. If the goal is merely to warm the floor in a room that already has heat, a thin electric warming mat can be laid between the subfloor and the tiles. Run by a timer, the mat can be set to warm the floor just enough to keep toes toasty. Mat systems are cheaper to install, but more expensive to operate.

In addition to delivering heat, it's critical to retain it. "In a bathroom, one of the most important things is to have the right insulation and vapor barriers," Silva says. "Make sure the insulation gets into all the spaces, like behind the shower or tub. Ridged foam can be cut to fit tight into the stud bays. A polyisocyanurate with a foil face will provide good insulation and a vapor barrier all in one. Spray-in foams are even more effective and will fill all the gaps—and with these, you don't need a vapor barrier," he adds. (For more about insulation, see page 62.)

vital ventilation

Though many homeowners pay little or no attention to it, "ventilation is the crucial element in a house, especially in a bathroom," Silva says. Most local building codes require that the bathroom be ventilated, and for good reason: Poor ventilation allows humid air to condense in the walls, where it can cause extensive structural rot in a short amount of time. "I've pulled relatively new bathrooms apart and found more mold and decay than you could ever believe—and all because there was no ventilation," Silva says.

You can reduce bathroom dampness by opening windows, but to ensure sufficient ventilation, you need an exhaust fan that's powerful enough to completely replace the air in the room at least eight times an hour. Every fan has a CFM rating, which tells you how many cubic feet of air it can move in a minute. To determine what CFM rating your fan should have, multiply the total cubic footage of the room by 8 and then divide by 60. The smallest fans on the market move about 60 cubic feet of air per minute, enough to clear moisture from a 5-by-8-foot bathroom. For bathrooms larger than 100

Hidden in the ceiling above, this powerful, quiet bathroom ventilator is also an attractive light fixture.

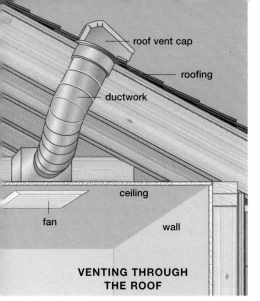

VENTING THROUGH THE ROOF

Labels: roof vent cap, roofing, ductwork, ceiling, fan, wall

square feet, the Home Ventilating Institute recommends a ventilation rate based on the number and type of fixtures present. Toilets, showers, and tubs require 50 CFM each; a whirlpool tub requires 100. (For more information about sizing a vent fan, visit the Home Ventilating Institute at *www.hvi.org.*)

Fans are sold in several types. The simplest turn on when the light switch is operated or from a separate switch. Noise may be an issue with these; compare sone ratings and look for the lowest at the correct CFM for your bathroom. A much quieter alternative is a central ventilation fan that can be connected to all the bathrooms. Its motor is in the attic, so the fan can't be heard inside the house. Both types of fans absolutely must be vented to the outside of the house, not into the attic. "Otherwise, you're dumping moisture on the underside of the roof," Silva says. To avoid cutting into the roof for the vent, or in cold winter climates, This Old House master carpenter Norm Abram advises venting through the soffit. Make sure that rigid insulated ducting is used and that an exterior damper to prevent cold air from blowing in is installed.

Your fan should be controlled by a timer switch or, even better, a humidistat switch that operates the fan when the humidity levels in the room require it. This will keep the fan on even after you've left the bath (it should be on for 15 to 20 minutes after a shower) without your having to remember to turn it off.

PREVENTING MOLD

Most homeowners hate the household fungus known as mold because it produces unsightly black spots on bathroom walls and ceilings. But mold is much more than a cosmetic problem. As it grows, mold produces volatile organic compounds (VOCs) that can cause health problems such as upper respiratory distress, chronic headaches, skin rashes, flulike symptoms, sinus congestion, and nausea. Excessive exposure to VOCs can damage the liver, kidneys, and central nervous system.

Mold thrives in warm, damp environments. The best way to combat it is to remove excess moisture from your house. When you're renovating the bathroom, install a plastic vapor barrier between the insulation and the drywall to prevent warm air from condensing inside the walls. Put in a ventilation fan to expel moisture from the room (see opposite page). And because paper is a food source for mold, you may want to choose nonorganic drywall with paperless facings. However, mold-resistant drywall is effective only when combined with good design, effective ventilation, and good building practices.

If you suspect that your bathroom has mold problems, take precautions before you start having the walls ripped apart. Mold is a living organism, and a single mold spore can reproduce trillions of spores within a few days. To keep mold from spreading to other parts of the house during your renovation, block off the construction area with plastic sheeting and keep the air moving out of the room. A fan blowing out the bathroom window will help create the necessary negative pressure.

Some contractors will not begin work until mold abatement is completed. If you don't want to do the job yourself, hire a professional. But beware: Mold abatement has become the fastest-growing segment of the environmental-remediation business, so watch out for disreputable companies. Also, insurance carriers can be skeptical, as so many claims have been filed; check to see that yours will cover the work before it begins.

defining a style

Vintage tub, tiled walls, a mosaic floor, and period fixtures and accessories create a Victorian look in this bathroom.

plumbing catalogs for salvaged and rehabilitated originals.

If your house doesn't have a definable architectural style, simply go with a look that you like, as long as it doesn't clash with adjoining spaces. You'll still need something to unify your design, so you might start with a color scheme, a piece of tile, or a vanity that you love, then look for other elements that will complement your choice. It hardly matters where you start, as long as you use the same motif throughout the room.

design elements

In the confined quarters of the bathroom, a balanced, visually pleasing design is especially important. Through skillful use of form, color, and texture, you can create a mood, camouflage flaws, and even make your bathroom appear larger.

After you've settled on a floor plan, you can begin to develop a decorating scheme. To give your design coherence, it helps to focus on a particular historical era, geographical region, or artistic movement—Victorian, Mediterranean, or Art Deco, for example. Then you can choose fixtures, materials, and decorative details that will evoke this look.

Begin by noticing characteristics that define the rest of your house. Though your new bathroom needn't mimic the existing architecture, it

should blend in. The TOH crew likes to stay faithful to the era when the house was built but add the best of new building technologies. Sticking to your home's original style is usually wise from a resale standpoint as well. Modern versions of period fixtures, fittings, and lighting are widely available. If only the real thing will do, you can search the Internet, home-restoration magazines, and vintage-

Blue is a great color for the bathroom. Here, sky-blue floor tiles match a faux-cloudy sky. The painted clouds lift the eye upward, accentuating the high ceiling.

ABOVE LEFT: Dark wood used in the trim and accessories contrasts nicely with this traditional bathroom's white walls and white and beige floor tiles. ABOVE RIGHT: Warm tones create a cozy feel in this guest bathroom. The faux-painted walls and decorative sconces add a sophisticated look.

Imagine that you're looking at your bathroom plan head-on (you can make a sketch, or elevation drawing, from this perspective). Study the different lines that characterize the design—the vertical lines of the shower stall, the horizontals created by cabinet tops—and imagine how they'll draw your eye through the space. Notice the interplay of shapes created by windows, doors, alcoves, and large bathroom elements. Finally, check to see that your fixtures and other major features are in proportion to the size of the bathroom. If space is limited, choose scaled-down fixtures that reveal as much floor space as possible—a wall-mounted sink instead of a vanity, for example.

Your color scheme needs to be integral to your design. Pale hues work well in a bathroom; they reflect light, which makes a room appear larger. Blues and greens also tend to create an illusion of extra space, and they seem especially appropriate in the watery environs of the bathroom. Dark shades, though they should be used judiciously, can make a narrow bathroom seem shorter or add drama to a drab one. Unless your bathroom is quite large, it's safest to stick with a monochromatic color scheme, especially if you want to create a restful mood or conceal a problem area.

The bathroom is chock-full of textures and patterns that can compete for attention in a small space. When you're considering how the various surfaces will look together, remember that natural materials such as wood and stone will contribute to the mix of patterns, as will the grout lines in a tile installation.

tip: head to the library
When you want to add an authentic finishing touch to a period decorating scheme, check out vintage home-decorating magazines. Norm Abram notes that large public libraries often have old issues of home-design publications, which will give you a sense of the wall colors and coverings that were fashionable when your house was built.

floors, walls, and countertops

Sheet vinyl serves as a floor material that is soft and warm underfoot.

Bathroom flooring must perform in wet, slippery conditions. The flooring section on pages 96–109 provides details on the many types available. As you consider the merits of each, pay special attention to moisture resistance and safety.

vinyl The most popular bathroom flooring material is vinyl, and not just because it's attractively priced. Properly installed, it offers excellent water resistance, even in a below-grade bathroom. It can be installed over any flat underlayment, including an existing vinyl floor. Its soft, skid-resistant surface helps prevent slips and cushions the blow from a fall.

linoleum and cork For a natural alternative, consider linoleum, which offers all the advantages of vinyl and then some, including superb durability and natural resistance to bacteria. Cork is another anti-microbial resilient flooring

derived from natural sources. Use cork tiles rather than sheet flooring, and caulk the perimeter of the room before installing the baseboard. A coat of sealant will protect cork from moisture.

tile Ceramic-tile flooring looks elegant and is watertight if properly installed. Smooth-glazed tile can be very slippery when wet, so consider a type with a textured surface, or use smaller tiles so that the extra grout

ABOVE: Neutral ceramic tiles create a clean look in a small bathroom. Here, they are also used as trim around the bottom of the wall, an excellent choice for a floor that will get wet. LEFT: A tiled linoleum floor is a stylish and eco-friendly choice.

lines will provide traction. Check the tile's porosity rating. Porous tiles may powder or chip if subjected to frequent moisture. Even if you choose a relatively impervious tile, keep it as dry as you can. Pooling water will damage grout and mortar, eventually loosening tiles. To stave off mold and make cleaning easier, use mildew-resistant or epoxy grout.

stone If you want natural-stone flooring such as marble, granite, limestone, or slate, choose cut tiles rather than flagstones (which have a free-form shape and varying thickness). Though their natural look is lovely, flagstones cannot be butted tightly together, so their resulting wide grout joints collect stains and bacteria. Stone tile with a glossy surface can be slippery, so look for a honed or rough surface. It's essential to protect stone flooring with a high-quality sealant so it doesn't absorb dirt.

wood and laminate Hardwood flooring can be used in a bathroom if it is installed without gaps and is sealed thoroughly (Tom Silva suggests putting two coats of sealer on the back side of the wood before installation). Because solid-wood flooring is very susceptible to moisture damage even when carefully finished, a flooded tub or toilet overflow can ruin a wood floor. If you want the look of wood with less risk of water damage, a better choice is engineered wood. Because of its multilayered makeup and factory-applied finish, it is far more durable in a wet environment. Some types of laminate floors, when professionally installed, also offer the look of wood with moisture resistance. It is essential that the installers follow the manufacturer's instructions to prevent dampness from seeping between the planks or joints.

ABOVE: A patchwork of naturally water-resistant slate tiles covers the floors and walls of this contemporary bathroom. LEFT: Hardwood flooring in a bathroom may require more maintenance, but its warmth and style are hard to beat.

tip: tiling over tile If you want to change a tile wall treatment, you needn't necessarily tear your bathroom walls down to the studs. Instead of starting over, you can sometimes tile over the existing surface, a technique known in the industry as TOT (tile over tile). Scuff up the existing tile surface with 80-grit sandpaper and level it with a coat of thinset adhesive. Then install new tiles as you normally would.

A pale wallpaper pattern creates texture without overwhelming the room.

walls

You can use any type of wall treatment in your bathroom that you'd use in the rest of your house. The key is to choose a water-resistant version and make sure it's properly applied or installed.

paint The most versatile and economical wall treatment for the bath is paint. High-sheen paints offer the most moisture resistance and are easiest to clean, but a gloss finish will magnify imperfections in the wall. A semigloss or satin finish will look more attractive and still protect the wall from dampness. Make sure the paint has a fungicide additive. Before installing new trim, prime the back to seal the wood. Avoid using the shower or tub before the paint has completely dried, as the humidity can cause adhesion problems. Allow plenty of time between applications so that each coat dries thoroughly.

wallpaper and wall coverings

If you choose wallpaper, use a water-resistant variety, and don't compromise on quality. Vinyl wallpaper holds up best in moist conditions. Avoid natural-fiber wall coverings, which will soak up moisture and stain. All types of wallpaper will perform best in a powder room or other infrequently used bathroom. If your bathroom isn't square, choose a wallpaper pattern that repeats diagonally rather than horizontally or vertically.

wainscoting

Wood wainscoting works well in a Colonial or country-style bath and has the added benefit of concealing any flaws in the wall. "Wainscoting is one of the things I love adding to a house," Silva says. "It protects the wall and looks good at the same time." Water can damage wainscoting, so be wary of putting it in a heavily used bathroom. Wainscoting should be primed and painted on both sides before installation to help ensure that condensation won't affect it. You can also choose MDF beadboard, or a panel system, which won't warp like wood. To finish off wainscoting, set it on a baseboard and cover the joint with a cap molding.

Wainscoting adds interest in a small bathroom and protects the drywall from hanging wet towels.

Used like wainscoting, cobalt blue ceramic tiles cover more than half the wall, providing dramatic color and moisture protection.

other materials Almost any material that's suitable for a bathroom countertop can also be used as a wall treatment. Ceramic tile withstands wet conditions and lasts for decades with little upkeep. Natural-stone tiles offer similar advantages. If price is no object, you can have stone slabs fabricated to serve as wall panels. Solid surface material can be made to fit any wall, and because it's seamless and watertight, cleaning is a breeze. No matter what covering you use, walls should be caulked wherever moisture might seep in. For this, Tom Silva recommends a tripolymer sealant or a premium-quality vinyl adhesive caulk.

countertops

Though a bathroom countertop doesn't have to stand up to kitchen knives and hot pots, it must be able to resist scratching, staining, and constant moisture. Any material that's suitable for a kitchen countertop will do the job (see pages 159–164 for more on countertop materials). Also consider cast polymers such as synthetic marble, which are typically formed with an integral sink. Some can be matched to the tub and shower.

Solid-surface materials perform even better in the bathroom than they do in the kitchen. Their ability to be molded into any shape makes them

ideal for a small or oddly configured bathroom. Veneers made of solid surfacing are much thinner but have the same look, feel, and warranty. They are glued to a substrate of fiberboard and typically cost 30 percent less than standard solid surfacing.

A ceramic-tile countertop is a time-honored and good choice for the bath, since it's virtually impervious to water and will complement the popular choice of tile for flooring and shower surround. Tile has definite drawbacks as a countertop material, however. It's unforgiving if you drop a glass object on it, and grout lines tend to collect dirt. But its flaws can

be minimized in a bathroom. Choose unbreakable cups and accessories, and keep grout lines thin and sealed.

Because bathroom countertops tend to be small, consider using materials that might otherwise be too expensive or impractical. Granite and marble countertops for kitchens made from a single slab of stone are expensive, but you may find a reduced-price remnant large enough to cover the top of a small vanity. Keep in mind, though, that marble is easily scratched and that both marble and granite finishes can be damaged by the oil and alcohol in many personal-care products.

Specialty materials such as copper and zinc, which require frequent polishing, may be manageable on a small area as well.

Synthetic stone countertops provide an upscale look on a budget.

bathroom **fixtures**

High-end replicas of old-fashioned claw-foot tubs create an antique look in a new bathroom.

Fixtures can make or break a bathroom. The sinks, tub, shower, faucets, toilet, and accessories give the room not only its visual style but its functionality. Beyond looking great, they must operate easily and reliably for many years.

tubs

Bathtubs are available in three types, according to how they are installed. Recessed tubs fit into an alcove or a corner, and they usually have two or three unfinished sides that are concealed by walls. Drop-in tubs are mounted on a platform or dropped into an opening in the floor, so they have no finished sides. Freestanding tubs such as the old-fashioned claw-foot tub are completely finished and usually have four visible legs. Within these categories, you can choose a whirlpool tub or a conventional one.

A standard bathtub is 60 inches long, but all tub styles are available in a variety of shapes and sizes. A tub with a higher rim will allow for deeper baths, a plus particularly for taller people. But bigger isn't necessarily better. Large tubs consume much more water, which requires more energy to heat, and they can be more difficult to clean. If you opt for a large freestanding tub, Tom Silva suggests a handheld shower unit for easier cleaning.

Before you buy a tub, make sure that it will fit through the bathroom door and that it's not too big for the room (there should be a space at least 5 feet long and 30 inches deep in front of the tub after it's installed). Also note the location of the tub's drain hole in case you can avoid having the bathroom drain rerouted.

Many of today's tubs are made of lightweight plastics such as acrylic. These tubs come in a huge array of shapes and sizes, and they're easy to transport and install. However, plastic surfaces easily scratch and become dull. Fiberglass-reinforced plastic, though less expensive, is even more likely to scratch. Tom Silva's top choice is the traditional enameled cast iron. "It's the one that will hold up the longest, and it can be refurbished if the surface ever wears out," he says. Enameled steel has a similar look, but its lightness makes it noisier, and its greater flexibility means that the enamel will chip more readily.

whirlpool tubs Most whirlpool tubs are prefabricated drop-in-style tubs made from molded acrylic, but you can also get a custom whirlpool tub or have an antique tub retrofitted with circulation jets. For the experienced do-it-yourselfer, there are kits for building a whirlpool or adding jets to your existing bathtub. However, most homeowners will be better off with factory-installed jets and a professional plumber. The most popular whirl-

Whirlpools come in a wide range of styles and can be fit into a corner or placed in the middle of the room.

Soaking tubs are deeper and larger than conventional tubs, and some can accommodate two people. They are made from stainless steel, acrylic, cast-iron enamel, copper, and even wood sealed with epoxy resin. Prices range from $400 to $900 or more.

One caveat: Soaking tubs can weigh up to 300 pounds and can hold an additional 500 or 600 pounds of water. Putting this kind of weight on standard floor framing is out of the question. Richard Trethewey suggests consulting a structural engineer about ways to bolster and disperse the tub's weight. "It can really ruin your day when the second floor tub ends up in the first floor hallway," he says. Options include sistering engineered lumber alongside existing joists, installing a steel beam beneath the tub, or adding a properly supported concrete pad. Since soaking tubs usually sit away from the wall, conventional faucets may have to be replaced with floor-mounted hardware, which necessitates tearing into the floor or ceiling to reroute plumbing.

Soaking tubs are a luxurious option. If you choose one, be sure your floor can be made strong enough to support it.

pools range from 5 to 7 feet long; the larger ones are wide enough to accommodate two people.

Some whirlpool jets circulate water into the tub, while others shoot air. Air jets are smaller and less powerful than water jets and provide a lighter massage. A tub that uses water jets typically has four to twelve jets, while a tub with air jets can have ten times as many. The jets are powered by a pump, which usually sits opposite the drain. You'll need access to the pump when it requires repairs, so either order a tub with a removable skirt or create an access panel. Site the tub so that the access panel is easy to reach. If your tub shares a wall with a bedroom closet, put the panel inside the closet. To combat pump vibrations, some pros set whirlpool tubs in plaster of Paris; rubber mounts also help.

A two-person jetted tub typically holds 50 to 70 gallons of water; some hold up to 90 gallons. The extra weight of that much water can send a tub crashing through an inadequately supported floor. If the total load exceeds 30 pounds per square foot when the tub is in use, you'll need to strengthen the framing. You may also need a larger water heater, or an extra one, to heat such a volume of water, though some tubs feature an inline heating element that heats the water as it enters the tub.

A deluxe whirlpool tub can cost $3,000 or more, while a regular white cast-iron tub costs from $400 to $900. In fact, even the most basic whirlpool will double your bathtub budget, and the price will go up if it requires an extra water heater, a dedicated electrical circuit to power the pump, or beefed up framing to support the tub's extra weight.

Framed into a dramatic nook, this one-piece bath-shower module creates a striking focal point.

showers

Nothing beats a shower when you want to "get clean and get on with life," as Richard Trethewey puts it. If you want your shower to do more, you can equip it to provide a steam bath or a water massage. Whether or not it doubles as a mini-spa, a shower must be solidly constructed and absolutely waterproof.

A shower stall can be prefabricated, assembled from manufactured components, or constructed from scratch. One-piece prefabricated stalls are watertight, simple to put in, and easy to clean. But because of their size, one-piece prefabricated stalls are usually a convenient choice only in new construction or if your remodel entails opening a large hole in a wall. If a one-piece enclosure isn't suitable for your bathroom, you can buy a modular manufactured shower surround that is assembled on site. Both modular and one-piece stalls come in rectangular and corner designs; many feature integrated soap dishes, grab bars, and other accessories. In order of increasing cost, they're available in fiberglass-reinforced acrylic, plastic laminate, and synthetic marble.

A custom shower, which can be surfaced with your choice of tile, stone, or any other material, is a step up in aesthetics. It also allows you to create a shower of any size and shape. It starts with a base (usually called a pan), which can be purchased or built from scratch. Constructing a shower pan is an exacting job best done by a professional tile contractor. The TOH crew typically uses a copper pan that must be cut, soldered, built up with mud (a mix of cement and sand), sloped precisely to the drain, and then tiled. Prefabricated bases are made of plastic, poured masonry, cast polymer, or solid-surface composite.

Once the base is in place, the adjoining walls must be waterproofed before being covered with the finish material. Norm Abram suggests having the walls stripped to the studs and covered with 15-pound builders' felt, then screwing in panels of cement backerboard all the way to the ceiling.

Building codes typically require a minimum width of 32 inches for a shower, but the TOH crew recommends at least 36 inches square. "Any less than that, you're really going to feel a squeeze," Silva says. Norm Abram cautions against putting a window in the shower. "Water invariably pools on the sill and seeps into the walls, nourishing mildew and rot," he says.

steam showers In a steam shower, a small yet powerful electric generator heats water from a dedicated supply line and then sends plumes of steam into the shower stall through one or more nozzles near the floor. The stall should be completely sealed with a tightly fitting floor-to-ceiling glass door so that steam can't escape. "Otherwise it'll peel the wallpaper off the entire top floor of your house," Trethewey says. A steam shower must also have a separate fan.

Though the steam generator is no larger than a carry-on suitcase, it requires additional space and a point of access for repairs. Typically, the generator is installed in a closet that abuts the shower area, or in the basement, "but the closer the better," Trethewey says. "To get the most steam, you want as direct and short a pipe run as you can get from the generator to the shower."

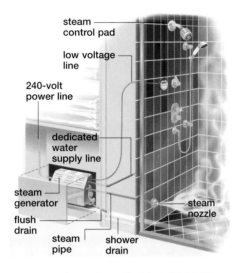

steam control pad
low voltage line
240-volt power line
dedicated water supply line
steam generator
flush drain
steam pipe
shower drain
steam nozzle

ANATOMY OF A STEAM SHOWER

The cost of the generator is based on the size of the shower enclosure. Outfitting an average-size shower can cost up to $4,000, and a shower lined with natural stone instead of ceramic tile will absorb steam more quickly and require a larger generator. For $1,600 to $6,000, you can buy a prefabricated steam-shower unit with the generator built into the fiberglass stall. A steam generator requires a dedicated 240-volt circuit, which can cost another $300 to $600. If your electrical panel won't accommodate the addition, the price will go up by $800 or more. However, in most areas, the electricity to run a steam shower for 15 minutes costs less than 30 cents.

SCALD-FREE SHOWERS AND TUBS

A shower or tub faucet that blasts you with scalding water whenever someone flushes the toilet is more than a nuisance; it's a serious hazard. Tap water heated to 140 degrees Fahrenheit (a typical temperature for home water heaters) can cause third-degree burns in seconds. You can guard against burns by setting the water heater at 120 degrees, but the only way to prevent temperature fluctuations is to install scald-free shower and tub valves.

Temperature fluctuations are caused by rapid changes in the pressure balance between hot and cold water. For instance, when someone turns on the washing machine, a loss of pressure in the hot-water pipes can turn the shower cold. Scald-free valves work in one of two ways. Pressure-balancing valves automatically adjust the mix of hot and cold water when there's a rapid change in water pressure balance.

Thermostatic valves self-adjust when the water being delivered no longer reflects a pre-set temperature.

Most states mandate the use of scald-free valves in new construction. Even if they're not required for your project, it's only sensible to take a precaution that costs so little and does so much to prevent injuries. A basic pressure-balancing valve begins at about $100 and is installed just like a conventional valve. "There's no downside," Trethewey says. "One of these valves will really keep you out of hot water—or cold, as the case may be."

shower spas By adding wall-mounted spray jets to your shower, you can create a "surround" design that provides a full-body water massage. Expect to pay between $2,000 and $12,000 for a spa-shower system, depending on its complexity. Add to that the cost of a higher-capacity water heater (or an extra one) and higher water consumption (a six-jet shower will use 50 gallons of hot water in five to ten minutes). Expect a higher energy bill, and don't forget that you'll need plenty of water pressure. "It's like putting a car wash in your home," Trethewey says. "When you have a shower spa, I like to see at least 50 pounds of pressure per square inch. If you don't have that, you might have to put in a new supply line all the way to the street."

You'll also need ¾- or 1-inch pipes in good condition running from the hot water heater to the shower valve.

Provide a shutoff valve for your spa system so you can take an ordinary shower, and make sure that the highest jets can be turned off separately so they won't spray short people in the face. To avoid the temperature and pressure fluctuations that can plague an elaborate multi-spray shower, you may want to have your system specially designed.

tub and shower fittings

Tub and shower fittings are difficult and expensive to change once installed, so it's worth buying the best you can afford. In both tubs and showers, the valve that controls the flow of water is concealed behind the wall, making repairs difficult and leaks potentially disastrous. To be safe, choose brass fittings rather than plastic ones and invest in a washerless valve (see page 216 for more about faucets).

Tub faucets can be deck- or wall-mounted. A tub requires a spout and a drain; a tub-shower

Water from this showerhead falls gently and covers a large surface area.

combination also requires a showerhead and a diverter valve. The diverter, which allows you to switch from one function to the other, can be positioned on the spout or between the upper and lower faucets. A tub-only package will sometimes include a deck-mounted hand shower in addition to a spout. Though solid-brass workings are a must, you can choose any finish that suits your taste (see page 216 for more on finishes).

When choosing shower fittings, focus first on the control valve that adjusts the volume and temperature of the water flowing from the showerhead. The capacity of the valve will determine how many spray options the system can include. The valve should include scald protection to prevent temperature fluctuations (see page 211). Look for a showerhead that has holes in the center as well as around the perimeter for the best spray pattern. You can add a ceiling-mounted "shampoo" shower to a conventional overhead system for a waterfall effect, or have wall-mounted spray jets installed.

In this spa shower, a hand-held showerhead, a rain head, and four body jets can be used in unison or individually, depending on how stressful your day has been.

Self-rimming

Low-flow showerheads, rated at 2.5 gallons per minute or less, are the law for new installations. In any circumstance, you may want to have one installed simply to reduce your water bill. Don't try to save money here; inexpensive models tend to deliver a mist of fine droplets that turn lukewarm before they reach you.

sinks

Bathroom sinks, or lavatories, come in a variety of configurations. Deck-mounted sinks are the most popular because they suit just about any decorating style. Most deck mounts are drop-in models made to sit inside a countertop cutout. Self-rimming versions that overlap the countertop are the least expensive and simplest to install. Undermount lavatories are

Concrete is an increasingly popular countertop option. In this bathroom, cast-in-place concrete was the ideal choice for an integral-bowl sink large enough for two people to use at the same time.

Undermount

recessed below the countertop, which makes them sleeker and the counter easier to clean, though they cost a bit more. For an especially striking look, you can choose an above-counter basin that perches on top of the counter like a piece of sculpture.

Deck-mounted basins are commonly available in fiberglass, enameled steel, vitreous china, and enameled cast iron, but you can get a variety of more unusual materials (see page 215). An inexpensive self-rimming fiberglass basin sells for less than $100; an above-counter sink of hammered copper or hand-blown crystal can set you back thousands.

integral-bowl Integral-bowl sinks combine countertop and basin in a single molded piece that sits on top of a vanity or cabinet. Because there are no seams or joints, a countertop with an integral bowl is easy to install and clean. Integral-bowl sinks are most often made from solid-

Above-counter

surface materials, but they also come in fiberglass, vitreous china, and cast polymers such as cultured marble, and concrete. Solid-surface materials, though expensive, offer the most durability and versatility. When shopping for a one-piece sink and countertop, make sure the bowl is deep enough so you don't get sprayed when the faucet is running full force.

A contemporary pedestal sink is a sleek space saver.

wall-mounted Wall-mounted sinks are fastened directly to the wall with hangers or angle brackets. Because they require no floor space, they're ideal for small bathrooms. Wall-hung sinks are typically made from vitreous china. Though they usually have a retro look, you can find contemporary versions featuring stainless steel, brass, and other high-style materials. If you choose a wall-mounted sink, be sure a support ledger is installed behind it.

Space-saving wall-mounted sinks are perfect for small bathrooms.

pedestal A pedestal sink consists of a wall-mounted basin and a stand that's secured to the floor. The stand, or pedestal, usually conceals the plumbing. Installation can be tricky. Measurements must be precise, and it's often a challenge to fit the plumbing into the pedestal. Most pedestal sinks are made from old-fashioned white vitreous china, and their traditional look blends perfectly with an old house or period décor. They occupy minimal floor space, which can help make the room appear larger. However, they provide no storage area and little or no deck space.

An elliptical console sink gives more deck space than a standard pedestal.

console A console sink is basically a pedestal sink with an expanded deck. Instead of a pedestal, it has two or four legs, which are usually made of porcelain, ceramic, or chrome (though you can get wood, bronze, stainless steel, or wrought iron). The basin is typically vitreous china, but high-end and custom models may be marble, stainless steel, solid surface, or even glass, and they may include storage below.

MATERIALS FOR BATHROOM SINKS

When shopping for a bathroom sink, pay attention to the materials it's made from. Listed below, generally in order from least to most expensive, are some common choices. But remember that prices will vary widely within each category of material, depending on size and whether the sink is self-rimming, above counter, or integrated with the countertop.

■ So-called fiberglass fixtures are actually acrylic, or less durable polyester gel, reinforced with a fiberglass backing. Fiberglass-reinforced plastic is inexpensive and lightweight, but it's less durable than other materials and is prone to scratching. Quality can vary considerably.

■ Cast polymers, the most common of which is cultured marble, are made from ground stone and polyester resin. Because these products are often made in small shops across the country, quality can vary significantly. Check that the product you buy meets quality standards specified by the American National Standards Institute *(www.ansi.org),* which permits them to be certified by the Cultured Marble Institute (CMI).

■ Enameled steel is light, maneuverable, and affordable. It looks much like enameled cast iron, but its lightness makes it noisy, and its greater flexibility means that the enamel chips more readily.

■ Vitreous china, made from kiln-fired clay, is virtually impossible to scratch or stain. However, it is susceptible to chipping and weighs a good deal more than enameled steel or fiberglass.

■ Stainless steel, once confined to the kitchen, is now being used for bathroom sinks and even tubs. High-quality stainless fixtures are made from at least 18-gauge stainless steel. Twelve-gauge is better. Stick with a matte finish rather than a mirrored one so water spots don't show.

■ Cast-iron fixtures are durable, beautiful, and classic. They are formed in molds, sprayed with an enamel powder, and then fired. The enameled surface is smooth and cleans easily. It resists chipping and cracking.

■ Solid-surface products are durable and easy to maintain. They lend themselves well to custom installations and integral-bowl sinks. But beware: Some lesser-known products are not as reliable as well-known brand names.

■ Brass, copper, and glass make for stylish sinks. However, they're expensive and require vigilant maintenance. They are best for seldom used guest baths or powder rooms.

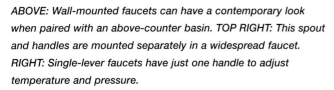

ABOVE: Wall-mounted faucets can have a contemporary look when paired with an above-counter basin. TOP RIGHT: This spout and handles are mounted separately in a widespread faucet. RIGHT: Single-lever faucets have just one handle to adjust temperature and pressure.

faucets

The quality of a faucet is determined largely by what you can't see. For a drip-free, durable faucet, choose a washerless model with solid-brass workings. Reliable, leak-free ceramic-disc faucets provide easy ergonomic control, smooth water flow, and usually a lifetime guaranty.

Faucets come in four basic styles:

■ Centerset faucets, the most common type, combine a spout and handles on a single base unit. Make sure the one you buy matches any pre-drilled holes on your sink or that it has a cover plate that conceals any extra holes.

■ Single-lever faucets, the only style suitable for universal bathroom design (see page 194), have one handle that's often part of the spout.

■ Widespread or spread-fit faucets have separately mounted spout and handles that sit directly on the sink or countertop.

■ Wall-mounted faucets, which are typically paired with above-counter basins, are installed in the wall.

Faucets, of course, are sold in many shapes, styles, and finishes. The most popular finish is polished chrome—a durable, easy-to-clean surface that's suitable for any décor. Other common finishes include brushed chrome,

which is easier to keep spot-free, and powder-coated enamel, available in many colors. If you want polished brass, look for a faucet that has a factory-applied clear coat for easier maintenance.

Bathroom faucets run from $40 to $400 (although at the upper reaches, you're also paying for style and trend). As a rule, you get what you pay for. Expect to spend at least $100 for a high-quality ceramic-disc faucet with solid-brass workings. Centerset faucets are generally more affordable than other types. You'll pay up to twice as much for a widespread model of comparable quality.

toilets

With toilets, "function should come first and fancy should come second," Trethewey says. "Plumbers often get bad-rapped for not being interested in color and styling, but, for us, those aren't primary concerns. A toilet that works is."

Unlike other bathroom fixtures, toilets are made in only one material: vitreous china. Fired at a very high temperature, it is normally all but indestructible (although the tank lid will break if you drop it). Toilets are available in two-piece and one-piece (sometimes called low-profile) units. Deciding between them comes down to aesthetics, "or as much aesthetics as there can be, considering you're talking about a toilet," Trethewey says. A one-piece model is sleeker, more contemporary in styling, and less conspicuous. "Put it behind a low divide at the end of a tub and it will disappear," Trethewey adds. One-piece toilets are also easier to clean because there is no gap between tank and bowl to collect dirt. The two-piece toilet, however, has a more familiar look, is available in more styles, and is less expensive. For either type, consider a model with an 18-inch high seat, which is designed to meet Americans with Disabilities Act standards.

Conventional toilets flush when water leaving the tank rushes into the bowl in a surge that carries waste down the drain. Traditionally, these toilets consumed a great deal of water—3½ to 5 gallons or more with every flush. But newer low-flow toilets required by law in all new and remodeled baths use no more than 1.6 gallons of water per flush. Still, not all low-flow toilets are created equal. "With early models, the reality was that they often needed two flushes to get the task done," Trethewey says. "But with today's low-flow toilets, they've solved that problem." For best results, choose a gravity-fed toilet with a large water surface in the bowl and a fully glazed trap that is at least 2 inches wide. You can also opt for a pressure-assisted toilet, which flushes more effectively but makes more noise. Pressure-assisted toilets also require professional attention if repairs are needed.

A toilet bowl may be either round or elongated. Many people consider elongated bowls more comfortable, but rounded bowls take up less space. Round-front toilets extend 25 to 30 inches from the wall. Most elongated models extend 2 or 3 inches farther, but you can find more compact elongated bowls.

Before you shop for a toilet, measure the "rough-in" distance from your wall to the center of the toilet drain. Most newer homes have a standard 12-inch rough-in, but your house may have a 10- or 14-inch rough-in.

Toilets vary tremendously in cost. A sculpted one-piece toilet with a power-assisted flush can set you back $800, while a basic gravity-action, two-piece model in white costs less than $150. Many of the extras you get when you pay more are cosmetic upgrades such as colorful finishes and specialty flush levers. If price is an issue, put your money into features that determine how well the toilet flushes and how easy it is to clean and maintain.

Today's high-quality toilets clog less and are far more water efficient than older models.

lighting

In the bathroom, as in the rest of the house, a good lighting plan includes "layers" of light from different sources—a mix of task lighting, general illumination, and decorative accent lighting.

Task lighting is important in bathrooms, since adequate illumination is essential for shaving, applying makeup, and other personal grooming tasks. It should be concentrated around mirrors, but the idea is to illuminate your face rather than the mirror. The best way to evenly distribute light is to put vertical fixtures or sconces at eye level on each side of the mirror, 36 to 40 inches apart, and a fixture above the mirror, 75 to 80 inches from the floor. Vanity-style lighting should be at least 150 watts, spread over a fixture that's at least 24 inches long.

The shower and other compartmentalized areas may also benefit from task lighting. Shower fixtures should be recessed and waterproof, with neoprene seals and glass lenses (plastic will yellow). Similar fixtures work well over a freestanding tub. If you have a small bathroom and your shower has a clear glass door, a dedicated fixture may not be necessary.

In a small bathroom, vanity fixtures can provide ambient illumination as well as task lighting. In a larger bath, a surface-mounted ceiling

Distribute bathroom light evenly by placing fixtures at eye level on each side of the mirror.

fixture is usually the main source of ambient light, while the low profile of recessed lighting is perfect for small rooms. Recessed fixtures can also be aimed to provide concentrated accent lighting. As a finishing touch, you can add low-voltage ambient lighting in the soffit or toekick.

Bulb selection is as important as the type of lighting. The full-spectrum light of a halogen bulb is best for lighting the bathroom mirror because it renders skin tones most accurately. Crisp, white halogen light is also excellent for highlighting architectural and decorative details. Fluorescent bulbs, once banished

from the bathroom because they gave a ghoulish cast to skin tones, are now available in good color rendering along with unsurpassed energy efficiency. You may even consider installing both fluorescent and standard incandescent fixtures—on separate switches—so you can see how you'll look in differently lighted environments.

Make sure that all light fixtures are UL-approved and suitable for use in damp areas. Fixtures placed within a certain distance of the tub or shower (usually 6 feet, though local codes vary) must be "wet" or "shower-location" rated.

accessories

Though often handled as an afterthought, bath accessories should be considered when you're planning your renovation. When your floor plan is complete, look it over to see where you want to install hardware. Note the location of studs so you can adequately secure towel bars and other accessories that must withstand frequent tugging.

Most bath hardware is made from brass, but you can also buy plastic, wood, and ceramic versions. "No matter what you're buying, you'll find it in basic, better, and best quality. Beware of basic," Trethewey says. "The entry-level products in the market are usually poor. You should

A ring of fluorescent lighting provides even grooming illumination from all directions. In some locales, fluorescent lights are required in bathrooms because of their energy efficiency.

get the better or best things in all cases, because the purchase cost is just a fraction of the installation cost." To be safe, stick to solid-brass construction and avoid plastic. If you're using ceramic accessories, have them on hand before you begin tiling so they can be installed in the wall.

When choosing a mirror, buy the largest one that will fit your space. A mirror that extends to the backsplash will help prevent water damage and make it easier to clean behind the faucet. It will also make the room seem more spacious.

Never use plastic wall anchors to install bath accessories. Toggle bolts will work for gently used hardware. Grab bars and heavily used accessories should be screwed directly to wall studs or 1-by-4 or 2-by-4 backing installed behind the drywall.

ABOVE: Make sure towel bars are anchored firmly to the wall. BELOW: Glass holders, soap dishes, and toilet paper dispensers provide the finishing touches in a bathroom. Choose mid- to high-end products that will stand up to heavy use over time.

cabinets and storage

Bathroom cabinets are similar to kitchen cabinets in construction and style (for more information on cabinetry, see pages 154–157). However, priorities are often different for the bath. If you have room for just a few cabinets, you may want to splurge on custom ones designed to make the most efficient use of your space. On the other hand, one or two cabinets won't constitute a major design feature, so you may decide to choose something off the shelf and spend your money on designer tiles or a whirlpool tub.

As in the kitchen, homeowners are currently opting for taller cabinets in the bathroom—up to 36 inches instead of the standard 32. Higher cabinets not only provide more storage but also keep tall people from having to bend. In shared bathrooms, you can mix heights to accommodate different users.

Stock bath cabinets are sold in a wide range of dimensions designed to make the most of a small space. If you find off-the-shelf models to be too low, you can raise them by having the toekick built up. Bathroom

ABOVE: No amount of space is too small for a storage opportunity in the bath. These two shelves fit nicely under a sloped ceiling. LEFT: Handsome built-in shelves utilize the space under a bathroom counter.

cabinets are also available in several depths, from 18 to 24 inches. Deeper cabinets will provide more storage and counter space, while shallower units will free up floor area.

Cabinets for the vanity now come with crown molding, fluted panels, and other details borrowed from fine furniture. You can buy a washstand that's made to resemble a piece of furniture, or customize a ready-made cabinet by adding legs or drawers. You can even convert a vintage bureau or cabinet into a base for a sink.

Since most items stored in a bathroom are small and risk getting lost at the bottom of a cabinet, choose a vanity with drawers. Add-on accessories such as baskets, shelves, and lazy Susans improve storage capacity and accessibility. A wall-mounted faucet liberates the countertop for toiletries.

As you plan, look for opportunities to add storage space. Build nooks into a room divider; fit a niche between wall studs; extend the countertop over

A shallow countertop extends over the toilet tank and into the shower for extra storage space.

This tall, glass-fronted cabinet and space-efficient base unit create convenient, generous storage.

Where space is at a premium, find fixtures that can do double duty, like this mirror that slides to reveal a medicine cabinet.

the toilet tank (either hinge the counter over the tank so it lifts for repairs, or choose a one-piece, low-profile toilet). Include some open shelving for easy access to items you use every day. If you have adequate floor space, include one or two freestanding storage units. Furnishings made for the bedroom or kitchen, such as an armoire or bar cart, can lend originality to your decorating scheme.

221

CHAPTER SEVEN

exteriors

MAKE YOUR HOME MORE BEAUTIFUL
AND SECURE WITH EXTERIOR IMPROVEMENTS

AS MOTHER NATURE DISHES OUT WIND, RAIN, AND SUN, season after season, paint peels, siding cracks, and roofs leak. When this happens, the appearance and the structure of a house begin to deteriorate.

That's where this chapter comes in. Here you'll find exterior improvements that make a house work harder and look better. From basics about painting to the particulars of installing new siding, windows, roofing, and more, this chapter will help you sort through the options and ensure that the work gets done through proven methods.

While anticipating how the house will look is important, focusing on providing shelter is primary. "Water is the ultimate enemy," says This Old House general contractor Tom Silva. "Wherever it can drip or trickle or seep inside your house, you're going to end up with big problems." Consequently, when Silva works on the exterior of a house, he is as concerned about blocking water as he is with visible craftsmanship. Because keeping the elements at bay is a house's ultimate job, Silva encourages homeowners to buy the highest-quality roofing, gutters, siding, windows, and doors they can afford.

siding

Vinyl siding, traditional clapboards, stucco, cement shingles—many kinds of siding are available, each with its own strengths and weaknesses. To make a wise choice, you'll have to compare several factors, including appearance, durability, maintenance requirements, ease of installation, and cost.

The price of new siding can vary widely depending on the quality of material you choose, whom you hire to install it, where you live, and the specifics of the job. For siding such as wood clapboard, fiber cement, vinyl,

White clapboard siding complements this traditional-style home. Despite its high-maintenance needs, sometimes wood is simply the right choice.

and metal, you'll most likely be quoted a price per square foot. Stucco can be priced per square foot or per square yard. Because wood shingle siding overlaps, the materials are priced per square, like roofing (one square equals 100 square feet). For materials and installation, expect to pay less for midgrade siding options such as wood clapboards, fiber cement, vinyl, and stucco (around $2 per square foot) than you will for metal ($2 to $4 per square foot), EIFS ($7 to $10 per square foot), or wood shingles ($450 to $600 per square). Here is a closer look at the main types of siding.

wood

As the iconic siding for American homes, wood is the standard by which other materials are measured. Most nonwood siding products aspire to imitate wood's natural beauty, but there is nothing like the real thing. "It's got a look you just can't match with anything else," Silva says. "And it's also the easiest material to work with, in terms of sawing and nailing it into place." Clapboard, a lap siding with a fairly narrow weather gauge, is the most popular type of wood siding. It goes on fast, sheds water well, and is easily repaired. It's expensive—twice the cost of vinyl—but high-quality clapboard can last for centuries.

For wood siding to last, it must be applied carefully and be meticulously maintained. To be protected from sun and rain damage, wood siding must be sealed and stained, or primed and painted, every four to eight years, typically. In addition, wood can split, burn, rot, and attract termites. Though expensive, premium redwood and cedar heartwoods have a natural resistance to decay and insects; and, because they are stable products, aren't prone to splitting and will hold paint well.

Board siding is milled in a variety of patterns, species, grades, and sizes. The two basic varieties are pattern siding and clapboard, or bevel siding. With pattern siding, the faces of the boards are milled with a pattern and the edges interlock with either tongue-and-groove or lap joints. With bevel siding, boards are sawn to a tapered profile that gains its weather tightness when each board is overlapped by

Stained wood-shingle siding is a classic choice for a Cape Cod-style home.

the one above. Both types come with a smooth (surfaced) face and a rough (sawn) face, but be aware that grading for bevel siding is commonly done on the smooth side, so it may show more defects if you install it rough side out. When you contract for siding installation, be sure to specify the grade of the material, which can affect the look, cost, and longevity of your siding dramatically. Grades vary by species, so ask to see samples before you buy.

wood shingles Wood shingle siding is another classic material, suited to architectural styles such as Craftsman, shingle style, Victorian, and Cape Cod. In general, wood shingles have the same key attributes and drawbacks as wood siding, with a couple of exceptions. Foremost, wood shingles can easily cover walls

that are curved, irregularly shaped, or slightly bumpy (in many cases, they can be applied over existing siding). Also, some wood shingles have been factory treated with preservative or a flame retardant that makes them less combustible.

Though you can buy shingles in more than one grade, it doesn't pay to cut corners on quality, considering the relatively high cost of installation. Choose No. 1 "blue label" shingles.

fiber cement

For siding that resembles wood but doesn't have the same maintenance requirements, the TOH crew likes fiber-cement siding, a gray product made from a mix of Portland cement,

sand, and cellulose. Available in both clapboards and shingles molded with a wood pattern, cement siding doesn't burn, melt, or rot; is unlikely to split; and is impervious to termites. In fact, most types carry a 50-year warranty. When applied over factory-coated primer, two coats of acrylic latex paint should last two to three times as long as paint on wood siding. However, installation is more labor intensive than for wood because the material is tough on saw blades, kicks up an irritating dust when cut, and weighs twice as much as cedar.

This Old House master carpenter Norm Abram chose cement clapboards to replace the wide cedar boards on his family's summer cottage, which his father had sided 50 years earlier. "The old claps were badly in need of paint" he says. "I considered putting up new cedar and using a stain instead of paint, but it would have been difficult to match the relatively wide boards my father used. Cement solved these problems nicely."

Fiber cement is a low-maintenance siding product that can resemble wood shingles or boards.

vinyl

Because of its durability and ease of maintenance, vinyl has become the most popular siding material in the country. Vinyl siding has made huge leaps since the flimsy varieties that first appeared decades ago. "If you use high-quality vinyl installed by a trained craftsman, you can end up with a great-looking house," says Silva, who has vinyl siding on his home. "But one warning: I would never recommend covering up an old, well-detailed wood exterior with vinyl," he adds. The reason: Subtle architectural details around windows, doors, and eaves are often eliminated. In addition, the thickness of vinyl will subtly change the relative proportions of windows and doors, permanently compromising the architectural character of a home.

Since thin siding is more likely to sag, choose siding that is at least .044 to .048 inches thick; some premium brands measure up to .055 inches thick. Stiffness is also important. A relatively deep profile and a folded-over, doubled nailing hem increase stiffness; the more bends the better.

As with cement board, vinyl siding comes with a product warranty, usually about 50 years.

metal

Both aluminum and steel sidings are tough, lightweight, and somewhat malleable. They come in a number of profiles and textures with factory-baked-on finishes. They won't rot, crack, peel, blister, burn, or be eaten by bugs. They will, however, dent and scratch, and steel siding will rust if scratched down to the metal. For maintenance, you just hose them off every year. They're relatively easy for professionals to install, although Tom Silva's warning about putting vinyl over a classic wood exterior applies here as well.

Unlike wood, vinyl siding doesn't rot or peel, so it requires very little maintenance. It is an excellent choice for waterfront homes that are exposed to heavy moisture and salt.

ABOVE: Metal siding looks good on traditional farm or ranch-style houses, as well as on contemporary architecture and urban lofts.

stucco and EIFS

Stucco siding has a universal appeal and finds itself equally at home on the walls of a Mediterranean revival, a Tudor revival, a French colonial, or even a Modernist house. Mixed from Portland cement, sand, lime, and water, stucco creates a pleasing, very durable, water-resistant (when painted), low-maintenance exterior finish that can withstand the worst extremes of almost any climate.

Stucco can be applied over wood-frame construction or masonry walls. It can be given a range of textures, from swirling arcs to a smooth, stone-like finish. It doesn't hold up well if water leaks in behind it, and because it is rigid, movement caused by settling or earthquakes can crack it, requiring repair. Expert installation, including proper flashing around windows and doors and at the tops of walls, is essential.

Stucco is the siding of choice for many styles of architecture, from Mediterranean to Modern or, in this case, English Tudor.

Many planned-community builders use stucco because the finish looks great in a wide variety of colors and textures, giving unique appearances to homes of the same style that are built with the same materials.

Engineered Insulation and Finish Systems (EIFS) resemble stucco but are more energy efficient, more resistant to cracking, and easier and faster to apply. With these systems, a latexlike material is applied over a base of rigid insulation board (see page 229). Because these systems can hide rotting sheathing and framing where moisture has found its way in, look for second-generation EIFS that include air space and weep holes behind the rigid board to drain any accumulated moisture.

UNCOVERING OLD SIDING

One person's improvement can be another's nightmare. In older homes, beautiful wood siding may have been covered by vinyl or aluminum somewhere down the line. Instead of re-siding a house where this has been done, you may be able to simply restore the original siding. Of course, you won't know what you have until you strip off the outer layer, but removing the siding on a portion of one wall will usually give you a pretty good idea.

If you're lucky, you'll discover siding that's in relatively good condition and with the kinds of architectural details that give a house  character. If you're unlucky, the siding may not be worth saving and/or original details may have been removed or destroyed. A good carpenter can usually reconstruct missing details. Though this can be expensive, it's often less expensive than completely re-siding the house with wood.

siding installation

When it comes to siding, "you can get a long-lasting exterior with any number of materials, as long as it's installed well," Silva says.

When re-siding an old house, Silva will first tap his hammer over the sheathing, listening for dull thuds that indicate rotten wood and loose boards. Solid thumps reveal studs. After all the punky boards are replaced, he shoots a few extra nails through the sheathing to tighten up the connection to the structure.

clapboard The trick to installing clapboard siding is to make sure it is aligned evenly and will shed water. If water gets behind clapboard, rot will run riot through sills and sheathing.

Beneath clapboard siding, a properly applied solid base of plywood sheathing offers a flat surface and helps prevent clapboards from cracking during nailing. For a barrier against air infiltration, today's construction practices often call for a layer of spun olefin housewrap to be stapled over the sheathing. But Tom Silva uses older (and much cheaper) materials—15-pound builder's felt or rosin paper—because he prefers to insulate with spray foam. "There's no air or moisture

Tom Silva believes that what goes on is never as important as how it goes on, so make sure you hire an experienced contractor.

passage to worry about," he says. And always, whether over felt, paper, or a wrap, Silva tacks up drainage strips before he hangs wood siding. "It needs an air space behind so it can dry out," he says.

All clapboards should have the same amount of exposure, and courses should line up at the top and bottom of the windows. Another quality-control issue has to do with the way two clapboards are butted end to end when one isn't long enough to run the entire length needed. In such a case, ask your installer to make a scarf or miter joint, an overlapping bevel cut made with a miter saw. The two meeting edges are embedded in caulking compound, then attached to the wall with a single nail driven through the top (overlapping) clapboard nearest the joint. "It's the only time I nail into the sheathing without hitting a stud," Silva says. For appearance and weatherproofing, two

end-to-end joints should never be lined up one directly above the other.

wood shingle Though wood shingles can be applied over a somewhat irregular surface, the flatter the base, the better they'll look. The best backing is ½-inch plywood, oriented strand board (OSB), or waferboard wall sheathing. Waterproofing membrane should be applied over the sheathing before shingling.

Shingles make a wall impervious to water because they're nailed so that they overlap. "Done right, there are always three layers of shingles at any one spot—just like the shingles on a roof," Abram says.

The method used to join shingles at exterior and interior corners will affect the look of the finished job and the difficulty of doing the work. The easiest method is to butt shingles up against a corner board and caulk the joint (all joints between shingles and trim should be caulked). Another method is to trim the corner shingles so they meet at a miter joint; this is very attractive, but the miters need to be caulked and may open up over time. "Weaving" the shingles is elegantly simple, relatively easy to do, and doesn't require caulking. With this method, the corner shingles are alternately overlapped and the overlapping shingles are planed flush.

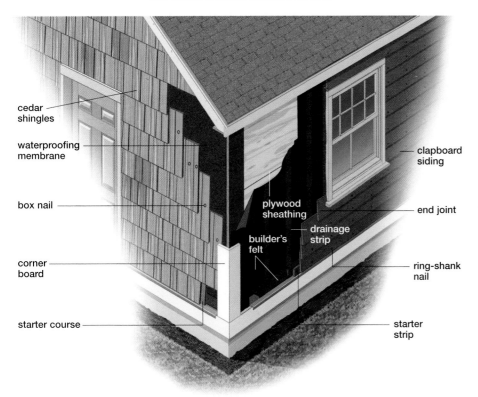

cedar shingles

waterproofing membrane

box nail

corner board

starter course

plywood sheathing

builder's felt

drainage strip

clapboard siding

end joint

ring-shank nail

starter strip

The biggest challenge to a shingle installation is evenly spacing the rows (or courses) of shingles and working out their positions so that shingles align at the tops of windows and doors.

vinyl and metal Vinyl, aluminum, and steel siding systems are designed for easy installation, but it takes extra time and care to achieve a result that really looks great. Find an installer who can add a little embellishment or detailing like the type you might find on a wood-sided house.

The backing must be smooth enough for the siding panels to lie flat. Typical bases are plywood sheathing, furring strips applied over clapboard siding, or $3/8$-inch foam board insulation. If insulation board is used, the siding nails must be long enough to go through the insulation and into the wall studs. Nails should not be driven in too tightly; the panels should hang from the nails without being so loose that they rattle in the wind. That's because vinyl needs room to expand and contract with changes in temperature; a 12-foot length of vinyl can expand $5/8$ inch with seasonal temperature fluctuations.

With these sidings, trim pieces are installed at corners, doors, and windows before the first length of siding is attached. Quality-conscious installers leave about $1/4$ inch of clearance at the end of panel courses and let the trim channels cover the gap. A good installer will also orient overlaps away from where they will be obvious.

stucco and EIFS Stucco requires a base of $3/4$-inch plywood sheathing covered with overlapping lengths of 30-pound roofing felt for moisture protection. Strips of diamond-pattern wire lath are nailed firmly to the sheathing, but they should not lie flat against the wall, as the wet stucco must penetrate the lath, not just sit against it. Stucco goes on in three coats, and each must be allowed to cure for at least a day before the next coat is applied. Because the look of stucco and the success of the finish are completely contingent upon the abilities of the applicator, be sure to find a seasoned pro for this work.

In a typical installation of EIFS (see page 227), polystyrene insulation board is secured to the wall's substrate—typically sheathing covered with builder's felt. A $3/8$-inch air space is maintained by spacers. Then a durable base coat of the latex stuccolike material is troweled over the surface. For reinforcement, a fiberglass mesh is immediately embedded in the base coat. Then a colorfast finish coat is added over the base. If you opt for an EIFS, find a qualified applicator who adheres to the complete description of recommended installation procedures of the EIFS Industry Members Association at *www.eima.com*.

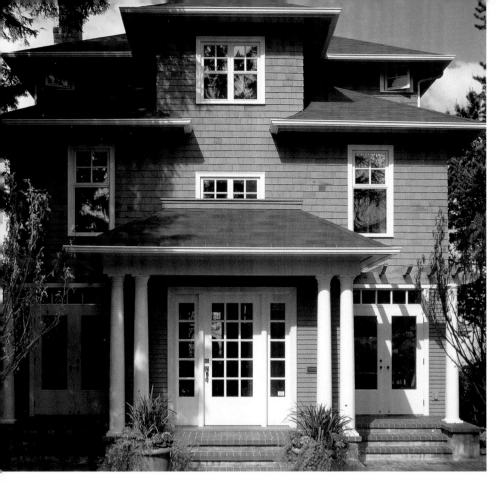

Windows are a crucial part of a home's exterior design. Here, muntins (the wood strips that divide windowpanes) add detail and interest to the front door and double-hung windows.

windows

In addition to allowing light, views, warmth, and fresh air into a house, windows serve as primary architectural features that help establish the home's overall design. Ideally, they should be as beautiful to look at as they are to look through. They should admit light while providing a barrier against drafts and energy loss—a heady task considering that a midsized home can easily have 30 or more windows.

Before jumping into a major window replacement project, be aware that you may not necessarily have to buy all new windows. Tom Silva advocates doing everything possible

to retain existing windows—they reflect the scale, detail, and period of an older home in ways modern replacements can't. In some cases, added weatherstripping or new jamb liners may be all your old windows really need (see page 233).

When you are shopping for new windows, the variations can be mind-boggling. To specify windows, you must choose the frame material and construction, the type of window, the shape and combination of operable and nonoperable units, the size, the color, the type of glazing,

and more. And when making these decisions, you should choose windows that complement your house's architecture.

Windows are sold in many sizes, from about 12 inches to 15 feet wide, and 15 inches tall to a full story and more. As a rule, only lightweight frame materials come in the largest of these sizes—but even these windows are exceptionally heavy because of the weight of the glass. Most stock windows have a standard jamb depth of $4\frac{9}{16}$ inches, sized to fit a conventional 2-by-4 wall, but may be ordered with extensions to fit thicker walls.

Sidelites and an arched transom window accent the two-story bay on this house.

Awning windows are often placed underneath fixed picture windows. They open only partway but can provide welcome ventilation even if the weather is slightly iffy.

window types and styles

There are a surprising number of window types based on whether and how they open. The main ones are fixed, double-hung, and casement windows. Additional types include awning, hopper, and transom windows.

A double-hung window has upper and lower sashes that slide up or down to open. A casement window has a sash that is hinged to the frame on one side and cranks open. Fixed windows simply admit light and views without ever opening. Awning and hopper windows are hinged at the top or bottom, respectively, to tilt out. Transom windows sit above a door or other windows. Some are operable, while others are fixed; most are shaped to provide an interesting accent.

In addition to choosing a window type for each opening, you must choose an overall style for your home. For example, varying the arrangement of muntins, the wood strips that divide the panes, can completely change the way a window looks. For a Colonial style, muntins are spaced in squares or rectangles. Diamond-patterned muntins create a more Victorian look. Irregular shapes or spacings imitate Arts and Crafts and Art Deco styles. The width of stiles and rails, the perimeter pieces of the window sash, and the trim around it also strongly affect the look of your windows and whether they're appropriate to the period of your home.

Windows must also be scaled to your home. Greek revival windows, for instance, are tall and narrow, echoing the style's high ceilings.

tip: accent windows Whether in the form of sidelites that flank a front door, or a curved transom that caps a picture window, accent windows can punctuate a wall with just the right decorative touch. The plain symmetry of a Colonial house, for instance, can be enlivened with the addition of a fan-light oval window. Narrow accent windows often can be installed in an existing wall without requiring structural changes—wall framing generally requires only slight modifications.

window materials

Though windows were once responsible for a significant part of a home's energy loss, new materials used for window glazing and frames have made today's windows both stylish and high in performance. "Today's windows are about as energy efficient as they can be. Now the advances are about better hardware, weatherstripping, and looks," Silva says.

The most significant improvement over recent years has been high-performance glazing, a combination of energy-efficient, double-pane insulated glass and transparent, heat-reflective low-E coatings. Though high-performance glazing costs 10 to 15 percent more, it reduces energy loss through windows by 30 to 50 percent, adding up to big savings over time. This glazing also minimizes fading of interiors caused by ultra-violet rays from the sun.

Frames have changed too, becoming less drafty and easier to maintain. Though the look of wood is still preferred by most people, particularly for interior frames, the entire frame isn't necessarily made from wood any longer. Because exterior wood surfaces require painting every few years, the best of today's windows offer natural wood interior frames but have exterior frames clad with a jacket of low-maintenance aluminum or vinyl.

In addition, the design of some aluminum and all-vinyl windows has been improved to include thermal breaks that minimize the conduction of heat through the frame. Plastic composites are also becoming a viable, low-maintenance alternative to wood.

When it's time to make a choice, strongly consider a solid wood sash with aluminum or vinyl exterior cladding, or a sash made of plastic composites; all are stronger (though

For the look of wood without the maintenance, choose a window with aluminum or vinyl exterior cladding. The exterior is detailed to look like wood, and the solid wood interior can be painted or stained.

pricier) than an all-vinyl sash. Also, with all-vinyl windows, insulated glass may fail, particularly on large windows, because of vinyl's expansion and contraction with temperature changes.

Look for the Energy Star label, evidence that the window has been tested to meet energy-efficiency criteria. Also check the spacers used to separate panes of insulated glass around the perimeter; these affect heat loss at the window's edges. The best ones are stainless steel with a thermal break.

Vinyl-clad windows are often used in new construction and work with a variety of architectural styles.

window installation guidelines

Regardless of the materials or construction, a new window is only as good as its installation. The biggest enemy that a window confronts is water, which can seep through invisible cracks between the frame and the rough opening. Leaks can warp and rot the window, sill, and framing. When you seal out water, you also seal out drafts, dramatically increasing the home's energy efficiency and comfort.

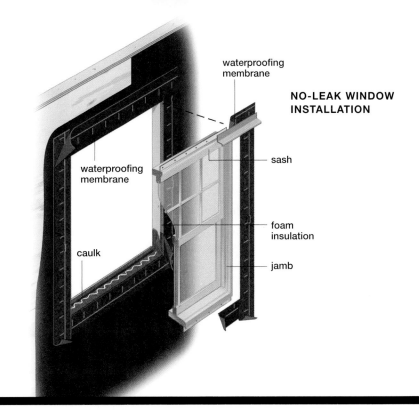

waterproofing membrane

NO-LEAK WINDOW INSTALLATION

waterproofing membrane

sash

foam insulation

jamb

caulk

REFURBISHING OLD WINDOWS

Advertisements for replacement windows recommend tearing out old windows and replacing them with new ones. "I wouldn't rush to do that," Silva says. "Old windows have a look all their own and can usually be salvaged." Of course, if windows are leaking and are badly rotted, it may indeed be time to replace them.

When the problem is draftiness, a better solution may be to repair them by adding weatherstripping. A good window restorer can stop drafts by removing the window sashes, carving grooves into the bottom of each sash and across the meeting rail, and pressing weatherstripping into the grooves. "Adding a new sash lock, or two on wider units, will make a tighter seal at the meeting rails," Silva says. He also recommends

installing insulation in the weight pockets, over the header, and under the sill, which can make a big difference in the efficiency of the window. The other reason for new windows is to get double glazing, but Silva is a big proponent of adding good storm windows for the same effect—after you fix up the original single glazing.

The channels that guide the sashes of double-hung windows on each side

eventually wear out to the point that the gaps can't be bridged effectively with weatherstripping. At this point, you have two options: replace the windows or install jamb liners made of vinyl, aluminum, or plastic to make the window more energy efficient by sealing the area between sash and jamb.

Installing the liners is a job for a pro. Once the liners are in place, the window sash may have to be trimmed by an inch or two and then pushed into place between the liners. If that's not possible, a new sash will be necessary. "Either way, the cost is going to be a lot cheaper than installing new windows," Silva says. One caution: In old houses, the modern materials used in the jamb liners may look out of place.

ABOVE LEFT: Tom Silva levels the windowsill, then measures the corner-to-corner diagonals. If they're within $1/16$ inch of the same length, the opening is square and the window will be plumb.
ABOVE RIGHT: If no preformed head flashing has been supplied with a window, Silva cuts and bends a piece that extends about 3 inches up the wall and overhangs the front and sides of the casing.

Inside the house, Silva applies a light bead of low-expansion urethane foam between the window and the framing.

To properly install a wood-framed window, Silva begins by painting the frame on all sides with an oil-based primer to preserve and protect the wood. He then staples a strip of building paper or fiber-reinforced polyethylene to the exterior sheathing around the opening in the wall. Also before the window is installed, self-adhering waterproofing membrane is applied on the bottom and sides of the opening. Then the window frame is placed and Silva makes sure it's square, level, and plumb so it will open properly. Silva uses rustproof screws, rather than nails, to fasten the window frame to the wall framing. These hold more securely than nails, especially as a window is opened and shut repeatedly. To make the window waterproof, he installs self-adhering waterproofing membrane on the top of the window and covers it with aluminum or copper head flashing, which forces any water to drip outward and seals the joint between the window and the wall. He also caulks the seam where the frame meets the exterior sheathing and the gap between the frame and the rough opening.

bay windows

On the exterior of a house, a bay window can add interest to an otherwise uninspired architectural style or a bland wall. Inside, it can awaken a room with natural light and a feeling of spaciousness.

Bay windows range from small projections that can turn the area above a kitchen sink into a mini-greenhouse, to large floor-to-ceiling bump-outs that can create reading nooks and sitting areas in bedrooms and living areas.

Installing a bay window can be very involved. "They're good-looking, but they can be very expensive," Silva says, mostly because of the structural and finish work involved. "You have to match everything from roofing

RIGHT: A bay window can add interest and depth to the outside of your home and extra living space inside. BELOW: Tom Silva builds a custom window seat along the bottom of this 150-pound prefabricated bay window. The structure is supported by a hidden cable system that can be adjusted to level the window.

outside to flooring and interior trim on the inside. What looks like 'just a window' can very quickly turn into a major project."

Traditionally, a ground-floor bay window can be supported on extended (cantilevered) joists that have been engineered into the design, or by a perimeter foundation or concrete piers. On a higher floor, wood knee brackets can be used underneath the bay to support it—and the weight of furniture and people it has to carry. A new alternative that Tom Silva has used and likes is a bay window that incorporates a load-bearing steel cable system that ties the cantilever to the house's structure; and can be used to level the window itself. Once in place, the cables are hidden by interior trim.

skylights

Because they're on the roof, skylights let in more light than wall-mounted windows—up to 30 percent more. "A skylight fools you," Silva says. "It gives the illusion of a bigger space." Most skylights cost only slightly more than an ordinary window of comparable size, and adding one takes a matter of hours in new construction or a couple of days in remodeling. "A good time to add one on an existing house is when you're re-roofing," Abram says. "You'll also be able to flash the skylight properly, which means your chances of living leak-free will be excellent."

Skylights are not in keeping with the style of some older homes. In those cases, it's better to opt for dormers with windows, or face the skylight toward the rear of the house, where it will be out of sight from the street.

skylight options

Both fixed and operable skylights are sold in many sizes and styles. Fixed units are less expensive, but operable skylights give another ventilation option—up high in the ceiling where heat rises. In fact, be careful that the size of skylight you choose and where you position it on the roof do not contribute to unwanted heating. "A standard 2-by-4-foot skylight might let in just the right amount of light when it's positioned on a roof with northern exposure, but put that same skylight on the south side and you'll be in big trouble," Silva says. Just as a skylight can fill a room with natural light, it can conduct a lot of heat, raising the room's temperature to uncomfortable levels.

Other factors that affect the right size of skylight to choose are the room's size, how reflective the surfaces and colors in the room are, and the depth of the shaft between the room and the skylight. "The final choice of the size of skylight is best left to a professional—preferably one who has done this many times before," Silva says.

Since skylights are often placed high up on ceilings, operable types may need to be opened and closed with a long cranking rod. Or you can

Installing skylights in a high ceiling creates a dramatic effect. Be sure they are placed in such a way that they let in sun when you want it without adding too much heat.

buy motorized skylights (right), operated by a switch, a remote control, or by a heat sensor that opens the skylight automatically when room air reaches a certain temperature. This type of skylight should also have a rain sensor that closes the skylight when it rains. If you want to be able to fine-tune the amount of sunshine and heat gain through a skylight, choose one with dual (or triple-pane) insulating glass with a heat-reflective coating, and consider the type that comes with built-in blinds that may be remotely controlled.

leak-free installation

Skylight installation requires cutting a hole in the roof—an obvious invitation to leakage. Modern skylights are designed to prevent this, but they're not fail-safe.

If a skylight leaks, the flashing around it is often the culprit. Proper installation is critical. Tom Silva likes to install a wide strip of bitumen-based waterproofing membrane all around the sides of the skylight and onto the sheathing. Then the flashing is installed according to the manufacturer's instructions. "Most brand-name skylights come with flashing kits specifically designed to match them," Silva adds. "Using these is probably the best way to avoid leaks."

Another source of leaks can be the seal between the glass and the sash. After enough freeze-and-thaw cycles, the seal will inevitably get brittle and crack. Seals shielded from sun and rain tend to last longer than those that are more directly exposed, as do those that are protected by high-performance glass that blocks ultraviolet light. Still, the seal requires regular inspection. If there's a problem, the glazing can be removed and the worn-down gasket or caulk replaced.

As a further measure to prevent leaks, occasional maintenance is important. "Whenever I clean gutters, I check the uphill side of the skylight and clear off accumulations of leaves, dirt, and shingle grit that can slow water down long enough to cause trouble," Abram says.

TOP: Metal flashing is crucial to leak-proofing a skylight. Here, Tom Silva slips a one-piece aluminum head flashing underneath the shingles to deflect water.
BOTTOM: To waterproof the skylight's sides, Silva uses step flashing. Beginning at the bottom, he aligns the lower edge of each piece of flashing with the lower edge of the overlaying shingle.

LEFT: Inside, Silva uses urethane foam to seal the gap between the framed opening and the skylight. Foam also insulates the metal on the roof from humid interior air, which can condense and stain the ceiling.

237

doors

An exterior door serves three major purposes: to present an inviting entrance, to keep out the ravages of weather, and to provide a barrier against would-be intruders. Doing all three jobs calls for great looks; solid, sturdy construction with a measure of insulation and effective weather-stripping; and strong, dependable locks and hinges.

door basics

Exterior doors tend to be wider and thicker than interior doors (see pages 114–117). "A standard exterior door is 36 inches wide and a minimum of 1¾ inches thick," Silva says, "but the sizes can vary hugely, especially in older homes."

These patio doors match the style of the casement windows around them, and allow the maximum amount of sunlight in.

In addition to size, what distinguishes exterior doors from interior doors is the variety of materials from which they're built: from solid wood and wood veneer to modern substitutes such as steel, fiberglass, and vinyl. All doors, including wood ones, can be built around a central core of rigid foam insulation, which increases energy efficiency.

While doors come in many styles, the overall appearance of an entryway is often determined by the trim and other architectural details that surround it. "You can take the same door and, depending on what you add around it, create a completely different look," Silva says.

Most new exterior doors are sold as parts of complete door systems that include the frame, hinges, sill, weatherstripping, and any sidelites or transom windows. "This simplifies the installation, because you have only one major piece to install rather than many smaller components," Silva says. Exterior door prices depend on region

and manufacturer, but the least expensive option is typically steel, followed by vinyl and then fiberglass. Wood and wood-clad doors carry the highest price tag. Beware of low price replacement wood doors; you may end up with shoddy work and low-quality materials.

steel Steel doors are clad with heavy-gauge sheet metal that is extremely tough, though it can be dented and it heats up in direct sun. They have an interior wood frame filled with foam insulation. The best doors have a baked-on polyester finish or a surface laminated with wood veneer that can be stained. The latter can successfully imitate the look of wood.

vinyl Vinyl is not as tough as steel or fiberglass. Though vinyl doors are often embossed with a wood texture, they tend to look like vinyl, not wood. They won't corrode, rust, or dent, and they do not require painting. On the other hand, prolonged exposure to the sun can make vinyl brittle and fade dark colors.

fiberglass Doors made of fiberglass and related composites are a good alternative to wood because they resemble wood but require far less maintenance. Top-quality models are embossed with a realistic wood texture and given a surface coating of cellulose that can be stained with a wood stain. They are very durable

The stained glass, iron muntins, and hardware on this front door reflect the Craftsman-style architecture of the home.

even in cold or corrosive climates. Most have a core of wood framing that has been filled with foam insulation.

wood Wood species used for doors include maple, oak, cherry, walnut, mahogany, redwood, cedar, and fir. These woods are stable enough to maintain their dimensions as they age and weather, and can stand up to dampness without decaying or cracking.

Even the sturdiest wood, however, needs to be protected from the sun or it will gray and deteriorate. Paint offers the ultimate protection, "but if you have a beautiful wood door, why would you want to cover it with paint?" Silva says. Instead, he prefers a marine-grade varnish containing ingredients that block ultraviolet light. However, the door will require

recoating yearly as opposed to every four to seven years if it were painted. If your preference is to paint the door, choose a top-quality, 100 percent acrylic primer and topcoat.

The quality of a door's construction is as important as the material. If the joints are simply butted and glued together, as they are in the least expensive wood doors, the parts

will soon separate. Far stronger are mortise-and-tenon joints. This traditional joinery uses a tenon (a projecting tongue) on one member that fits snugly into a slot (called a mortise) on the other. This makes for an extremely strong, sag-resistant connection. Most manufacturers today reinforce joints with dowels tapped into holes in the wood filled with glue. "This is what you should look for to make sure you're buying a good door," Silva says. "Even if you can't see the dowels, you'll know they're there because the door will be significantly more expensive." Pre-hung exterior door systems range from about $400 (standard) to $2,500 (custom). A complete array with sidelites and a transom can run from $1,000 to $7,000.

Strong, durable, mortise-and-tenon joinery is the most common method used to construct custom doors.

locks and hardware

However solid a door may be, the security it provides depends on the hinges, locksets, and fasteners that hold it in place. "Buy the heaviest doorknobs and hinges you can find," Silva says. Among the many varieties available, the best locksets are made from solid forged brass and are mortised into the door's edge. Tubular or key-in-knob types (also called bored locksets because they fit into two intersecting holes bored into the door) are the most common, but are not as strong.

tip: the keyless option Not all locks need be opened by keys. Check out keyless locks that can be opened with a keypad code, a magnetic card, or a silent signal from a remote control like the type used to unlock car doors. Some high-end locks even use a fingerprint. The ultimate in security, these can be programmed to allow entry only to certain people at certain times.

All deadbolts operate by key on the exterior, but Silva says to make sure you choose one with a thumb knob on the interior. "If there's an emergency, you want to make sure you and your family can get out of the house fast, without fumbling around looking for a key to open the deadbolt," he says. Better still are interior levers that simultaneously unlock the deadbolt and the doorknob's latch bolt as they're the simplest of all to use.

With the best hardware and a solid door, the next link in the chain of security is the screws that hold the hinges to the door frame and the door, and the latch plate to the frame. If the screws are less than 2 inches long, the door can easily be kicked in. Silva drives screws that are at least 3 inches long through the jambs and into the rough framing for a solid hold.

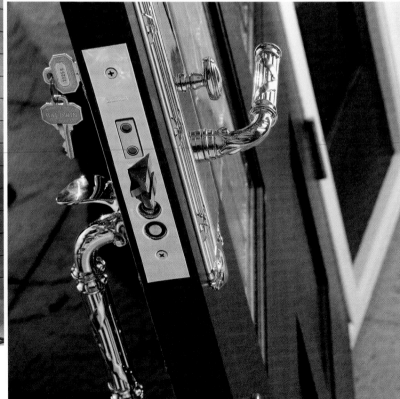

LEFT: Try to match the finish of your exterior door hardware to kick plates, entry lighting, and house numbers. BELOW: This lockset features an easy-to-use thumb knob and hand lever combination. A key is needed only to enter; the hand lever unlocks the deadbolt when operated from the inside.

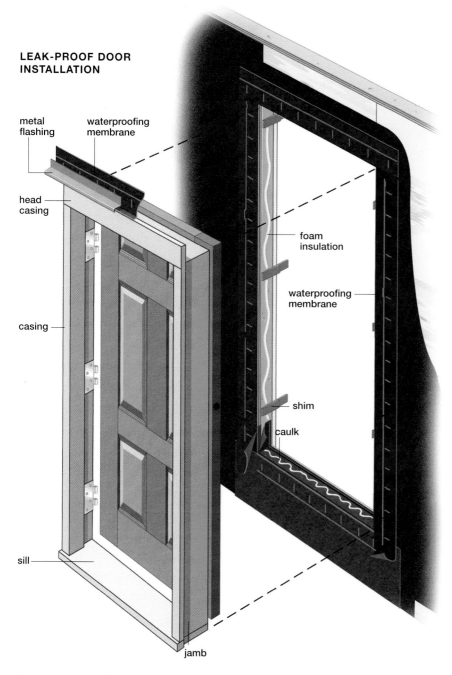

LEAK-PROOF DOOR INSTALLATION

metal flashing

waterproofing membrane

head casing

foam insulation

waterproofing membrane

casing

shim

caulk

sill

jamb

Once the door opening is weatherproofed, Tom Silva inserts the jamb and threshold assembly.

door installation guidelines

Besides looking good, an exterior door must close smoothly, latch securely, and provide a draft-free and waterproof barrier. Pre-hung doors, because they are mounted as a unit into the wall framing, require precise installation to ensure weather tightness. After years of experience, Tom Silva has developed the following techniques.

First, he applies wide strips of a bitumen-based waterproofing membrane over the sill and 4 to 6 inches up each side of the rough opening. Then he staples long strips of 30-pound building felt vertically to prevent water that might get between the siding and the door casing from penetrating.

He then runs a bead of tripolymer caulk under the threshold and tips the door frame into place. Using shims, he makes sure that the jamb is precisely plumb, level, and square. When everything checks out, he drives long screws through the jambs and into the trimmer studs at the shimmed spots.

Because the biggest source of air infiltration around a door is the gap between the jamb and the framing, Silva fills the crevice with a squirt of low-expansion urethane foam, which seals far better than fiberglass insulation and also acts as a vapor barrier. To create a tight seal around the door itself, he uses weatherstripping consisting of a continuous strip of foam wrapped in rubberized nylon.

roofing

A solid, strong, weathertight roof is fundamental to a house's primary purpose—providing shelter. And because the roof is often the largest, most visible surface, it plays a key role in establishing the home's overall look.

materials

From asphalt shingles to metal, there are lots of choices. Regardless of the product or type, all shingles or panels must overlap or interlock to shed water effectively, and they must be durable and flexible enough to withstand severe weather and temperature fluctuations.

Of course, price is likely to be a major factor in your choice of a new roofing material. As discussed below, the cost per square (one square equals 100 square feet) can vary dramatically from high-end materials such as tile and slate to more moderately priced roofing such as asphalt shingles. "Roofs get very expensive very quickly for anything other than asphalt," Silva says. "That's why I like asphalt so much—it's a great value." Still, whether for reasons of aesthetics, architectural style, or historical purity, some homeowners prefer other materials.

Tom Silva suggests that homeowners also pay attention to the color of the roof they choose, as "dark roofs can add a lot of heat to the inside of the house." Here is a brief guide to the most popular options.

asphalt Though asphalt shingles were once the Model T of roofing shingles—simple and inexpensive but offering little variety—they have evolved significantly. They are now available in many styles, colors, textures, and weights.

Generally, the more you're willing to spend, the better the features and appearance and the greater the longevity. Basic three-tab shingles might last 20 years and cost up to $150 per square installed. But if you live in a damp, humid climate, consider paying about 25 percent more for algae-resistant shingles. Or in any climate, for two or three times the cost of basic shingles you can purchase laminated, or architectural, shingles with a thicker texture that mimics the look of slate or wood. One caution: Shingles labeled "30-year" or "40-year" will not necessarily last that long. "If you've got an asphalt roof that's 20 years old, no matter what the shingle is, you've got an elderly roof on your hands," Silva says.

Asphalt shingles come in a number of colors and shapes, making them an excellent choice for any style home.

Wood shingles and shakes have a natural feel and look great with wood siding.

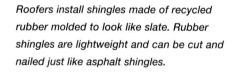

Roofers install shingles made of recycled rubber molded to look like slate. Rubber shingles are lightweight and can be cut and nailed just like asphalt shingles.

wood shingles and shakes

Sawed into shingles or split into shakes, cedar, redwood, southern pine, and other woods were once ubiquitous on rooftops. Now they are nearly always Western red cedar. In fire-prone areas, wood shingles must be treated with fire retardant and sometimes aren't allowed to be used at all. Wood shingles are expensive, from $250 to $500 per square installed. They're typically laid over skip (spaced board) sheathing so that the underside of the shingles can breathe. "They're definitely a luxury in every sense of the word," Silva says.

slate and look-alikes

A material that's both beautiful and durable enough to last for centuries, real slate, unfortunately, is extremely expensive—up to $1,000 or more per square installed. It's also very heavy, so it requires a beefy, engineer-approved roof structure, which can add even more to the final tab. However, several slate alternatives mimic the look at a fraction of the price. Plastic shingles are expected to last 40 years or more and cost less than half the price of slate. In addition, they're much lighter—less than a tenth the weight of slate. Fiber cement shingles, which range from $250 to $500 per square installed, come with a 50-year warranty and weigh half as much as slate. Tom Silva likes rubber shingles, which are made from recycled materials and cost half as much as slate. "They don't break, they're easy to install, and from the ground they look just like the real thing," says Silva, who installed them on his brother's house.

tile In some Southern climates, tile roofing is a popular option that is consistent with the Spanish- and Mediterranean-style homes often seen in the region. Concrete and clay tile roofs are heavyweights at about 900 to 1,000 pounds per square (though lightweight concrete tiles are available at about half the weight). They will last 50 years or more but are prone to cracking under any pressure. They are also fireproof. Expect

TOP: A multicolored tile roof is paired with metal on this Spanish-style home. BOTTOM: In some states, a metal roof can lower your homeowner's insurance because of the increased protection it provides in hurricanes, tornadoes, and fires.

UNDERNEATH A FINISHED ROOF

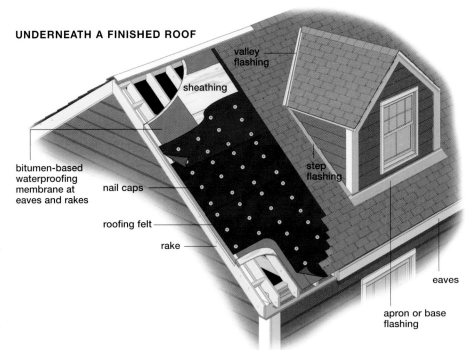

valley flashing

sheathing

step flashing

bitumen-based waterproofing membrane at eaves and rakes

nail caps

roofing felt

rake

eaves

apron or base flashing

to pay $200 to $700 per square installed, or more if the structure requires reinforcement.

metal Because it resists fire, rot, insects, and mildew, metal roofing has become a popular choice for many homeowners. On the downside, metal roofs readily conduct heat, can be noisy in a hailstorm, and are easily dented or scratched. Made primarily from steel and aluminum, metal roofing is manufactured as large metal panels, imitation shakes, and tile and slate look-alikes. Installation methods vary; all types should be installed by a professional who is familiar with the particular material. Metal-panel roofs have a distinctive rural or commercial look. They are not appropriate for all types of architecture, so consult an architect or experienced designer before opting for this material.

the roof deck

A leak-proof roof begins below the shingles at the sheathing, which is typically a layer of plywood panels fastened to the rafters. Building codes specify the minimum thickness of sheathing, but Tom Silva prefers to go one better. Where codes allow for $\frac{1}{2}$-inch-thick roof sheathing, he'll install $\frac{5}{8}$-inch; where $\frac{5}{8}$-inch is allowed, he'll install $\frac{3}{4}$-inch. A heavier sheathing can take an extra heavy load of snow (or workers on the roof) without deflecting between the rafters.

Sheathing is typically covered with a layer of 15- or 30-pound roofing felt, which protects the roof during installation of shingles and acts as a secondary water barrier. In areas with ice and snow, Silva recommends applying a 6-foot band of bitumen-based waterproofing membrane along the eave line, underneath the roofing felt.

Counterflashing is inserted into the mortar joints between this chimney's bricks.

flashing

"A 50-year roof requires 50-year flashing," Silva says. Flashing is used to form a watertight seal at roof intersections and around protrusions such as dormers, skylights, chimneys, and plumbing vent stacks. "The flashing basically takes water that comes off a shingle and kicks it away so it won't be driven back under the shingles," Silva says. Flashing is generally held in place by nails. Any nail heads that are exposed (most won't be) should be covered with roof mastic to prevent them from leaking. When new roofing is installed, the flashing should be replaced as well.

Faulty chimney flashing is a very common source of roof leaks. Properly weatherproofing a chimney requires a three-layered approach that combines a sticky waterproofing membrane, flashing, and counterflashing. Chimneys low on a roof can also benefit from a deflecting sheet-metal structure called a cricket on the highest side.

tip: hiring a roofer First, check at least half a dozen references. Then visit two or three job sites to gauge the quality of the work. "Take a pair of binoculars with you, and look at the roof for evenness and uniformity," Silva says. Above all, be sure the contractor will tear off the old shingles, not just lay the new ones on top.

A WELL-FLASHED CHIMNEY

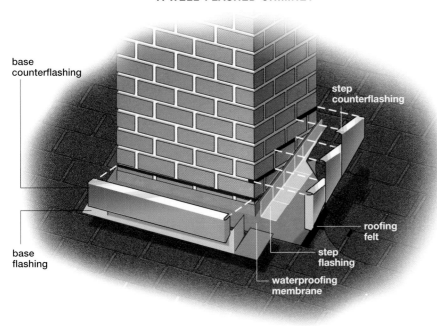

base counterflashing

step counterflashing

base flashing

roofing felt

step flashing

waterproofing membrane

TEAR OFF OR COVER?

All roofing materials eventually wear out. If you are experiencing roof leaks, however, the cause may be an isolated problem with the flashing. But if the roof looks worn and leaks in more than one place, it probably needs replacing. A professional roofing contractor can determine which it is with an inspection.

When new roofing is needed, Tom Silva never recommends adding a new layer of shingles over the old one, even where building codes allow it. "That's a little like sweeping dust under the rug and calling the house clean," Silva says. Tearing off the existing shingles and roofing felt gives the contractor a chance to inspect and, if necessary, replace any rotting, loose, or damaged sheathing panels and to install a new layer of roofing felt. The result will be a new roof that is far less likely to leak over time—and that puts less of a burden on the roof framing. Tear-offs cost between 10 and 25 percent more, but that is well worth the peace of mind. "But be warned: It's a messy job," Silva says. "Make sure the contractor protects your plants, positions the waste bin as close to the house as possible, and uses a magnetic sweep to pick up any stray roofing nails left behind."

A proper gutter system safely redirects rainwater, protecting your foundation and walls from water damage.

gutters

Though gutters and downspouts can look a bit ungainly, they perform a vital role—helping to preserve a home by safely directing rainwater. Without gutters, water draining directly from a roof causes splashback when it hits the ground, wetting the lower part of exterior walls or seeping down into the base of the foundation. This, Silva says, "is a recipe for rot and wet basements or crawl spaces." While a home in the desert Southwest may not need gutters, they make sense on homes in most of the country.

materials Gutters can be installed in sections or in continuous pieces that are custom-fitted to the house. The fewer the seams, the lower the chance of leaks.

Tom Silva prefers aluminum or copper gutters. Aluminum is most commonly used because it combines strength and durability with affordability. Silva urges homeowners to

"buy the thickest stuff you can afford." Generally, aluminum for gutters should be at least .032 inches thick.

Copper is a beautiful, long-lasting option. Nothing else looks quite as good, especially on an old brick or Colonial home. But at about $3 to $5 per linear foot, it is more than twice the price of aluminum.

Though wood, galvanized steel, and vinyl were once common, they are seldom used today. Wood, which must be protected by a finish, is extremely high maintenance. Galvanized steel rusts and corrodes over time. Vinyl gutters tend to leak at the connection points and are made from a flimsy material.

If sections of your roof lie beneath tree branches, you may want to consider leafless gutter systems, though they can be quite expensive, and some systems make your gutters much more difficult to clean. Leafless gutter

For gutters to work properly, they must be clear of debris. By cleaning your gutters twice a year, you can help keep the rest of your home free from water damage.

systems can be installed along with a new roof or retrofitted to existing gutters. They are especially useful on two- and three-story homes, where gutters are not easily accessible.

installation Gutters work by virtue of a gentle slope—1 inch per 20 feet of run is sufficient for water to flow to the downspout. Without this slope, the gutters will hold water and debris, and the weight alone can tear them from the house. (Clogged gutters can also cause snow to back up and form ice dams.) Gutter lengths must be carefully cut and measured before being installed with fasteners attached to the eaves. Gutter seams should be sealed with butyl caulking, which prevents leaks. "It's messy stuff to work with, but it stays pliable even when the gutter expands and contracts," Silva says.

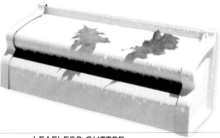

LEAFLESS GUTTER SYSTEM

exterior painting

Paint protects exterior surfaces from moisture and the damaging effects of ultraviolet light. While no paint job endures forever, it can last eight years or more if high-quality paint is applied correctly to surfaces that are properly prepared. To ensure an easier repainting job, don't wait until the previous coat has begun to peel, crack, or flake.

evaluating painting needs

If there are no clear signs of peeling and flaking, one sure way to discover whether existing paint must be scraped and sanded before repainting is to use Tom Silva's "duct tape test." Press a piece of duct tape against an inconspicuous section of siding and then peel it off quickly. "If the tape is clean, it's safe to repaint after washing the surface," Silva says. If not, a more aggressive approach will likely be needed.

If certain serious house problems are at work, a pro can discover them by reading clues from a paint surface's texture. When moisture becomes trapped behind wood siding, for example, the siding can expand and contract with temperature changes, pushing paint away from the surface. Bulges or flakes at the top of a wall may indicate gutter or roof leaks. Paint peeling on the exterior wall

of a bathroom may mean that condensation is building up inside the wall, indicating the need for improved bathroom ventilation. Caulk applied along the bottom edges of clapboards in a misguided attempt to make a house energy efficient can cause an entire wall to peel because of trapped moisture.

The symptoms of paint problems (right) point to various causes. Alligatoring results from the natural aging of paint, but it can also occur when the top coat is harder than the base coat, which happens when oil-based or alkyd paint (see page 250) is applied over latex. Cracking and flaking result from low-quality or overly thinned paint, or poor surface preparation. Peeling often signals an incompatibility between paint layers—for example, when latex is used over multiple coats of oil-based paint—because the two types of paint expand and contract at different rates. Peeling can also be caused by moisture in the wall or, with oil-based paint, if the surface was wet during painting. Finally, wrinkling can occur if uncured paint became wet as a result of rain or humidity. In each of these cases, the surface must be scraped, sanded, and re-primed.

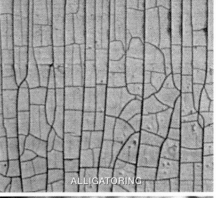

ALLIGATORING

CRACKING/ FLAKING

PEELING

INCOMPATIBILITY

WRINKLING

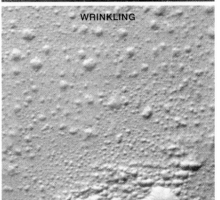

Painters clean a house using a mixture of bleach and water, a sprayer, and a stiff-bristled brush. The mixture eliminates mold and mildew in addition to dirt.

To protect against paint drips, he covers plantings and surfaces within about 10 feet of the house with 12-by-15-foot canvas tarps supported by planks and temporary framing or sawhorses. He recommends against using plastic sheeting. "On a hot, sunny day, you can kill a shrub in 30 minutes or less by covering it with plastic," he says.

Next, to kill any mildew and clean the exterior surfaces and shutters, a chlorine bleach solution diluted with four parts water is applied (particularly bad areas should be scrubbed and then washed with the solution). "If you paint over mildew, it will look good for a few months, but the mildew will eventu-

Paint will not adhere well to weathered, gray wood. A quick swipe with a sander uncovers wood that looks fresh as new and will take paint far better after priming.

paint preparation

It bears repeating: The key to a good paint job is in the preparation. Slap a coat of paint on a poorly prepared surface and it will soon peel off, leaving a bigger problem than before. Prepping a surface can devour about 75 percent of the time and effort required for a good paint job, but,

as This Old House painting expert Jim Clark says, "it's like plumb-and-square to a carpenter."

Clark follows a painstaking approach to preparation. He begins by removing shutters and labeling them for easy replacement. Then he repairs or replaces rotted or damaged sections of siding and window frames.

tip: hiring an exterior painter Ask prospective painting contractors for references, and then check the houses out firsthand—particularly ones that have the same siding material as your house and that were painted a few years ago. Most importantly, ask what the painter plans to do on your house and get it in writing. Will the crew wash the house first, then do minor scraping and spot-priming, or will they need to do extensive scraping and priming? Be sure all details of the work are included in your agreement.

ally grow right through the new paint," Silva says. Though Clark uses a pressure washer to clean the house, both Tom Silva and Norm Abram caution homeowners against using one themselves. "I've seen too many instances where people literally blasted a hole through the siding or forced water behind it and into the wall," Silva says. After washing, the surfaces must be thoroughly rinsed with clean water.

The next step is to remove any paint that is unstable or has failed so that it won't continue to peel. In some cases, paint has to be taken down to the bare wood, a difficult task that can be complicated by the possible presence of lead in old paint (see below).

Some painters use chemical strippers along with scraping and sanding. Because of the vastness of the surfaces involved, power sanders, including pad and random-orbit sanders, work especially well. Stripping and scraping can leave an uneven finish, so instead Clark uses 100-grit aluminum oxide paper to sand sound paint, which smoothes its edges and provides for better adhesion. Near trim and architectural adornments, a heat gun is helpful for softening the paint so it can be peeled away with a hand scraper. This process should not be used with paint that contains lead; and because a heat gun can ignite combustibles such as wood siding if

Here, Jim Clark scrapes off 10 layers of old paint after using a chemical stripper.

held too close for too long, a fire extinguisher should be close at hand.

Even after it is stripped and sanded, a wood surface may not yet be ready for painting. Any holes or cracks must be filled with epoxy putty, which hardens quickly and can be sanded smooth when it dries.

BEWARE OF LEAD IN OLD PAINT

Before scraping or sanding any surfaces that may have been painted prior to 1978, consider this: Dust or particles from lead paint, when airborne, present a serious hazard. They are especially dangerous to children and pregnant women. Lead, once commonly used as an ingredient in house paints, was banned from use by the federal government in 1978. If you suspect that your home's old paint may contain lead, it's important to have the paint tested before any scraping or sanding is begun. Though home test kits are available, the Environmental Protection Agency warns that these tests are not always accurate and should not be relied upon before you make renovations. Contact the National Lead Information Center (NLIC) at 1-800-424-LEAD for a list of certified lead-removal professionals in your area.

choosing paint

Because labor accounts for most of a paint job's cost—typically over 90 percent—it makes sense to buy the highest-quality paint you can. Generally, the price of paint is a pretty good indicator of quality because better ingredients are more expensive.

There are two main kinds of exterior house paint: oil-based and latex. Oil-based paint is also called alkyd paint because of the alcohols and acids used to make the synthetic oil. Latex derives its name from the rubber that it used to contain, though it is now made from acrylics. Both types of paint consist of a pigment, a solvent that makes the paint smooth enough to brush on, and a binder that glues the pigment to the surface as the paint dries.

After oil-based paint dries, it forms a tough, inflexible film; latex paint is more flexible, making it less prone to cracking. Oil-based paint generally adheres better to problem surfaces because its solvents seep into the wood or microscopic openings, even through slightly chalky, old

When it's time to repaint an older house, do some research to find a historically accurate color palette.

paint. A surface painted with latex, however, has tiny gaps that allow water vapor to pass through, making it less likely to peel off homes with excessive interior moisture. It also cleans up with water, unlike oil-based paints, which require a solvent. "For trim, I like to use oil-based paints because of their durability and sheen," Silva says. "For the siding, latex works well, and I appreciate the ease of cleanup."

A color chip just isn't big enough to make a color choice for a large area. Tom Silva helps a homeowner decide on a color combination by looking at sections painted on the side of the house.

A good painter will use a brush near the trim work for more control.

a latex-based primer and cover it with either oil-based paint or latex-based paint," Silva says. "But if you use a latex-based paint or have a coat of latex on the house, then you need to follow it up with another coat of latex. Otherwise, the paint could peel."

Paint should be applied from the top down so that any drips won't mar the completed work. Painting with a brush instead of a spray gun offers more control and ensures better penetration. To maintain a smooth and seamless finish, the painter should work with a wet edge, meaning that each new stripe of paint overlaps the previous one while it is still wet. Painting over a drying surface produces messy brush strokes that do not smooth out. Last, the trim is painted, using a smaller brush to bring the paint neatly to the edge.

painting techniques

Painting is a fair-weather project only and should ideally be done during a warm month, when the wood is dry. Tom Silva likes to coat bare spots on the wood with paintable water-repellent preservative, which not only keeps out water but also prevents the wood from expanding and contracting. "That's one sure way to control flaking later on," he says. Next comes the primer, which provides a better surface for the first layer of paint to take hold. "In general, you can use an oil-based primer or

resource directory

associations and organizations

Kalt Associates, Architects
248-594-7385
4871 Haddington Drive
Bloomfield Hills, MI 48304
design and architectural services

Pacifico Associates Inc.
248-399-3348
www.parch.com
300 E. Fourth St. Ste. 6
Royal Oak, MI 48067
3D architectural rendering and
virtual reality services

**The Rohm and Haas
Paint Quality Institute**
www.paintquality.com
exterior and interior painting resource

building materials

Andersen Windows
888-888-7020
www.andersenwindows.com
windows, patio doors, and artglass

Armstrong
800-233-3823
www.armstrong.com
vinyl, ceramic, hardwood, and
laminate flooring

Certainteed
www.certainteed.com
roofing, insulation, and siding products

Forbo Flooring/Marmoleum
866-MARMOLEUM
www.forboinoleumNA.com
linoleum flooring

James Hardie® Siding Products
888-JHARDIE
www.jameshardie.com
fiber cement siding products

Jeld-Wen Windows and Doors
www.jeldwen.com
windows and doors (patio, interior,
exterior, garage)

Ludowici Roof Tile
800-917-8998
www.ludowici.com
variety of tile roofing products

Marvin Windows and Doors
888-537-7828
www.marvin.com
windows and patio doors

USG Corporation
800-874-4968
www.usg.com
manufacturer of building materials,
including drywall

fixtures and hardware

American Standard
800-442-1902
www.americanstandard-us.com
bath and kitchen fixtures, faucets,
and accessories

Baldwin
800-566-1986
www.baldwinhardware.com
locks, hardware, bath accessories, lighting

Broan-Nutone
800-558-1711
www.broan.com
ventilation, ceiling fans, heating

Elkay
630-572-3192
www.elkayusa.com
kitchen sinks and faucets, specializing
in stainless steel

Kohler
800-456-4537
www.us.kohler.com
bath and kitchen fixtures, faucets,
and accessories

Moberg Fireplaces
223 NW 9th Avenue
Portland, OR 97209
503-227-0547
www.mobergfireplaces.com
specializing in cast-iron, porcelain, stucco,
soapstone, and clean-burning fireplaces

Rejuvenation
888-401-1900
www.rejuventation.com
period-authentic lighting and hardware

Swanstone
800-325-7008
www.swanstone.com
sinks for kitchen and bath, countertops,
shower and bath surfaces

surfaces

Nevamar Company
800-638-4380
www.nevamar.com
decorative laminate surfaces

Wilsonart
800-433-3222
www.wilsonart.com
laminate and solid-surface
countertop products

appliances

Brita
800-24-BRITA
www.brita.com
water filtration systems

General Electric
800-626-2000
www.ge.com
kitchen appliances, lighting,
and electronics

Kitchenaid
800-422-1230
www.kitchenaid.com
kitchen countertop and major appliances

Miele
800-843-7231
www.miele.com
kitchen appliances

credits

photographers

courtesy of American Standard: 208, 213 TR, 213 BR, 214 R, 215 BR, 216 TR, 217, 219 (3); courtesy of Andersen Windows: 231 L, 231 M, 236; courtesy of Armstrong: 204, TL, 100 L; Scott Atkinson: 45; Bernd Auers: 55 T; courtesy of Baldwin: 240; Andre Baranowski: 91 B, 190, 191; Noel Barnhurst: 51 BL; David Barry: 245 T; Paul Barton/Corbis: 44; Matthew Benson: 116 B, 146 T; Pascal Blancon: 6, 12 T, 13, 117 B, 121 B, 142 T, 144 T, 155 TR, 175 T, 222, 248, 251 T; courtesy of Bomanite Corporation: 108; courtesy of Brita: 185 B; courtesy of Broan: 200 B; David Carmack: 46, 52, 60, 63 B, 87, 91 T, 111 T, 145, 155 B, 157 T, 193, 196, 228, 234; courtesy of Certainteed: 226 BL; Webb Chappell: 68 T; Kindra Clineff: 48, 82 T; courtesy of Craft-Art: 163 B; Grey Crawford: 50 B; Grant Delin: 188 TR; Scott Dorrance: 113; courtesy of Elkay: 169 BR; Phillip Ennis: 50 T, 86, 90 T, 106 B, 126, 167 B, 171 B, 180 T, 202, 203, 206 T, 227 B, 230 B, 239 T; Scott Fitzgerrell: 49, 89 (3), 91 M; Emily J. Followill: 139 B; courtesy of Forbo Linoleum: 103 T; courtesy of General Electric: 180 B; Tria Giovan: 88, 94, 95, 106 TL, 112, 135 B, 167 M, 186, 189 B, 209 B, 220 TR, 226 BR, 244 B; Rick Gomez/Corbis: 31; Jay Graham: 131; John Granen: 16, 51 TR, 220 BL; Noah Greenberg: 188 BL; Art Grice: 101; Michael Grimm: 71, 233 B, 243 ML, 243 MR; John Gruen: 15 BR, 22 T, 23 B, 194; Ken Gutmaker: 96; Darrin Haddad: 62, 161 BR, 237 TL, 246 M; Jamie Hadley: 87 TL, 120 B, 121 T; David Hamsley: 211 B; Craig Harris: 93, 239 B; Philip Harvey: 157 (2), 215 L, 218; Alex Hayden: 137; Tom Haynes: 99, 102, 103 B, 105, 106 M, 107; Michael Heiko: 140 T; courtesy of Ernst Hofmann: 22 B, 23 T, 23 M; courtesy of James Hardie: 225 B; Frances Janisch: 136, 165 M, 178 B; courtesy of Jeld-Wen: 114, 116 T; Spencer Jones: 79 T; Richard Kalt, AIA-Kalt Associates: 28; Michael Keller/Corbis: 35; Keller & Keller: 20 T, 21 B, 37, 66 B, 72 BR, 79 B, 83, 122, 124, 129 B, 142 B, 235 B, 241 R, 249, 250 B; Grant Kessler: 72 TL; Muffy Kibbey: 40 T, 41 B; Nathan Kirkman: 246 B; courtesy of Kitchenaid: 178 T; courtesy of Kohler: 168, 169 BL, 170 (2), 209 T, 210, 214 L, 216 L, 216 BR; David Duncan Livingston: 74, 98, 110, 123, 128, 153 T, 166 B, 204 M, 205 B, 207 T, 213 MR, 224, 227 T, 246 T; courtesy of Ludowici Tile: 244 M; Mark Luthringer: 184; Janet Mesic Mackie: 158 MR, 169 TL, 171 T, 173 T, 176 B; courtesy of Marmoleum: 204 B; courtesy of Marvin Windows: 231 R, 232 T, 238; Stefano Massei: 65 B, 89 B; Bill Mathews: 129 T, 160 T; Joshua McHugh: 8 B, 164 T; E. Andrew McKinney: 10 T, 85, 90 B, 132, 161 T, 166 T, 173 M, 173 B; Shelley Metcalf: 59 B; courtesy of Miele: 175 B, 176 T, 177; Melabee M Miller: 100 R; courtesy of Moberg Fireplaces: 119 B; Keith Scott Morton: 158 B, 172 T, 179, 181; Michael Myers: 237 (3); courtesy of Nevamar: 159 T; Wendy Nordeck: 221 T; Benjamin Oliver: 251 B; Bradley Olman: 92, 109, 167 T, 183 B, 235 T, 242 B; Gabe Palmer/Corbis: 42; Gary W. Parker: 11 T; Ellen Pearlson: 219 TL; Pluriel Phototheque/Superstock: 30; Erik Rank: 155 (7), 160 B, 162 B, 163 B, 163 M, 164 B; courtesy of Rejuvenation: 117 (3); The Rohm and Haas Paint Quality Institute: 247; Lisa Romerein: 40 B; George Ross: 17 T, 17 BR; Eric Roth: 127 B, 135 T, 138, 139 T, 147, 149, 150, 158 TL, 161 BL, 162 T, 165 B, 170 T, 172 B, 183 T, 185 T, 206 B, 207 B, 212 TR, 219 MR, 225 T, 227 M, 243 T; Royalty-Free/Corbis: 27, 29; Mark Rutherford: 36, 65 (4), 66 T, 69 B, 198; Jeremy Samuelson: 10 B; Susan Seubert: 38, 140 B; Casey Sills: 182; Ariel Skelley/Corbis: 43; Michael Skott: 230 T, 232 B, 250 T; Kolin Smith: 9 T, 14 T, 39, 57, 58, 59 T, 78, 80, 81, 146 B, 152 T; Ben Stechschulte: 144 B, 197; Thomas J. Story: 19 BR, 26, 221 (2); Tim Street-Porter: 192, 205 T; courtesy of Swanstone: 169 TR; courtesy of USG Corporation: 76, 77, 82 B; Brian Vanden Brink: 84, 97, 118, 120 T; Dominique Vorillon: 18 T; David Wakely: 213 B; Bevan Walker: 33; Jessie Walker: 127 T, 130, 134 B, 152 B, 153 B, 156 T, 156 B, 158 TR, 164 M, 165 T, 174; courtesy of Watts Heatway: 200 T; Burt Welleford: 55 B, 73 TL; Paul Whicheloe: 212 BL; Chris Whitehead/Getty Images USA: 47; courtesy of Wicanders Cork Flooring: 104; Brian Wilder: 24, 115; courtesy of Wilsonart: 159 B; Joe Yutkins: 243 B

designers

Angela Grande Associates with Claus, Architect: 167 B; Stephen Blatt, Architect: 97; Butler's of Far Hills/Jeff Haines: 180 T; Bradley, Klein, Thiergartner: 203 L; Erica Broberg, Architect: 220 TR; Linda Brown: 153 B; Thomas Buckborough: 139 T, 149; John Buscarello: 50 T; Cambria: 161 BR (B3); Tom Catalano Architect: 183, T, 225 T; Lo Yi Chan: 118; Andrew Chary and Associates, Architect: 171 B; Decorating Den: 167 T, 183 B; Gail Drury, CKD, CBD of Drury Design: 174; Dale and Susan Frens, Architects: 112 R; Fran Murphy & Associates: 126, 230 B; FTR Designs: 106 B; Richard Gibbs, Architect: 244 B; Chris Grandmontagne: 129 T; Interior Consultants/Denise Balassi: 206 T; Chris Kimball: 135 T; Laura Langworthy: 162 T; Mark Hutker and Associates, Architects: 120 T; Lisa Melone: 100 R; Michael Whaley Interiors: 86; J.R. Miller: 189 B; Valerie Moran: 88; Neff Design Center: 158 TR; Opacic Architect: 227 B, 239 T; Sandy Oster Interiors: 202 B; Adolfo Perez, Architect: 219 MR; Jonathon Poore: 150; Amy Sandack of Drury Design: 165 T; Sandvold Blanda Architecture & Interiors: 226 BR; Elizabeth Steimberg: 203 R; Jean Stoffer: 156 B; William Stubbs: 90 T; Tres McKinney/Richard Witzel & Associates: 90 B; Christina van Cleef: 202 T; Susan Victoria: 183; Jim & Jean Wagner of WoodFellows: 152 B; Walton Design Interiors, Lisa Mermis and Glenna Walton: 160 T; Sally Weston, Architect: 84; Workshops of David T Smith: 130, 134 B, 156 T; Zodiaq: 161 BR (T)

photo stylists

Marlana Cole: 152 T; Sarah Dawson: 140 B; James Day: 138 T; Gloria Gale: 129 T, 160 T; Joji Goto: 83; Mary Scott Himes: 8 B; Linda Humphrey: 137; Gia Russo: 10 B

index

Page numbers in **boldface** refer to photographs.